TREES

Adam and Eve, by Albrecht Dürer (1493)

Trees

Woodlands and Western Civilization

Richard Hayman

Hambledon and London
London and New York

Hambledon and London

102 Gloucester Avenue
London, NW1 8HX

175 Fifth Avenue
New York 10010

First Published 2003

ISBN 1 85285 299 2

A description of this book is available from the
British Library and from the Library of Congress.

Typeset by Carnegie Publishing Ltd, Lancaster.
Printed and bound in Great Britain by The Bath Press.

Distributed in the United States and Canada exclusively
by Palgrave Macmillan, a division of St Martin's Press.

Contents

For Lucien, Alexis and Wendy

Illustrations

Plates between Pages 118 and 119

1 *Landscape with the Finding of Moses*, by Claude Lorrain
(1604–1682). (*Prado, Madrid / Bridgeman Art Library*)

2 *Charles I*, by Anthony van Dyck (1599–1641).
(*The National Gallery, London / Bridgeman Art Library*)

3 *Portrait of the Artist with his Wife and Daughter*, by Thomas
Gainsborough (1727–1788). (*The National Gallery, London /
Bridgeman Art Library*)

4 *Cornard Wood*, detail of painting
by Thomas Gainsborough (1727–1788). (*The National Gallery,
London / Bridgeman Art Library*)

5 *The Cenotaph to Reynolds' Memory, Coleorton*, by John Constable
(1776–1837). (*The National Gallery, London / Bridgeman Art
Library*)

6 *The Menin Road*, by Paul Nash (1889–1946).
(*Imperial War Museum / Bridgeman Art Library*)

7 Green Man, bench-end in Crowcombe church.
(*Richard Hayman*)

Text Illustrations

Preface

Woodlands are wild places that give us a sense of infinity, a sense of timelessness in a society organized on an increasingly short-term basis. Thomas Vaughan, the seventeenth-century hermeticist, recommended that we should 'walk in groves, which being full of Majestie will much advance the soul'. When the American Henry David Thoreau went to live in the woods of Walden in 1845, he did so not to learn out about trees but to discover himself. In personal terms, I can trace the origin of this book back to the 1980s when, as a photographer, woodlands became my primary interest, and the wooded landscape surrounding the upper Neath valley in South Wales my main subject matter. Brought up in the Ansel Adams school of landscape, I wanted to distil some elusive essence of nature in an image or icon. It never worked – a heightened visual experience in the field can seem curiously dead when it is reduced to a still image – but I did learn that ultimately it is not the image that matters. What I had achieved was engagement with the subject, the going out and looking and thinking.

Trees begins from the assumption that nature remains in itself the same, but that different societies see it differently. It charts some of the ways that trees have been seen in western society. Environmental history has usually been written in terms of loss, but I wanted to contribute to a growing corpus of literature that champions a more positive relationship between nature and humanity. It is a commonplace that society has become alienated from nature, and that there was a time when human beings lived in greater harmony with the natural world. The source of that alienation has variously been ascribed to the rise of Christianity, the rise of science and the industrial revolution. Whatever the cause or nature of our alienation, our relationship with nature is an indispensable component of what makes humans human, and it needs to be reconciled with the world we live in now. If we cannot articulate our need for nature in the present there is little hope that future generations will treat it any better.

1

Roots and Branches

No living things have had more impact on human sensibility than trees. Trees are special. They are bigger than us both physically and metaphorically, but we couple our reverence for them with a relentless destruction of forests that epitomises a fundamental human ambivalence to nature. William Blake complained that 'a fool sees not the same tree that a wise man sees', because for many of his contemporaries a tree was 'only a green thing', raw material at the service of utility. But we never tire of expressing our love of trees, of recalling how refreshed and inspired we feel in their presence.

We love trees both for their physical nature and their symbolic potential. A tree's roots, trunk and branches, bearing fruit and changing with the seasons, have an inherent attractiveness to symbolic and associative thinking. Trees span many lifetimes and have always been used as historical markers, bringing the past closer to the present, and ensuring that trees planted in commemoration of some event or person will outlive those who have planted them. We project many of our thoughts about the world onto objects in the external world. Trees are one example of this, and in turn they reveal truths about nature. Trees are evocative and evoked through the medium of cultural memory and imagination. Nature, as Blake observed in his *Songs of Innocence*, is the echoing green that resounds within us and around us. So at the end of it:

> Old John with white hair
> Does laugh away care,
> Sitting under the oak
> Among the old folk.[1]

Trees have roots in the ground and reach up to the sky, linking earth with heaven, a rich potential that has been tapped by nearly all of the world's mythologies. Trees are a universal symbol of the divine. Of these trees of the imagination, none have influenced the western world as profoundly as those of Eden. The Garden of Eden had been planted by God, and its first inhabitants enjoyed some of its trees for their beauty and others for their fruit, as God intended. In paradise, God himself walked among trees. The destiny of Adam and Eve was determined by two trees at the centre of the garden: the tree of life promised eternal life to those who ate its fruit, while the tree of the knowledge of good and evil brought death. By eating from the tree of knowledge the eyes of Adam and Eve were opened. Embarrassed by their nakedness, they hid behind the trees when they heard the approaching footsteps of God. Banishing them, God placed a cherubim and a flaming sword at the entrance to the garden, barring the way to the tree of life.

In Norse mythology the gigantic ash Yggdrasil was the cosmic tree that overshadows the whole world. According to the *Prose Edda*, written in the early thirteenth century by the Icelandic aristocrat Snorri Sturluson, Yggdrasil had three separate roots – one in the realm of the gods, a second in the land of giants, and a third in the land of dark, cold and mist known as Nifelheim. Its trunk stretched up to the sky where its branches spread out over the whole universe. An eagle perched on the top of the tree and between its eyes sat the hawk known as Vederfolnir. The eagle was at war with a dragon known as Nidhogg who gnawed at the third root of the tree in Nifelheim, symbolizing the conflict between higher and lower, heavenly and earthly realms. A squirrel stirred up enmity between the eagle and the dragon by running up and down the tree passing on malicious gossip. Meanwhile four harts nibbled its leaves and innumerable serpents destroyed its branches. Yggdrasil symbolized the condition of nature and the interaction of its species:

> The ash Yggdrasil
> Endures more pain
> Than men perceive,
> The hart devours it from above
> And the sides of it decay,
> Nidhogg is gnawing from below.[2]

Beneath the tree were springs of destiny and of wisdom and understanding. The gods sat in judgement by the spring of destiny, the water from which nourished two swans who, like Adam and Eve, were the ancestors of all their species. Odin, recognizing that wisdom could only be gained by sacrificing to it, hung for nine days and nine nights on its branches to learn hidden knowledge. Yggdrasil was the guardian tree of the world. All of life was contained within the tree, unifying all the creatures of the world within its shade.

As individual trees have been mythologised, so have forests. Forests are the promised land in much early medieval Irish literature, such as the *Voyage of Bran*, written in the late sixth or early seventh century, where a mysterious woman appears in the hall of Bran, bearing the branch of a marvellous apple tree and promising to take him to land 'without sorrow, without grief, without death, without sickness, without weakness'. In the *Voyage of St Brendan* the monks visit a thickly wooded island where the trees bear grapes the size of apples and perfume so sweet as to tempt them from their fasting. *The Journey of Tadg Son of Cain* has a similar tale of an island whose perfumed trees satisfy the hunger of the travellers just by inhaling, and where there is a never-ending crop of apples, hazelnuts and heavenly birdsong.

In the much more familiar Greek pantheon, Artemis was the goddess of the grove, an enigmatic deity whom no human set eyes upon. Aeschylus tells us that she suckled wild animals and Homer called her the mistress of the hunt. But she was cruel too. When Agamemnon killed a stag in one of her sacred groves, she demanded the sacrifice of his daughter Iphigenia. The youthful Hippolytus was devoted to her, but even though he brought her flowers from a meadow that only he could enter, he could only hear her voice but not set eyes upon her. She was the elusive, unobtainable deity whose virginity stands for the inviolate forests. Dionysos, although a prodigious hunter like Artemis, was her symbolic foil. Dressed in animal skins and wearing a wreath of ivy, he had a retinue of dancing nymphs and a reputation for licentious revelry. Initiates of Dionysian mystery cults believed themselves to be transformed during their dances into satyrs, men of the woods. Artemis and Dionysos represented in turn the enigmatic ideal and the primal urges that come from the depths of the inner self, mirrored in the depths of the forests.

Woodlands play an equally important role in secular histories. When the plough and pasture superseded the woodlands as our primary source

of food, primeval nature acquired a past. Woodlands represent the world
as it would have been without humans, a world beyond society. Many
cultures, therefore, have origin myths based on or among trees. As
uncultivated places outside the boundary of the normal everyday world,
woods still have connotations of freedom that few other natural places
enjoy. In his *The Making of the English Landscape* published in 1955, the
historical geographer W. G. Hoskins charted and explained the role of
the plough, pastoralists, road builders and industrialists in altering the
character of the landscape, and in his telling phrase explained how the
landscape was 'made', contrasting with the 'un-made' landscapes such
as the woods. 'England must have seemed one great forest before the
fifteenth century, an almost unbroken sea of tree-tops, with a thin blue
spiral of smoke rising here and there at long intervals.'³ Such unbroken
stretches of woodland were places where, as Wordsworth put it in his
Guide to the District of the Lakes, we can only imagine 'the primeval
woods shedding and renewing their leaves with no human eye to notice,
or human heart to regret or welcome the change'. Hoskins was thrilled
by the prospect of being able to see the natural world 'through the eyes
of men who died three or four thousand years ago'.⁴

The idea of original woodland is universal and its prominence in
creation myths shows how woodland is an important element of how
a society sees itself and its relation to the natural world. In modern
society comparison of the contemporary landscape with original woodland tells how successful the human race has been at pacifying nature,
or how arrogant it has been at destroying it, depending upon your point
of view. If the leafy shade was the primeval habitat, then the people
who first inhabited it lived either in the garden of delight or the savage
wilderness, again depending upon your point of view. Assuming that
the human race had been born perfect and descended into corruption
by engagement with its baser instincts, the biblical Eden and Greek
Arcadia have been the archetypal landscapes. A more prevalent view is
that the woods were the haunt of primitive people with primeval urges,
who were closer to the beasts of the wild until their gradual ascent to
civilization. One early exponent was the Roman poet Lucretius:

> They [the first inhabitants] dwelt in the woods and forests and mountain
> caves, and hid their rough bodies in the underwoods when they had to escape
> the beating of wind and rain. They could not look to the common good,

they knew not how to govern their intercourse by custom and law. Whatever prize fortune gave to each, that he carried off, every man was taught to live and be strong for himself, at his own will ... And by the aid of their wonderful powers of hand and foot, they would hunt the woodland tribes of beasts with volleys of stones and ponderous clubs, overpowering many, shunning but a few in their lairs; and when night overtook them, like so many bristly hogs, they just cast their savage bodies naked upon the ground, rolling themselves in leaves and boughs.[5]

The concept of original savagery could also be turned on its head. Primitive societies could be a stick to beat civilization. Tacitus criticized Rome in his description of the forest-dwelling Germans, while Lucretius pointed out that primitive men died of starvation, whereas the civilized Roman died of overeating. Gradual pacification of the wild by building huts and manipulating fire gradually raised men above the level of the beasts. Change was the result of human agency. By itself, nature was not quite static, but certainly stable, representing circular time in contrast to the linear time of progress. This is an old idea and one that has enormous implications for the imaginative and emotional investment that we make in the natural world. Graduating from the woods may have been a sign of progress, but a certain simplicity was lost that we have been trying to rediscover ever since, whether through hunting, rambling, camping or poetry. Society's ambivalence to the forest life is expressed in a mixture of sympathy and disgust, in attitudes to outlaws like Robin Hood and more recently to gypsies. The paradox embedded in the concept of society and nature is one that the past has wrestled with no less than the present.

Rome, the eternal city of Western civilization, was born of the forests, according to Virgil and Livy. The twins Romulus and Remus, the sons of Rhea Silva and the god Mars, were foundlings suckled by a she-wolf, growing up in the forests of Latium. Virgil compared Latium with Arcadia and gave its forests a rich cultural significance. Latium was the place where Saturn sought shelter after his displacement as leader of the gods. Here he brought unruly men down from the trees, gave them laws, and governed them throughout the Golden Age. The name Latium is said to derive from *latere*, or to hide, and it was in this safe haven that Romulus and Remus founded the city of Rome, which they turned into an asylum for the vagabonds and refugees living there. The boundaries of the Roman Republic would in the future be the edges of the uncultivated forests, defining a clear boundary between civilization and the *locus neminis*, 'the place of no one'.[6]

Rome was not the last civilization to place its origin in the forests, giving its subsequent history the stamp of organic growth, and justifying its imperial schemes as the natural way of things. The German architect Joseph Decker (1677–1713) imagined Gothic architecture as the inspiration of nature, its tall columns and vaults like an avenue of trees. This became a cliché in eighteenth-century Germany and Britain, where routinely cathedrals were praised as nature-inspired and Gothic splendour was cited to praise the awesome qualities of woodland trees. Goethe, for example, described the interior of Strasbourg Cathedral as 'like sublime, overspreading trees of God, whose thousand branches, millions of twigs and leaves ... announce the beauty of the Lord, their master'.[7]

Any individual can achieve a certain amount of fellow feeling with the past by wandering in wild places. As we walk in an ancient wood our attitudes to it can be reflected back to comment upon the constructed world that we ourselves live in, and how we have come to be there. We see woodland in the context of society.

2

Gods

In the 1880s the Scots anthropologist James Frazer embarked on a study of the priesthood of the Roman goddess Diana Nemorensis. A work that began on the shore of Lake Nemi in Italy grew into a global study of magic and religion, one of the most ambitious historical studies ever undertaken. The thirteen volumes of *The Golden Bough* (1890–1915) are an encyclopaedia of ethnography as it was understood at the end of the nineteenth century, orchestrated as an account of early religions by the prevailing notions of late nineteenth-century thinking.

In the sacred grove at Nemi the matter of the priesthood was settled by mortal combat. To become the priest of the grove pretenders had to murder the existing priest, a practice Frazer found so barbarous as to be alien to the refinements of classical civilization. He therefore explored more primitive cultures for clues as to the origin of the custom, on the basis that 'recent researches into the early history of man have revealed the essential similarity with which ... the human mind has elaborated its first crude philosophy of life'.[1] The implication here that cultures develop sequentially from savagery to barbarism to civilization would hardly have raised an eyebrow in Victorian Britain. In practical terms, it led Frazer to consider that the first crude philosophy of life was the worship of nature, specifically the worship of trees, and that he could recover vestiges of it in the dying rural cultures of Europe.

Frazer's methods may have become unfashionable, but he was asking legitimate and important questions: what role did natural features such as woodland play in early societies and how could this be found out? It remains an open question whether Frazer's folk practices had an ancient ancestry, or whether such material should only be used as a source of ideas as to what might have happened in the distant past. Certainly no one would now support the notion of a timeless rural culture dismantled by the industrial revolution, although this was the

bane of folklore studies for most of the twentieth century. It has been
argued, however, that universal primal religious impulses can be
identified. These constitute fundamental religious experiences upon
which all subsequent religions have been built. They include a sense of
kinship with the plants and creatures of nature, humility in the face
of more powerful forces, and belief in the existence of gods or other
supernatural beings, our relationship with which continues after death
and is activated in a ceremonial setting. One of the implications of the
theory is that the transition from one belief system to another does not
involve a complete rupture of ideas. Continuity means that ancient
beliefs are embedded within modern religions. The difficulty is in how
to identify them.

One of the key processes in human history was the creation of a
landscape by the introduction of farming and the building of villages.
This gave an altered perspective as to the nature of wild places. If the
gods do not inhabit the everyday world then they must be sought beyond
its boundaries. In Europe the landscape of the first farmers coincided
with the erection of the large funeral monuments of the early Neolithic
period. On the face of it, nothing could be further from secluded
woodland haunts than these highly visible structures. Such monuments
were intended to say more about inter-human relationships than about
nature – humans worshipping other humans, either ancestors or 'divine'
rulers – while the placing of monuments in the landscape was a state-
ment of ownership, or dominion over territory and time. In later
Neolithic southern England are large-scale landscape features like Avebury and Silbury Hill in Wiltshire, or the six-mile linear earthwork
known as the Dorset Cursus, which could only have been set up in
relatively open country that offered distant prospects. But these open
landscapes had boundaries. There is archaeological evidence to show
that people visited wild and uninhabited places and that such places
were accorded a special significance. The existence of rock art, the
carvings found on natural rock surfaces often far from any habitation,
is perhaps the most accessible example. Votive offerings in bogs, or
those found in caves from Scandinavia to the Mediterranean, are another. These are contexts in which evidence can be recovered.
Unfortunately for our purpose, relationships with the natural woodland
world are largely beyond recovery, although their importance need not

be doubted. There is evidence that artefacts took on a significance derived from their place of origin, for example the production of stone axes from the exposed rocks of remote and inaccessible Lake District fells and, more famously, of stone from the Preseli Hills for Stonehenge. Might not wooden carvings have derived some significance from the place where the wood was cut?

Supporting evidence is largely indirect. Woodland trees and shrubs bore nuts and fruit, and they provided shelter for wild animals, but killing a stag was not simply a matter of food. Skill and courage in the killing of wild animals conferred status. Control of the spirit world was established by shamanic priests who wore antler head dresses to imbibe supernatural powers. There is plenty of evidence that stags were widely invested with a significance beyond the mundane, as they are commonly found as ritual deposits associated with Neolithic and Bronze Age ceremonial and funeral sites. Burials were often accompanied by sprigs of hawthorn and hazel nuts, perhaps collected from special trees, with a context beyond that of physical nourishment. Nature cults interlocked human existence with the natural rhythms of life such as the cycle of seasons. This is where we might expect trees to have played a significant role. A glimpse of one-such nature cult is found inscribed on a Bronze Age urn lid from Denmark, a country whose landscape was otherwise inscribed by conspicuous monuments. The round sandstone lid from Maltegard is engraved with matchstick lovers, he aroused and both with arms reaching to embrace across a central perforation which has an obvious sexual connotation. Behind them is a tree, while the whole composition is framed in a wreath of leaves. Trees also appear in fertility scenes in Scandinavian Bronze Age rock carvings, notably at the famous site of Bohuslän. The oneness of human with other forms of life is an aspect of animism that is also found in the activities of later centuries in Europe.

The woodland ways of the British Celts are best known from the works of classical authors. These contemporary accounts promise a great deal but are in many respects disappointing, revealing as they do not fertility rites but how forests and barbarians were used as crude political symbols. Greek and Roman authors played up the importance of woodland or other informal shrines erected by the native British, and their reasons are clear. Many classical authors characterised societies on the

Engraving on the lid of a Bronze Age cremation urn from Maltegard, Denmark.

periphery of the known world as progressively more savage the further they were from the Mediterranean. To write of distant peoples worshipping in the depths of the forest rather than in formal temples echoed contemporary prejudices. For example, the Greek geographer Strabo described Britain as similar but simpler and more barbaric than Gaul, while Ireland was more primitive still.[2] Strabo betrays an ambivalence towards nature that is far from alien in later European history. Essentially, however, he set up nature as the opposition to culture, where civilization represented the escape from the wild. People who inhabited or worshipped in the woodlands are portrayed by classical authors as barbaric. The reverse of Strabo is the use of nature as a moral corrective, that the woodland worshippers were untainted by the barbarities of civilization. At its root were contrasting views of the rise or fall of mankind, a question fundamental to most religions and philosophies and one that may well have exercised prehistoric societies in Europe.

A broad range of classical sources suggest that in the centuries before Roman domination woodlands, and often individual trees within them, were sacred places in barbarian Europe, in addition to the few formal temples that have been identified by archaeologists within villages or fortifications. Pliny the Elder placed the veneration of trees in a European context and established that it was a universal custom. The development of civilization could be seen there, from the basic natural resources of fruit and wood, with cave dwellers sleeping on beds of leaves, to the development of more sophisticated pleasures represented by vines and olive trees. Romans like Pliny were also haunted by the primeval German forest, which they envisaged as a vast and impenetrable expanse of oaks. Classical literature also provides the earliest instance of the German forest infiltrating the culture of Britain, an influence that was to continue much later through the popular fairy tales of the Grimm brothers and German economic forestry. Although Pliny devoted comparatively little attention to Britain, he described the cult of mistletoe that was associated with the Celtic priesthood, the druids. According to Pliny, the name druid was derived from 'drys', the Greek word for oak. Their sacred rites were performed in the presence of oaks and often using oak leaves, while anything growing on an oak tree was believed to be divine and heaven sent. In fact, mistletoe grows on the oak but has no roots in the ground, and its leaves remain green when the host tree is bare, so it is understandable how it could be deemed to have divine properties. Pliny wrote improbably of white-robed priests hailing the moon and cutting mistletoe with a golden sickle, presenting their rites as an innocuous but primitive superstition.[3] Other writers were less charitable, notably Caesar and Strabo, who wrote gruesomely of human sacrifice inside wicker images, or of druids dismembering their sacrificial victims in sacred groves.[4]

Tacitus wrote the earliest surviving account of the German forest, an earlier history of the German wars by Pliny the Elder being lost. In it he wrote of the Suebi, who performed human sacrifice in a hallowed grove. Specific places within woods had special meanings built up over time. In the hallowed place where the tribe was thought to have been born lived the tribe's presiding deity. Here, in the natural world, was the gateway to the underworld of spirits that was unlocked by ritual. Tacitus suggests that trees were not worshipped for their own sake, begging the question of what the oak and mistletoe really meant to the druids. According to Tacitus, the Langobardi had a hallowed grove on a small island in the centre of a lake, a remote natural location to which only the priest class had access, and significantly a place set apart from the everyday world. Amongst Germans the bodies of famous men were also burned with special kinds of wood, reaffirming their bond with the forest and associating beech, oak and ash with human characteristics.[5]

The Britons performed similar rites. Tacitus tells us that Mona, or Anglesey, was a stronghold of the druid order until Suetonius, the Roman governor of Britain from AD 59–61, rounded off his campaign in Wales by conquering the small island, where his troops were said to have been initially frightened by cursing druids and black-robed torch-bearing women. While the description is close to caricature, Suetonius is said to have deliberately destroyed the groves on the island in an attempt to wipe out the druid order. According to Tacitus the groves were host to most despicable rites: 'It was their religion to drench their altars in the blood of prisoners and consult their gods by means of human entrails.'[6] Here a Roman author is describing imperial expansion as a civilizing influence, as destruction of their temples implied the defeat of the Celtic gods. He portrays the groves as the meeting point between the secular world and the supernatural world of the gods.

The limitations of classical accounts of barbarian cult practices can be demonstrated by comparison with the *Periegesis*, the guide book to contemporary Greece written in the second century AD by Pausanias. Pausanias illuminates a lost world of ritual that was not centred upon or confined to the familiar stone-built temples. Nor were the rituals confined to an elite priesthood. Rural Greek cults were set in a world of shrines and festivals, of woodland deities and the general deification of the natural world. Lakes, rivers, trees, mountain passes and the craters of volcanoes, all of these places feature as important cult sites, while special reverence was accorded to natural springs, where water emerged from the Earth. Writing of Boeotia in northern Greece, Pausanias describes the Plataean festival of Daidala, held to commemorate the reconciliation of Hera and Zeus. In an oak wood worshippers set out a piece of stewed meat, then observed which tree the crow that picked the flesh alighted upon. This tree was then felled and a figure of a bride was carved out of the trunk. The figure was taken to a mountain-top altar of wood, placed on a brushwood pyre and burnt with a sacrifice of a cow to Hera and a bull to Zeus.[7] Another passage, about Achaia, describes a Patrean festival dedicated to a statue of Artemis. A fenced altar of green logs was set up in a circular enclosure of logs. After a procession, all manner of live animals, together with fruit from orchard trees, was thrown on the altar, which was then set alight. None of these animals represented husbandry, as all of them were wild beasts of the woods – game birds, boars, bears, wolves and deer.[8] This sacrificial pyre bears a striking resemblance to the sacrificial groves of the Celtic and Germanic peoples of Europe, and is similar to the woodland clearings of northern Europe described in the late nineteenth century by James Frazer.[9]

Images carved out of selected trees dedicated to the divinities were a common feature of the period. In the remains of ancient Corinth Pausanias found a wooden image of Dionysos carved out of a tree worshipped in honour of the god. Similar trees at Rhodes were dedicated to Helen of Troy, who was hanged from a tree. An oak at Dodona was dedicated to Zeus, a myrtle tree at Boiai was sacred to Artemis, while at Aulis Pausanias found a fragment of a plane tree described by Homer. These trees were not strictly speaking divinities themselves, but they shared some of the ambiguities of medieval Christianity, about which it was claimed at the Reformation that images of saints and relics were worshipped rather than revered. The difference is a subtle one but may be significant in the interpretation of so-called tree worship in the rest of Europe. A similar context is provided by Pliny for rustic Roman provinces. According to Pliny, trees were also the temples of the deities. Even in his time trees of exceptional height were dedicated to gods. A more common practice was to associate individual species with specific divinities (not dissimilar to the German practice already described), such as the dedication of the bay to Apollo, the myrtle to Venus, the poplar to Hercules and so on.[10]

The association between individual trees and people has a long history, surviving into the nineteenth century with the character of John South in Thomas Hardy's novel *The Woodlanders*. The best evidence for such ancient associations, however, comes from early medieval Ireland. As in the Old Testament, specific sacred trees in Ireland were associated with the inauguration of kings. The Maguire kings were inaugurated under hawthorns at a hill fort known as Lisnaskeagh in Fermanagh, while similar inauguration trees are known in counties Antrim, Clare and Galway. According to the eleventh-century *Vision of the Phantom*, a 'marvellous tree' is said to have sprouted on the day when Conn Cétchathach (Conn of the Hundred Battles) was born. The spiritual and temporal authority of pagan kings was mediated through such trees, and it was at these places where the divine authority of the ruler was established. Desecration of an inauguration tree was the ultimate insult and a taboo that invited retribution. Accounts of inauguration ceremonies describe a rod, or wand, usually in the form of a branch cut from the sacred tree, which symbolised the king's authority and his special relationship with otherworld deities or with God. Such branches were also later associated with clergymen and poets, acknowledging their own special relationship with the spiritual world.[11] It was similar to the use of laurel leaves as an emblem of honour in classical civilization, which is the root of the modern term Poet Laureate.

Accounts of barbarian Europe by Pliny and others provide largely general information and say nothing of the common interaction with trees, confining their descriptions to the priestly class. What riches might Pausanias have uncovered had he toured Europe with the same diligence that he employed in Greece? In fact, when looking closer at the place of trees in preliterate cultures, we are not much better placed in our sources than James Frazer. Like Frazer, we are dependant upon a miscellaneous collection of material that must be drawn upon in order to look beyond the immediate information that the classical authors provide.

There are sporadic references to tree worship in early Christian documents. A charter of 854 describes a boundary in Somerset in terms of 'the ash tree which the ignorant call holy'.[12] Why is not known, but the reference is a good example of how it was not simply woodlands that had a special significance but individual trees within them. The church intermittently issued orders forbidding any heathen practices associated with them, significantly grouping tree cults with veneration of other natural places like springs and stones, the other most common foci of traditional cult practice. For example, Theodore of Tarsus, appointed archbishop of Canterbury in 668, undertook a visitation of most of England in 669, after which he forbade worship at trees, wells, stones and 'enclosures'. In the late seventh century both St Aldhelm and Archbishop Theodore issued orders condemning the new year tradition of dressing up in animal skins, specifically as horned stags. The horns may have signified a new year's growth and have been a symbol of the renewal of life. Despite their association with shamanic ritual, the custom may have been Roman in origin, or have been one of those occasions when men dressed as animals or women and the normal rules of the world were turned on their head. (One of the manifestations of the tradition escaped suppression and survived into modern times as the horn dance at Abbots Bromley in Staffordshire.) [13]

Viking immigration to the north of England brought a fresh wave of pagans in need of proselytising. Archbishop Wulfstan of York issued a series of directions between 1000 and 1002 outlawing necromancy, auguries and incantations, and sanctuaries around wells, stones and trees, of which the elder was the most significant. Wulfstan's code was adopted by Canute, the first Danish king of England, who in 1018 forbade heathen worship 'of any kind of forest tree', along with the sun, moon, fire and water. During the middle ages the cults associated with wells flourished and became Christianized, but those focused upon trees and woodlands appear to have declined, if the decline in references to them is a reliable guide. There were exceptions, such as the extraordinary event at Frithelstock Priory, Devon, in 1351. The priory had already attracted the attention of the bishop for its lack of discipline, but in 1351 a group of monks set up an altar in the woods near the church and in parody of the church placed upon it 'a proud and disobedient Eve'.[14]

Uncritical acceptance of this kind of evidence has often been cited to prove that Christianity, worshipping in the artificial enclosed space of a church, was somehow antithetical to nature, with the honourable exception of the Celtic church. The Bible does not, however, corroborate such a view. There is a clear tradition of sacred trees, wells, rivers and mountains in the Old Testament. Often, as in the case of Abraham sitting in the shade of the oaks at Mamre, they mark the place where God revealed himself to the ancestors or prophets of Israel. When Gideon met an angel, made food offerings and built an altar under the oak tree of Ophrah, he was only doing what Christians would do centuries later, sanctifying a place in nature which had a special relationship to the divine.[15] Christ himself prayed in the temple at Jerusalem, but also in the open air in the hills of Galilee, giving His followers ample reason to follow suit. Wells are the most obvious example of natural open-air sanctuaries being adopted by Christianity, a religion where holy water is an integral part of one its main sacraments, that of baptism. Christian disapproval of veneration at natural sanctuaries was directed at the worship of false gods rather than at nature. The ability of Apostles to convert Jews and Romans and, later, of missionaries to convert pagans, was the ability to make the new religion intelligible within existing mental and cultural horizons. It was not a cultural revolution that obliterated the past. The image of St Patrick praying in the forests and mountains was equally relevant to Christian and to pre-Christian religion.

Indirect evidence of the veneration of trees comes from the lives of the saints, but it need not always be taken at face value. St Boniface (c. 675–754) was an English monk born in Crediton, Devon, who travelled to Germany as a missionary. In Geismar, Boniface felled a sacred oak tree, challenging the traditional belief that desecrating a holy object would bring retribution upon him. But a dead tree cannot fight back, raising the question of who or what was supposed to enact the retribution. There is a parallel with Pausanias's Greece and Pliny's Rome, where the tree was not worshipped in its own right but was host to or was closely associated with a deity or supernatural force. No supernatural force harmed the triumphant Boniface and subsequently many pagan Germans are said to have been received into baptism. The tree provided the timber to build a chapel dedicated to St Peter, while an axe became one of the saint's emblems.[16] Nevertheless Boniface was fortunate, for James Frazer quoted draconian penalties imposed by 'old German law' for damaging a sacred tree. If the bark of such a tree was peeled the culprit's navel was to be cut out and used to cover the blemish in the tree, while his intestines should be wound around the trunk. Only in that way could the tree be healed.[17] What the story of Boniface establishes is that in woodlands a distinction was made between its sacrosanct part, to be preserved as sites of special spiritual interest, and its secular part, to be harvested for utilitarian purposes.

A similar story is told of St Patrick in the Wood of Fochloth, the exact location of which is unknown although it was undoubtedly a real place. Patrick had a dream in which the people of Fochloth were calling to him. Later, while on his missionary journeys and performing baptisms at a well, he overheard two people talking of Fochloth and persuaded them to take him there. His eventual arrival was greeted not by kings and warriors but by two hundred druids. In a short confrontation Patrick called down curses upon the leader of the druids, who instantly fell down dead, to the horror of his fleeing fellow priests. Many people were received into baptism that day, and a monastic church was founded in the wood in the fifth century that was still a thriving community at the end of the seventh century.

Other monastic foundations in the woods of Ireland show that it was not nature that was vanquished by Patrick, but that woods were a suitably divine setting for the religious life, whether pagan or Christian. St Columba (c. 521–97) founded monasteries in the oak woods of Derry (546) and Durrow (c. 556). The woods of Derry were famous enough for the *Annals of Ulster* to record the destruction of trees there in storms in 1146 and 1178. The trees were sacrosanct and a taboo forbade the felling of them: in 1188 a man is said to have died chopping wood there after accidentally cutting his own foot. The monks of Derry are also said to have followed a rule whereby wood was left for nine days after it was cut, then divided up among the good, the bad and the poor. Other churches were built in association with individual trees, including the monasteries at Kells and Kildare, associated with oak trees, and the chapel of the hermit Oengus, who chanted psalms under a sacred tree.[18]

The sacred places of Britain also often became the sites of churches. There is indirect evidence that some of these sacred sites were associated with or focused upon trees. Place names hint at the former presence of sacred groves. Holy Oakes in Leicestershire appears in Domesday as 'Haliach' (meaning Holy Oak), while Hollytreeholme in the East Riding of Yorkshire was known in a twelfth-century charter as 'Halitreholm', meaning island with a holy tree. In the life of Wulfstan, bishop of Worcester between 1062 and 1095, is the story of a church at Longney-on-Severn in Gloucestershire which had a nut tree in the churchyard. The tree was so large that it darkened the church with its shadows and Wulfstan ordered it to be cut down. But the bishop met local resistance and the only way he could overcome it was to curse the tree so that it grew barren. The supernatural force inhabiting the tree was the Devil.

The yew tree is one of the longest lived of native trees and is common in English and Welsh churchyards. For this there is a mundane explanation, as most of them were planted in the nineteenth century in the wake of J. C. Loudon's *On the Laying out, Planting and Managing of Cemeteries*, published in 1843. Quite apart from the association of the evergreen with eternal life, the yew is a tidy tree that does not drown surrounding gravestones in rotten leaves every autumn. But a number of yews are venerable trees and may have influenced the siting of churches. They are very difficult to date, hollow middles, like the famous examples at Much Marcle in Herefordshire and Crowhurst in Surrey, being one of their chief characteristics.[19] The churchyard yew at Totteridge in Hertfordshire had a girth of twenty-six feet in 1662. Some are even larger, like that at Llanerfyl in Powys with a girth of thirty-five feet.[20] John Evelyn remarked upon the venerable age of the Crowhurst yew in the 1660s. Attempts to date the trees have not always been scientific and have tended to err on the side of antiquity, on the dubious basis that the older a tree is the more historically significant it is. Two or three millennia is not an unusual guess and could of course indicate that such yews were at one time woodland trees. If the estimates are accurate then yews may have influenced the siting of up to five hundred English and Welsh churches.[21]

Ireland has many examples as well – place-names such as Killure and Killanure are said to derive from 'church of the yew'. Although the Columban monastery at Durrow was founded in an oak wood, a ninth-century poem refers to 'a tall bright glistening yew' outside the sanctuary, which may have influenced the exact siting of the church within the wood and suggests that mass was originally said under the tree. Yews had other associations that contradict the over-emphasis placed on the oak in Celtic religion by classical authors. The Yew of Ross was one of the five *bileda*, or sacred trees, of Ireland. It stood near Leighlenbridge, on the River Barrow in Leinster, and when it fell in the seventh century branches from it were distributed among the Irish saints. It was probably not a young tree when it fell, which makes it likely that reverence for it was of pre-Christian origin. Such sacrosanct trees were often protected by taboos – in the twelfth century, Anglo-Norman archers are said to have been struck down by pestilence after they cut down sacred yews and ashes belonging to the abbey of Finglas.[22]

Woodlands do not feature directly in Christian sacraments but trees are as rich in symbolism in the New Testament as they were in the Old. Christ was nailed to a tree. In the Book of Revelation the Tree of Life yielded fruit every month, while its leaves were for the healing of nations. These, however, were abstract concepts that did not derive from and require contact with trees in a tactile sense. (Perhaps the most famous of Christian trees – the Christmas tree – is of pagan origin, but could be comfortably incorporated into a Christian festival without subverting it.) Apart from their funereal context, Christian ritual incorporated trees on Palm Sunday, commemorating the day when Christ entered Jerusalem and His way was strewn with palm fronds. As the evidence from Ireland suggests, in waving branches at Christ the multitude was acknowledging his spiritual authority. Since palms could not be grown in Britain, a variety of alternatives such as willow, box and yew were used instead, fronds from which were blessed and made into crosses in conjunction with processions and gospel readings. The hallowing of fronds is known from the early eighth century and was a well-established custom in the ritual calendar of late medieval Britain.[23]

In certain contexts, trees were regarded as having magical properties over a long period from the end of the middle ages to the nineteenth century. Blessed fronds from Palm Sunday were kept by the laity on account of their supposed protective powers. Another tree invested with the Holy Spirit was associated with Joseph of Arimathea's reputed visit to Glastonbury, where his staff sprouted into a thorn tree, many cuttings from which are said to have been taken. When Celia Fiennes visited Glastonbury in 1698 she found offshoots of the original tree in most of the town's gardens.[24]

To describe an individual tree as sacred or sacrosanct says little more than the fact the tree is special and should not be felled. The important question is whether there was ever such a thing as tree worship, or whether trees and woods were simply the places where the gods or ancestors dwelt in supernatural form. The latter is much more likely. It is graphically illustrated in an episode in the Irish Fionn cycle, describing the exploits of the warrior Fionn mac Cumhaill and set in the third century. While Fionn was walking in the woods

> He saw a man in the top of a tree, a blackbird on his right shoulder and in his left hand a white vessel of bronze, filled with water, in which was a skittish trout, and a stag at the foot of the tree. And this was the practice of the man, cracking nuts; and he would give half the kernel of a nut to the blackbird that was on his right shoulder, while he would himself eat the other half; and he would take an apple out of the bronze vessel that was in his left hand, divide it into two, throw one half to the stag that was at the foot of the tree, and then eat the other half himself. And on it [the tree] he would drink a

sip of the water in the bronze vessel that was in his hand, so that he and the trout and the stag and the blackbird drank together.[25]

The figure resembles a Hindu deity bearing the symbols of his identity – fish, bird, stags, water, apple and nuts – that represent earth, water and air and an otherworldly banquet. The figure has a recognizably religious character and probably represents the kind of pagan deity that was worshipped and whose presence was signified by certain trees.

The fronds from Palm Sunday did not derive their supposed protective powers from the innate properties of vegetable matter. They first had to be blessed, a ritual that drew nature under divine influence. In Pausanias's Boeotia a tree was just a tree until a certain crow rested on its branches, when it was felled and an image was carved into its trunk. Only then did it have special properties, drawing nature into a view of the world that is essentially anthropocentric. In Tacitus's German forest the Suebi worshipped not trees but the spirit of the tribe. The woodland location acknowledged the home of their ancestors and was the correct place in which to pay homage to it.

Ritual was the means by which supernatural powers were invoked or pacified. Antler-clad shamans and the druids were a priest class that controlled access to the spirit world. Pausanias also described popular rituals that involved whole communities. In both cases, trees and woods only gained supernatural power through human agency. All of the practices cited also represent a sophisticated relationship with woodland places. The taboo against the felling of trees may have been based on the notion of retribution, but not for destroying nature, as that would be impossible among people for whom wood was a basic raw material and ironic given the long history of woodland clearances. Tacitus suggests that the German forest was not an impenetrable wilderness, but that its clearings or groves required an intimate knowledge of unculti-vated places that was more significant than the search for food. Woodlands were one type of wild place where the boundary between the natural and supernatural worlds could be crossed, as it could be at caves or springs. The nature of woodlands, with their green canopies, clearly had different connotations to mountains open to the sky. They were, in effect, a gateway between secular and supernatural worlds, and in classical literature to the underworld.

3

Harts and Boars

Friedrich Nietzsche claimed that men who live by social contract need the wilderness to unleash the beast within. He might well have been thinking of the opposing domains of court and forest that structured aristocratic life in the middle ages, and of men like Edward, duke of York, the brother of Henry IV. Edward had been a favourite of Richard II, served Henry's army in Gascony and Wales, and subsequently led the van of Henry's army at Agincourt in 1415, where he was killed. His greatest achievement, however, was neither at court nor on the field of battle. The duke was the author of *The Master of Game*, the most famous treatise in English on hunting, and his views epitomized the longing of aristocrats for a humble life. Hunters, he claimed, were the most contented men on earth. To them were given the simple pleasures of sunrise and the freshness of dawn that helped to make a man virtuous, virtues would ensure the care of their souls after death – 'and therefore be ye alle hunters, and ye shal do as wise men'.

Despite the implied humility of the huntsman's life, hunting was the sport of the most sophisticated men of medieval society. As long as these men conducted their business at court they needed the freedom of the woods. For an Englishman like the patriotic Andrewe Borde, 'there is not so moche pleasure for Harte and Hynde, Bucke and Doe, and for Roo-Bucke and Doe, as is in England'. Venison

> is a Lordes dysshe, and I am sure it is good for an Englyshman, for it doth anymate hym to be as he is: which is stronge and hardy ... for it is a meate for great men. And great men do not set so moche by the meate, as they doth by the pastyme of kyllynge it.[1]

Venison was as good for the soul as it was for the stomach.

The landscape of hunting was the forest, a word of medieval origin largely encompassing woodland landscapes. The term forest probably derives from the Latin *foris*, meaning outside or out of doors, and in the medieval imagination conjured up the uncultivated wilderness beyond the bounds of civilization, although it was originally coined as a legal term defining an area under a jurisdiction separate from the common law. The history of woodland in the medieval period was dominated by the institution of forest law, which structured the art of hunting and provided the context for the place of the outlaw in English culture.

Hunting in England, however, had a far earlier pedigree than the Norman kings. Techniques of hunting with dogs had already been established throughout Britain by the time of the Roman conquest, at which time greyhounds were a noted British export.[2] A thousand years later the *Colloquy* of the monk Ælfric, an exercise in Latin usage written in the late tenth century for novices at Winchester Cathedral, provides the first detailed account of hunting in England, and specifically the work of the king's huntsman. The profession was evidently well organized in Anglo-Saxon England and had developed sophisticated techniques. The huntsman was able to catch deer in nets, could bring them down with dogs, and could also kill a boar with a spear.[3] Both hunting and falconry were popular pursuits with the ruling classes. King Alfred practised every kind of hunting, and personally instructed his falconers, hawkers and kennelmen. Anglo-Saxon law specified that every man had the right to hunt on his own land and there is no reason to suppose that men did not enjoy exercizing that right. Some animals were caught for their meat, such as deer and sometimes hares; others were either pests or were caught for their coats – wolves, foxes, beavers, otters, wildcats and martens.[4]

William I (1066–87) introduced the concept of the royal forest as a legal entity from continental Europe. Forest Law protected the habitat of wild animals, and as such began as a deliberate conservation policy. It also gave the king the right to hunt on land he did not own, overriding the rights of landowners, for which reason it was widely regarded as oppressive. Landowners also took exception to the manner in which the law was manipulated to raise revenue for the royal household, at the same time restricting their own rights as owners. Common people, meanwhile, resented the manner in which grazing sheep, pigs and cattle, and cutting wood, was subject to 'fines', a term disguising what was essentially a form of taxation. The *Anglo-Saxon Chronicle* includes a bitter attack on the implementation of the new laws upon an oppressed people, Saxon landowners having to 'follow the king's will entirely if they wished to live or hold their land'. Forest Law came to be regarded as the acme of Norman despotism.

The term forest did not originally specify a wooded landscape, even though the majority of forest was wooded. The term simply denoted an area set aside for hunting, and therefore defined a place of deer rather than a place of trees. Woodland was the most favourable location for a hunt, and so wooded areas were the most common form of forest, but there were exceptions, Exmoor Forest and the entire county of Essex being cases in point. By contrast, some well-known wooded areas, including the Forest of Arden, were never subject to Forest Law. One of the most resented acts of William the Conqueror was the creation of the New Forest, although Walter Map, archdeacon of Oxford, was perhaps embellishing popular myth when he claimed that the creation of the New Forest entailed the demolition of whole villages, the extermination of their inhabitants and the destruction of three dozen churches.

The area covered by Forest Law expanded under William II (1087–1100) and Henry I (1100–35), but the institution weakened during Stephen's reign (1135–54), during which the throne was in dispute. It was re-established by the first of the Plantagenet kings, Henry II (1154–1189), who continued a policy of afforestation well beyond the pretence of providing hunting ground for his own use. Revenue for the exchequer was its aim, the fighting of wars on many fronts its ultimate cause. The following century saw increasing use of the forest as a source of revenue and less as a reserve for the king's hunting, but only after the power of the monarch had been curtailed. King John (1199–1216) tried to exact still more revenue by stricter enforcement of forest laws, a policy that was curtailed by the compromise of Magna Carta of 1215 and in the 1217 Forest Charter. The latter established the respective rights and responsibilities of the barons and the king, and allowed landowners a greater share in the commercial potential of the woods.

Forest Law attempted to regulate the ordinary business of the forests while preserving the hunting for the king. In doing so it gave the lie to the myth that English woodlands were an uninhabited green wilderness. With its special language, Forest Law brought with it a self-contained sub-culture reflecting the specific activities within the woods. The laws distinguished between transgressions against the 'vert' (the woods) and the 'venison' (the animals). Transgressions against the vert were little more than an opportunity for swelling the royal coffers. Woodlands were well-trodden places where firewood was cut, cattle, horses and sheep were grazed (herbage), while during the autumn months pigs were fattened on acorns and beech mast (pannage). Occasionally land was cleared to create farms (assarts), or trees were felled for timber. Strict terminology was developed to describe the condition of trees in a forest. For example, according to Richard Fitznigel, 'if woods are so severely cut that a man, standing on the half-buried stump of an oak or other tree, can see five other trees cut down around about him, that is regarded as "waste"'.[5] More specialized economic activities, such as mining and ironmaking, were controlled by royal licence, while tanners, who used oak bark for tanning leather, were not allowed to inhabit a forest immediately outside a borough. Edward I (1272–1307) sold timber when he needed to fund his military campaigns. Henry III (1216–72) also raised large sums in this way. For example, in 1261 he sold 2545 oak trees from Northamptonshire, 3121 oak trees from Rutland, 39 from Bere and 824 from Savernake forest in Wiltshire, for a total of £442.

Harsher regulations governed the venison, the most definitive state-ment of which is found in the Assize of Woodstock of 1184, when Forest Law had reached its widest geographical extent. Possession of bows, arrows and spears in a forest was forbidden and it was also required that the toes of dogs should be clipped in order to prevent them bringing down deer. In the late sixteenth century the practice of lawing, as it was known, was described by John Manwood as a very precise operation: 'a mallet, setting a chisel two inches broad upon the three clawes of his forefoot, at one blow doth smite them off'. For the first two trans-gressions against the venison a safe pledge was to be taken, while the third offence was punishable by execution.

In an assize of 1198 the punishment was modified. Instead of execution for the third offence, the punishment for killing deer became, in theory at least, mutilation by removing the offender's eyes and testicles. In practice there is little evidence that this extreme punishment was ever carried out, and in any case the death penalty and emasculation were replaced by fines in the 1217 Forest Charter. But the association of cruelty with Forest Law became ingrained in English culture because it implied that the life of a wild animal was worth more than a human life. William of Newburgh wrote of Henry I after his death that 'he cared for wild animals more than was right, and in public punishment he made too little distinction between a person who killed a deer and one who killed a man'.[6] Nigel Wireker, in his satire of the laws written around 1180, picked up on the same draconian penalty for killing a deer:

> And man, though in his maker's image made
> Who all, that is, created, yet is paid
> By princes less regard than beasts of earth,
> Ay, all our race is held of lesser worth.
> How many are hanged on cruel gallows tree
> For taking flesh of beasts! More savagely
> Sicilian tyrants could not well ordain
> Than that for slaying beasts a man be slain.[7]

Adam of Eynsham, the biographer of St Hugh of Lincoln, was equally critical. He portrayed the royal forest as a place where all norms of civilization were turned on their head, a moral chaos in which the virtuous and villainous were interchangeable, the context that nurtured the legends of Robin Hood and the other outlaws. But criticism was not levelled at the king or his huntsmen. The chief culprits were the hierarchy of officials administrating the laws:

> The worst abuse in the kingdom of England, under which the country groaned, was the tyranny of the foresters. For them violence took the place of law, extortion was praiseworthy, justice was an abomination and innocence a crime. No rank or profession, indeed, in short, no one but the king himself, was secure from their barbarity, or free from the interference of their tyrannical authority.[8]

The principal foresters were appointed by the king, although the offices tended to be hereditary. The Esturmy or de Sturmy family were hereditary foresters of Savernake in Wiltshire. The Croc family could trace their origin in forestry to 1094, when Croc the huntsman received a charter from William Rufus. Subsequently Raoul Croc was forester in Wiltshire and Walter in Warwickshire. Matthew Croc was responsible for several small forests in the period 1155–83, while Elias Croc was responsible for the same forests in the period 1190–1209.

The most unpopular officials were the king's chief foresters. Alan de Neville was appointed chief forester in 1165. The chronicler of Battle Abbey wrote bitterly that 'this Alan so long as he lived enriched the royal treasury, and to please an earthly king did not fear to offend the king of heaven'. It is said that Henry II, on being told of Neville's death by the brethren of a monastery, pronounced that 'I will have his wealth, you shall have his corpse, and the demons of hell his soul'.[9] In John's reign Alan's nephew Hugh de Neville was chief forester, although he lost the post when he joined the revolt against the king. The office of chief forester lasted until 1229, when it was replaced by the appointment of two justices of the forest, who had geographically separate remits.

Forest Law was policed and enforced by wardens and the foresters they employed, although many were less than conscientious and used their office simply to ensure immunity from prosecution for their own poaching. It was their task to apprehend poachers, a largely futile business at the best of times. Draconian punishments failed to act as a deterrent when the chances of being caught 'red-handed', with blood-stained hands after the unmaking of a deer, were slim. Poaching was rife and well organized, with men often working in gangs. To apprehend a handful of men wielding bows and arrows and leading packs of dogs could therefore be a dangerous proposition. In the thirteenth century, for instance, a poacher Robert de Gernon kidnapped a forester and demanded a ransom when two of his greyhounds were killed. Meanwhile William Bukke, said to have been an habitual poacher, was shot and killed by a forester when trying to evade arrest.[10] Even if the officials did apprehend poachers it was not the end of the story. In 1276 John de Lascelles, a steward of Sherwood Forest, arrested two men carrying bows and locked them up at Bledworth. During the night an armed band of men broke in and freed them, beating their guards in the process. None of the gang was brought to justice following an inquest into the affair.[11]

Not all of the malefactors were lowly men, and poachers were not outcasts in the manner of modern criminals. Many communities were complicit in the black market for venison, while monastic houses such as Tintern Abbey in the Wye valley provided refuge for poachers and a market for their product. Knights such as Walter Capel and Richard de Sollers hunted illegally in the Forest of Dean in the late thirteenth century as a regular part of their social life. Hamo L'Estrange, sometime sheriff of Shropshire and Staffordshire, was convicted of several offences in Cannock Forest between 1255 and 1270. In the same forest in 1262 Archbishop Boniface of Canterbury and Archbishop Fulk of Dublin were both found guilty of taking deer illegally while passing through Staffordshire.[12] The most common transgressions against forest law, however, were minor matters like cutting wood, sometimes for private sale, and pasturing animals in contravention of the rules. Even so, and although such demands were not a central plank of the peasants' demands, the right to hunt freely was one of the demands made by Wat Tyler during the Peasants' Revolt of 1381.

Justice was administered at forest 'eyres', periodic visitations by justices acting in the king's name, who employed their own officials. Of these officials, the duty of verderers was to attend forest courts and to present evidence, which might include the bones of slaughtered deer. Regarders, of which there were usually twelve per forest, were supposed to 'regard' the forest every three years, requiring them to investigate potential transgressions such as assarting. Forest eyres were at their peak in the thirteenth century but were infrequent, to the extent that many men summoned had transgressed so long ago that they were already dead. If inefficiency characterized its operation, Forest Law nevertheless remained an important source of revenue for the treasury. The level of fines reflected not the seriousness of the offence but the transgressors' ability to pay. An exceptionally good year for the exchequer was 1275 when, in theory at least, £12,305 was raised through forest law fines, although in practice less than this was collected because some of the transgressors were fugitive, penniless or dead.[13] But the infrequency of eyres made them an arbitrary application of the law. In the fourteenth century they were supplanted as the centre of forest administration by inquests, which were held in most years. The first inquest was held in 1245. They were subsequently regularized under Edward I (1272–1307) and received permanent recognition in a statute of 1306.

The justices of the forest were political appointments. Edward II (1307–27) made his favourite, Piers Gaveston, justice of the forests south of the Trent, but when the king turned to the barons needing to raise revenue through taxes, the removal of Gaveston was the price of the deal. Nevertheless the economic importance of the forest to the king declined during the fourteenth century because more revenue was raised through direct taxation. The gradual breakdown in its administration also meant that malefactors remained unpunished. For example, the regards declined and ended south of the Trent after 1387. By the time John Manwood wrote his famous *A Treatise and Discourse of the Lawes of the Forrest* in 1598 the legal significance of the forest had all but lapsed.

Forest Law spoke indirectly of woodlands alive with wood cutters, charcoal burners, grazing animals and the like, but the image it projects is probably more innocuous than the reality. Ælfric's *Colloquy* reminds us that 'all sorts of wild animals live in the woods' and that the huntsman must be able to overcome his fear of them. Hunters may nevertheless have needed the illusion of primeval woods, and in doing so were aided by contemporary romance tales which in turn drew upon hunting scenes. Hunting was adventurous, brought prestige to those who excelled in it, and was generally regarded as one of the definitions of manhood, especially for aristocrats. The thrill of the chase was insufficient to satisfy the medieval hunter who also needed the thrill of the kill. Even so, hunting was an indicator of moral worth because it was a sport for men of action, and men of action would never themselves be ensnared by that formidable hunter of souls, the Devil. Gaston Phoebus, a French authority on hunting, was only repeating a commonplace when he advocated the benefits of hunting on the basis that 'all sin springs from idleness', for when a man has nothing better to think about his thoughts incline to the Devil and the pleasures of the flesh. Meanwhile Pero Lopez de Ayala, the greatest Spanish authority on falconry, argued that a man who fails to exercise his limbs will find his bodily humours grow stale, leaving him subject to sickness and disease.[14]

We know far more about hunting in the later middle ages than that of earlier periods, based on the evidence found in various treatises and romances and upon visual art. Apart from numerous continental sources, one of the earliest treatises on hunting was *Le art de venerie*, of *c.* 1325 by William Twici, a huntsman employed by Edward II. This, however, came long after the twelfth-century heyday of the royal hunter. The best-known work is *The Master of Game* of 1406–13 by Edward, duke of York, a translation with some additional material of the *Livre de chasse* by Gaston Phoebus. The first printed book on hunting was

The Boke of St Albans by Dame Julyana Bernes, published in 1486, followed a century later by Sir Thomas Cockayne's *Short Treatise of Hunting* of 1591.

All huntsmen needed expertise in the training and handling of dogs, of which various breeds were employed for their specific attributes. In *The Master of Game* it was recommended that boys should begin their hunting education at the age of seven or eight by learning about hounds and how they should be kept. 'Brachet' was a general term for hounds that hunted by scent in packs, a related breed being the limehound, or 'lymer', that was usually employed singly. Sleek greyhounds, larger and more powerful than the modern racing dogs, and burly alaunts, were running hounds that hunted by sight. Greyhounds, in conjunction with the bow and arrow, were the most common adjuncts of both legal and illegal hunting. Mastiffs were used for protection of the huntsman and for killing wolves, although they could also bring down red and fallow deer. Other hounds, such as the self-explanatory hart-hounds, otter-hounds and buck-hounds, were more specialised. A pack of hounds was said to need a minimum of twelve running hounds and a lymer, but the scale of a huntsman's kennels depended upon his master's status and resources.

The most common method of hunting, especially popular in medieval England and Scotland, was known as 'bow and stable' hunting, or more primitive versions of it. Deer were taken en masse, being driven to an ambush where they were killed either with arrows or brought down by dogs. It required a scenting hound to locate the herd, and hounds followed by mounted huntsmen to drive the deer to a predetermined location where camouflaged archers dressed in green waited silent and motionless. The technique could be practised by as little as half a dozen men and was therefore a viable strategy for poachers. An alternative, used by poachers and huntsmen when venison rather than sport was required, was for the deer to be chased into nets and for their throats to be cut at leisure. Larger-scale hunts made use of the 'stable', that is to say a line of unarmed men who were placed to drive the deer along a pre-planned route by waving and shouting. James IV of Scotland (1488–1513) was known on one occasion to have made use of over three hundred men for the purpose. The commandeering of such large numbers of beaters for the stable increased the spectacle of the hunt and was a mark of status. The deer were best shot head on, as they were a more elusive target if the archer had to aim to the side. Aiming to the side was also dangerous to other archers in the line, and was the most frequent cause of accidents during the hunt. Deer that escaped unscathed or were merely wounded by arrows were brought down by hounds waiting behind the line of archers.

The leader of the hunt would not necessarily have joined the line of archers. He is more likely to have followed the chasing hounds on horseback, although he may also have carried a bow with him. William the Conqueror is said to have been strong enough to draw a bow while spurring on his horse. Shooting from a fast-moving horse while both hands were on the bow required dexterity, physical strength and courage, all attributes highly valued by warrior kings. The end of the hunt was marked by the ceremonial laying out of the deer and dividing up of the carcasses according to established rules. A large bow and stable hunt would see venison distributed among local gentry, clergy and huntsmen, while offal was given to the hounds. A more ostentatious gift was made annually from 1275 by Sir William le Baud to the dean and canons of St Paul's, London. A fallow doe was given on the day of the conversion of the saint and a buck on the saint's commemoration day. The carcass was offered before the high altar to the canons, who wore garlands of flowers on their heads, while the antlers were borne around the cathedral on a spear to the accompaniment of hunting horns.[15]

The noblest form of hunting proceeded *par force de chiens*, 'by the strength of hounds'. It differed from bow and stable hunting in that it hunted a single quarry and the place of killing was not fixed, as it depended upon the skill of the hunter and the wit and stamina of the beast. Hart, boar and fox were taken in this way. On the eve of a planned hunt a single suitable beast was harboured, using a lymer, by noting animal tracks and excrement. In this way prey such as a hart could be established and distinguished from other lesser deer. This was followed by a gathering, a partly social occasion where the huntsmen agreed on their strategy for the morning. According to the location of the prey, small packs of hounds were positioned in separate relays according to the probable flight of the animal when the hounds were set upon it. This required specially acquired skills in anticipating an animal's movements and intimate knowledge of the lie of the land. The hunt proper began when the senior huntsman, the master of game, was taken with the lymerer and his hound to relocate the prey, with a pack of hounds behind ready to be uncoupled once the beast had been found. Success now depended upon the hounds, but the huntsmen could convey information to other relays of hounds by blowing of horns, which increased the general euphoria and was intended to encourage the hounds already in pursuit. When a hart was pursued, the animal's physical resources gradually ebbed away until it could run no further. The final confrontation occurred when it turned 'at bay' to confront the hounds, which was signalled by the huntsmen blowing horns, telling others who had not kept up with the chase to gather for the kill. The killing was usually postponed until the lord, or master of game, was present. At this point an exhausted hart was still capable of killing a hound. Killing it with a sword required considerable courage from a dismounted huntsman. To lessen the danger it was sometimes hamstrung first, with the huntsman approaching from the rear while the hart was preoccupied with the hounds, and severing one of the main tendons in its rear leg. When the hart lay dead the hunters blew the death.

In pursuit of a boar more hounds were recommended, due to the boar's ferocity, and the kill was a far more dangerous proposition. Once the boar had been cornered, or driven into a stream, the huntsman dismounted. A short duel followed that required more courage than jousting and quicker wits. The boar charged and was usually killed with a spear thrust into his head, although the huntsman risked death or serious injury if he missed his target or only managed to wound the beast. Of the other animal commonly hunted *par force*, foxes were taken down by the hounds.

The unmaking of a slaughtered beast was one of the most ritualized aspects of hunting. A hart was not simply handed to a butcher for dismembering. A nobleman's hunt had social and political connotations far exceeding the quest for food, and these had to be acknowledged in the hunting protocol. Moreover, the carcass was treated with the care and respect accorded to a worthy opponent that had usually tested the wit and the stamina of the hunters and hounds. The English method described in *The Master of Game* saw the hart turned on its back with its antlers in the earth, when the throat was slit up the length of the neck and flaps of flesh were cut on each side. At the blowing of the death the hounds bayed the dead animal and then were briefly allowed to tear at the flesh of the neck before being coupled up again. The purpose of the 'abay' was to reinforce the hunting instincts of the hounds. The dead animal was carefully cut up, using special hunting cutlery, into joints of meat, while the offal was kept separate. The ritual rewarding of the hounds was known as the *curée*, the origin of the English word 'quarry'. Hounds were fed the offal and bread soaked in blood. The lymer was rewarded separately and was usually allowed to gnaw flesh from the head. The unmaking of a boar proceeded slightly differently. Its head was severed and the blood retained. It was then trussed up over a fire to burn off its bristles before its testicles were removed. Then its belly was sliced and the internal organs extracted. Offal was sometimes reserved for the kitchen but was rightly the reward of the hounds, although (unlike deer's flesh) the offal was usually cooked before it was fed to them.

Kings have always enjoyed a reputation for being passionate hunters, especially during the eleventh and twelfth centuries, up to the accession in 1189 of Richard I, a crusading rather than a hunting king. Walter Map described Henry II as 'most knowledgeable about dogs and birds, and a keen follower of hounds'. Gerald of Wales described him as 'addicted to the chase beyond measure. At crack of dawn he was off on horseback, traversing the wilderness, plunging into woods and climbing mountain tops.' More critical was William of Newburgh, who said that Henry II 'delighted in the pleasure of hunting as much as his grandfather, and more than was right.'

Hunting was dangerous and the forests claimed the lives of a number of the aristocracy. Richard, the second eldest son of William the Conqueror, was killed in a hunting accident probably in his late teens in the early 1070s, and before he had been knighted. The accident occurred while chasing stags, and was possibly caused by collision with the low branch of a tree. Another Richard, the grandson of William the Conqueror and the bastard son of Robert, duke of Normandy, was also killed in the New Forest.[16] According to Orderic Vitalis, a monk of St-Evroul, Richard was part of a large party hunting deer by 'bow and stable'. He was accidentally struck by an arrow fired by an unnamed archer, who is said to have fled immediately to the Cluniac priory of Lewes where he became a monk, in part to expiate the sin of killing a man, but also to protect himself from the revenge of Richard's kinsmen.

The most illustrious victim of the New Forest was William the Conqueror's third son William Rufus, king of England from 1087 to 1100.[17] William was hunting in a wood with an entourage that included his younger brother and successor to the throne, Henry. They were hunting stags by the 'bow and stable' method, and were probably dismounted. Apparently William was pierced through the heart by a stray arrow, although a more mundane but less plausible explanation, offered at the time by Eadmer in his *Historia novorum in Anglia*, is that he stumbled and fell on the arrow. William of Malmesbury, writing in the period 1118–25, was the first author to name the killer as Walter Tirel, the count of Poix and a visitor from France. Because Walter fled in fear, and no one else saw the exact circumstances of the event, speculation was encouraged that William's death was contrived, perhaps a baronial conspiracy to promote the interest of Henry. Henry, however, did not reward Walter for any 'mistake'.

It was said that William II had died without having confessed or having been shriven, a fate worse than dying in battle. According to William of Malmesbury, the death had been foretold by a monk and was told to Robert Fitzhaimo, one of the king's barons, but the portent failed to dissuade the king and his entourage from going out into the woods. Orderic said that, immediately before William set out on his fateful afternoon's hunt, a letter written by Abbot Serlo of Gloucester arrived saying that the king's imminent death was intended by God as a punishment for his treatment of the church. The scene, if true, portrays William in the guise of the knight of popular romance who is warned of his impending fate, but for whom retreat was unthinkable. William II's death in the New Forest was also popularly attributed to divine retribution for the unjust manner in which the forest was created by his father. But by comparison with other fatalities in the woods, the death of William II was unremarkable. For example, the earliest accounts of his death are similar to accounts of the death in 1143 of Miles of Gloucester, the new earl of Hereford, also shot through the heart by an arrow fired by a companion, who died immediately without the chance to confess his sins.

Hunting was a man's world. Women were occasionally known to

shoot stags with longbows in game parks, but many huntsmen were dismissive of so contrived a pursuit. Women took a greater part in falconry. The woman's role in hunting was otherwise peripheral and was usually to be presented with the spoils. Hunting was a form of escape that stimulated male comradeship and confined women to the realm of the court. The erotic symbolism of the chase and the predatory nature of the hunter also had obvious sexual connotations, but these confirmed it as essentially a male rite and as a test of manhood. Richard Fitznigel, in his *Dialogue of the Exchequer* written in the late twelfth century, described the forests as

> the privy places of kings and their great delight. Thither they go for hunting, and having laid aside their cares, to enjoy a little quiet. There, away from the continuous business and incessant turmoil of the court, they may for a little time breathe in the gracious freedom of nature.[18]

Hunting was an attractive pastime for men who liked male company. Variations in the style and jargon of a hunt also bespoke a man's social status. In hunting class would invariably out:

> all men of worshyp may discover a jantylman frome a yoman and a yoman from a vylayne. For he that jantyll is woll drawe hym to jantyll tacchis [habits] and to folow the noble customys of jantylmen.[19]

Kings were drawn to the hunt in part to assert mastery over nature and its wild beasts. Contemporary literature is peopled with heroes like Arthur and Beowulf grappling with monsters and giants, and medieval kings and the aristocracy inherited and lived up to this tradition. The complex rituals that accompanied the hunt, in contrast to the matter of fact approach to hunting and poaching of common men, set the formal hunt apart and elevated the huntsman to a more noble status. Dominion over the forest placed kings at the head of the natural order, and set them apart from other men as divinely ordained individuals. They also hunted to test their mettle and to hone their martial skills. Classical authors such as Xenophon had regarded hunting as important training for war and medieval authors reiterated the parallel. It built up men's stamina for marching and for bearing arms, it hardened them to operating in inclement conditions, and familiarized them with working according to a collective strategy that was an essential requirement of military fieldcraft. Hunting developed the attributes of hardiness, courage, mental alertness, strategy and physical fitness. Hunting boars reproduced individual combat in a context of real danger.

The minority of voices that disapproved of hunting reveals an ambivalence towards nature in the medieval mind. By the twelfth century the church officially disapproved of hunting as a low pursuit, even though many senior clergy had aristocratic backgrounds and were hunters by inclination and upbringing. Hunting bespoke a warrior king not a philosopher king. The church may have had its own axe to grind, in its dislike of restrictive forest laws and the overriding of its rights as a landowner, but the degree to which clergymen could despise the hunter is demonstrated by the *Policraticus* of John of Salisbury, completed in 1159. Huntsmen were condemned by John as semi-beasts, like centaurs, and little better than the animals they hunted. Huntsmen, he claimed, were notoriously coarse in behaviour and never sober: how could a man who combined such behaviour with butchery, beheading his victims and hoisting them on sticks as a trophy, aspire to rule a realm of civilized beings? Furthermore, how could a king be so presumptuous to claim that the trees and wild animals in the forest were his private property, since only God could claim dominion over nature? [20] John was not arguing as a modern conservationist might, since clergymen did not doubt that wild beasts were put on the Earth for men to eat. He was attacking the king's delight in what was gruesome and unbecoming. Hunting revealed men as beings of nature, but so bloody a sport pursued gratuitously beyond the need for nourishment contradicted civilized values.

In the medieval imagination stags and boars represented more than simply venison and bacon. All beasts were imbued with moral attributes in the anthropomorphizing medieval mind, and to all beasts were attributed mythical or magical properties, as set out in the bestiaries. It is not difficult to understand medieval antipathy towards the wolf and the fox, both of whom devoured domesticated animals and fowl. Wolves were also reputed to eat children and devour corpses strewn on battlefields. The bestiaries went further: 'The wolf is the Devil, who is always envious of mankind, and continually prowls round the sheepfolds of the church's believers, to kill their souls and to corrupt them.' It was believed that a wolf's eyes shone in the dark, a reminder that to blind and foolish men the Devil's works look beautiful.[21] The fox was similarly associated with the Devil by interpretation of its behaviour. For example, it never ran in a straight line, typical of the Devil's devious ways, and it feigned death in a ruse to attract unsuspecting prey, just as the Devil ensnared the souls of unwary men.[22] One of the common representations of the fox in medieval art is found on misericords at Bristol Cathedral and bench-ends at the church of Brent Knoll, Somerset. A fox dressed in clerical garb is preaching to gullible ducks and geese, a typical ruse to catch unsuspecting prey and a satire on deceitful preachers.

It has been argued that the boar was a cult animal in the Germanic areas of pre-Christian Europe and that the association of the boar's head with Christmas is a relic of that earlier cult. It may have been believed that a man would take on the strength of the boar by eating him, and that a man consuming the boar's testicles would inherit the beast's rapacious sexuality.[23] Some of this may have persisted in the middle ages, but the boar was an antipathetic creature in Christian doctrine. Again, according to the bestiaries, the boar's moral disposition was detectable in his behaviour. His fierceness meant that he was equated with the Devil, and he lived in the woods because he was wild and unruly by nature. The boar's tendency to root in the ground symbolized those who sought earthly pleasures, and wallowing in mud symbolized those who wallowed in sin, neglecting the spiritual cleansing of penance.[24] Other animals had virtuous qualities. When pursued by huntsmen, a beaver would bite off its testicles and throw them in front of the hunters, thereby cutting itself off from shameless deeds and throwing vice in the face of the Devil.

The noblest of the woodland beasts was the hart, which was a stag over five years of age that bore at least ten tines on his antlers. A solitary animal during the hunting season, the hart was considered to combine innocence with guile and to provide the huntsmen with a cerebral as well as physical challenge. Its virtuous qualities posed a contradiction in the desire to hunt and kill it. The hart was supposed to have a bone in its heart (in fact a mass of gristle) that prevented it from dying of fear. (This was given to pregnant women or children as an amulet.) The hart's flight from the hounds symbolized the escape of men from the Devil, while the ten branches on its antlers recalled the Ten Commandments. The wounded hart was also associated with Christ's passion, which identified the hunters with persecuting Jews. A hart is central to the apocryphal story of St Eustace, one of the most popular of medieval saints. A Roman general called Placidas was separated from his fellows when he saw and pursued a smooth and shining hart that led him deeper into the forest. Here the hart revealed himself as Christ through the image of a bright shining cross between his antlers. Placidus was immediately converted and renounced his former life by changing his name to Eustace. In the later medieval period the same legend was attributed to St Hubert, an eighth-century bishop of Maastricht and Liège. Both Eustace and Hubert were patron saints of hunters.[25] In a related story David I of Scotland (1124–53), while hunting in the Forest of Drumselth, was attacked on his horse by a hart. Falling to the ground the king clasped a cross between the hart's antlers and was unharmed. In thanks for his deliverance he founded Holyrood Abbey on the very spot.[26]

A popular myth repeated in hunting treatises was that a hart could live for centuries and was capable of renewing itself. Nicholas Upton, a fifteenth-century canon of Salisbury and Wells, claimed that a stag killed in Windsor Forest bore a collar with the name Julius Caesar.[27] Its longevity entailed the ability to eat a snake then hasten to a spring and drink from it, which would revitalize the hart by restoring its youthful appearance. This drew the religious comparison that the hart was Christ himself and the serpent was Satan.

In an environment where a hart possessed magical powers, a medieval hunter might not have been surprized to encounter another beast, the unicorn. In medieval art the unicorn's habitat is invariably wooded. The animal had been described in the *Physiologus*, a Greek work compiled in Alexandria between the second and fifth centuries, from which the bestiaries took much of their information on the more exotic creatures of the world. The mythical unicorn, portrayed as a small goat-like creature with a horn in the middle of its brow, was said to be impossible to capture by conventional hunting techniques. The only successful strategy was to leave a virgin in the forest. As soon as the unicorn saw her he laid his horn in her lap and went to sleep, allowing the hunters to creep out from behind the trees and take him. In the bestiaries the surrender of the unicorn to the maiden symbolized the Incarnation of Christ in the Virgin's womb. (The sexual connotation of the virgin and the unicorn's phallic horn is a twentieth-century interpretation.) At the same time the vulnerability of Christ as the hart was signified by the fact that he was hunted down and killed by the Jews, here represented by the huntsmen.

Attitudes and beliefs about the mythical unicorn and the hart reveal the many-layered meanings of the medieval world, and the facility of the medieval mind for assimilating conflicting symbolism. The hart represented venison, a cerebral and physical challenge, and was killed despite its strong identification with Christ. In literature it was a beast into which humans were regularly transformed. White harts were usually supernatural beings – Richard II (1377–99) adopted the white hart as his personal badge, following his mother whose badge was a white hind. The hart was at the same time real, supernatural and magical, and the forest was where these states of being coexisted and interacted, and where men met their most daunting challenges in pursuit of them.

4

Exiles

The theme of the forest as the threshold to the otherworld is amplified
by medieval romances, where woody places are the landscape of adventure and self-discovery. Typically a knight errant in the forest rose
to the challenge or surrendered to his fate, and those men who emerged
again were different from the men who entered it. The forest in these
romances is poised between reality and imagination, a place where
medieval authors mixed up the commonplace and strange in order to
exile their heroes from the here and now into a realm of uncertainty.
Medieval authors did not need to rely on their direct experience of
trees and woods, however, as the symbolism of the forest was informed
by external influences such as the Bible and classical literature. Biblical
sources helped to define the significance of wild places in a Christian
society. Christ spent forty days and forty nights in the wilderness, a
rocky desert beyond the boundary of cultivation and exterior to society.
The desert was the opposite of the city, just as in medieval Europe the
forest was the opposite of the court. Medieval authors therefore treated
the uncultivated woods as the equivalent of the biblical desert, which
added a spiritual dimension to native woodland as a place of exile,
solitude and divine inspiration.

Lives of saints such as Paul, and the 'desert fathers' such as Anthony,
tell of hardships endured in the biblical desert, and of robbers and wild
beasts, while their hagiographer Jerome described such places as the
haunt of madmen.[1] St Matthew's Gospel describes the desert as the
home of the Devil and it therefore became a place where a man could
overcome the ultimate temptation. The life of isolation and physical
hardship tested a man's faith and ultimately could lead to greater
spiritual enlightenment. Such people were considered to be closer to
God. St Augustine wrote of enormous forests 'full of snares and dangers',
where 'many are the temptations which I have cut off and thrust away

from my heart'.[2] William of Malmesbury described these shaded places as where the Devil confronted travelling men, a theme which Chaucer drew upon in the 'Friar's Tale'. A corrupt summoner falls victim to the Devil's hunt after encountering in the woods

> A gay yeman, under a forest syde.
> A bowe he bar, and arwes brighte and kene;
> He hadde upon a courtepy of grene,
> An hat upon his heed with frenges blake.

It is a cautionary tale that warns how the Devil can entrap unwary souls by his disguises. The idyllic woodland setting was typically fertile ground where the devout could be caught off their guard, and therefore should be approached with special vigilance. The summoner rides off with the huntsman 'under the grene-wode shawe', which turns into an other-world where the summoner falls victim to the Devil:

> Thou shalt with me to helle yet to-nyght,
> Where thou shalt knowen of oure privetee
> Moore than a maister of dyvynytee.[3]

Belief in exile and hardship for the health of the soul inspired early monastic orders. The fifth-century Celtic saint Brioc is credited with founding a monastery in an isolated forest in his native Ceredigion. In his Life we learn that he and his brethren cut down trees, rooted up bushes and tore out brambles and tangled thorns to create a clearing in the forest. Here the self-contained, alternative society of the monastery was established. Followers of eremitic lives were equally drawn to the exile offered by the woods, but it did not represent a return to nature as we would understand it today. Living in a cave or a tree, or in the case of Simon Stylites atop a pillar, or even on an island off the windswept Atlantic coast of Ireland, in a regime of strict asceticism and divorced from human society was not a natural way of life. As a way to spiritual fulfilment it took a mystical rather than an intellectual path. Bernard of Clairvaux, founder of the Cistercian Order, wrote that 'you will find something more in the forests than in books'.[4] The middle ages saw hermits and anchorites take to the woods in search of closer communication with God. The Benedictine abbot St Romuald (c. 950–1027) was said to have been drawn to the eremitic life by his delight in the freshness of the forests.

These men needed practical skills as well. The eleventh-century St Theobold of Provins, who later became the patron saint of charcoal burners, built himself a cell in the forest in Luxembourg, living a life of simplicity and undertaking manual work for local villagers.[5] The best known of the English woodland hermits was Robert of Knaresborough (1160–1218), who lived for most of his life in a cave, although he was given land by King John free of tithe and lived for part of his life with a companion. Hainault and Writtle Forests in Essex both had official hermits by the twelfth century. Henry II endowed a solitary Cluniac monk in Writtle Forest, later adding a second. They were granted a small farm and were required to beseech God for the salvation of the reigning king and to pray for the souls of departed kings.

As a locus of exile, escape, penance and vision the forests were taken up by medieval Christian authors. King Nebuchadnezzar had been banished to the wilderness to live as an ox, a punishment for his overweening pride, but the desert was transposed to the forest in the version of the story included in the *Confessio Amantis* by John Gower of 1390. Ælfric's sermon on the Epiphany describes John the Baptist in exile living on wild honey and the fruits of the forest and not the diet of locusts and wild honey described in the Gospel of St Mark. In Geoffrey of Monmouth's *Life of Merlin* of *c.* 1150, Merlin was a king of South Wales who withdrew to the forest in remorse for his comrades slain in a battle with Peredur, king of North Wales. Grief-stricken and overcome by madness, he hid in the forest and fed on its fruits and berries. Disillusioned with the world of men, his exile represented a penance for the failures of a society whose flaws only Merlin had recognized. His rehabilitation began after his meeting with a minstrel, music being a common symbol of order and thus civilization in the wilderness, but on his return to the court he was still troubled by its hypocrisy and corruption. Merlin therefore established an alternative court in the forest, where proximity to nature and its moral lessons nourished his spiritual revival. Originally alone, like a hermit, Merlin's hall was the secular equivalent of a monastery and therefore his experiences embodied both the communal and solitary incarnations of the Christian wilderness tradition in a British greenwood setting.

In bringing a moral interpretation to woodland territory the biblical desert therefore made its most important contribution to the medieval romance tradition. Authors of these romances were avid readers of classical literature, particularly Virgil in the early medieval period and Ovid in the later. Platonic and neo-Platonic philosophies had linked forests with primordial matter and chaos, and further equated them with evil, in opposition to an ordered cosmos. It was a version of the forest that could readily be adapted to Christian thought. The allegorical association of the forest with savagery and untamed passion contingent upon this philosophy would also have been familiar to contemporary readers of Virgil.

Virgil's *Aeneid* was one of the most widely read classical texts in the medieval period. Virgil introduces 'the forest-clad mountainside, mysterious and dark' as the place of exile where Aeneas and his fellow Trojans land on the African coast after their escape from Troy. Here, in the dense forest, the goddess Juno orchestrates the lovemaking of Aeneas and Dido: they are out hunting when a storm breaks, scattering their retinues of hunters and beaters. They take shelter in a cave, a narrative device allowing the author to parallel the hunting of stags with an erotic quest.[6] But their brief passion is only possible in the forest refuge and soon Aeneas leaves Carthage on his quest to find Rome, leaving the distraught Dido to commit suicide. Later Aeneas visits the forest of Avernus, and is led by the doves of Venus to the Golden Bough, which he plucks in order to be admitted to the underworld. As in medieval texts, the forest is the place where a boundary is crossed to the underworld, although in the classical forest events are orchestrated by the gods, and in the medieval forests by lesser supernatural beings.

The gods also intervene in the forests of Ovid's *Metamorphoses*, where the characters are transformed into natural objects or animals, blurring the distinction between humans and nature. Actaeon, for example, mistakenly strays into Gargaphie, the sacred hunting ground of Diana, and sees the goddess of the wild woods bathing in a spring. Diana transforms him into a stag and plants fear in his heart, then sets him free but, before he has come to terms with his metamorphosis, he senses his own hounds in pursuit. Trapped inside his new body he is unable to tell them that he is their master and is torn to pieces.[7] Ovid's forests are places where protagonists fall prey to random misadventure, drawing on the Platonic concept of chaos. Elsewhere they are the settings of divine inspiration, populated by maenads and Muses, the equivalent to which in medieval romances are the supernatural fairies and dwarfs and their antics.

The influence of distinctly native concepts of the woods in English and Celtic romances, a highly stylised form of literature, is more difficult to pin down, apart from an intimate knowledge of hunting. But the influence of classical forms pervades nearly all native literature. The forest is not a central motif in *The Mabinogion*, yet it is the setting for pivotal events. Pwyll, prince of Dyfed, for example, is hunting in his own woods when he comes across the hunt of King Arawn, ruler of the underworld known as Annwn, where Pwyll sojourns for a year. Like the classical texts, the forest provides the setting for chance encounters that take the protagonists away from their everyday lives. Woodland is the gateway to a parallel reality of the underworld, but it is also a refuge where the real world is held in limbo. Like Aeneas and Dido, Tristan and Iseult find love in a forest refuge in one of the best known native Celtic tales. Tristan, the nephew of King Mark of England, is sent to Ireland to bring back the king's intended bride, Iseult. On the passage to England both Tristan and Iseult drink a love potion, intended for the king and his bride, and fall in love. Unable to conceal their affection at court, they are eventually exiled. In the two earliest known versions of the story, written in Old French in the second half of the twelfth century by Thomas and Beroul respectively, the exiled lovers take to the woods. They live freely in them having lived a lie at court. Symbolically their idyllic sojourn in the forest highlights the impossibility of their love at court, or in the real world. Love in the forest is like a holiday romance where normal rules are suspended, which parallels the romance of Aeneas and Dido.

As a literary motif the forest of medieval romance was fully developed in the works of Chrétien of Troyes, writing in the last quarter of the twelfth century. Chrétien's knights actively seek adventure in the forest in pursuit of personal fulfilment and their chivalric ideals. Chivalry is achieved by overcoming obstacles in the successful completion of a quest, desires that in the real world were satisfied by the Crusades and other foreign wars. Romance and crusading may have influenced each other, as romance inspired knights to look beyond the prosaic here and now in search of adventure.[8] In Chrétien's *Yvain*, the hero's quest is to win the hand of Laudine, but he cannot do this until he has proved himself in the forest. Calogrenant, one of Arthur's knights and Yvain's cousin, tells of his adventure in the Forest of Broceliande where he had met a wild man tending a herd of wild bulls, a pastoral scene which paralleled an everyday occurrence in the real world. In Calogrenant's description, the wild man is a kind of medieval Tarzan, untutored, hirsute and hideous, the antithesis of civilized man and the social contract of the court. He cannot understand Calogrenant's adventure in search of prowess and bravery because the wild man's own prowess and bravery are beyond question – he is able to grab a bull by the horns and have him meekly pleading for mercy. Up to a point the wild man is the knight stripped of his social graces, the essence which Calogrenant and Yvain are intent on discovering within themselves.

The wild man directs Calogrenant to a magic spring where he is challenged by a knight, Esclados le Roux, who chases him away. Seven years later Yvain takes the same path through the forest and avenges his cousin by mortally wounding the keeper of the spring. Yvain then woos and marries the widow of Esclados, Laudine. But by becoming engrossed in the tournaments of the rival court of Arthur, Yvain is accused of disloyalty and treachery to his wife. In his distress, Yvain immediately seeks the refuge of the forest, tearing his clothes off as he flees in a symbolic shedding of his courtly skin, and lives as a wild man of the woods. In his madness Yvain lives in the forest on a diet of raw venison, while metaphorically the forest echoes the desolation in the hero's own mind. This degeneration allows him to confront the beast at the core of the knightly self and is the prelude to Yvain's second quest to prove his love for Laudine. Once he has shrugged off his madness he becomes empowered, more heroic and virtuous than ever, battling against demons, and rescuing a lion by killing a serpent. Yvain tames the lion and becomes, in the subtitle of the story, the *Chevalier au Lion*, just as the wild man tended his herd of bulls, the difference between them being that Yvain's prowess has a moral bearing. Yvain's return to the court also fundamentally separates them. For a knight the forest can never be more than a temporary abode, and overcoming the challenge of the forest rehabilitates him for his proper domain, the court. The solitude of the forest therefore ultimately serves to confirm that man is a social being.

Hunting features as a central device in another of Chrétien's Arthurian romances, *Erec et Enide*. The story begins at Easter with Arthur's desire to revive an old custom, the hunt for the white hart, in which the knight who kills the hart is rewarded with a kiss from the fairest maiden. Erec, however, is waylaid by a knight, a lady and a dwarf, whom he follows with predictably unpredictable consequences. Hunting was also central to English romances such as *Sir Gawain and the Green Knight* and Malory's *Morte D'Arthur*. The anonymous tale of *Sir Orfeo*, written about 1330, is a retelling of a tale of Orpheus by Virgil and Ovid. It begins with the abduction of the wife of Sir Orfeo by the king of Faery, an abduction that takes place in a garden rather than a forest. In his grief Orfeo exiles himself to the lonely life of the forest, lives on fruit and grass, and sleeps in the hollow of a tree, while his body grows hairy like a wild man. As a penance, his exile is an eremitic withdrawal.

The forest is not, however, merely the landscape of exile. It is at the same time the parallel world of Faery where Orfeo sees the king of Faery enjoy pleasures in the forest: a landscape of sport with hunting horns, hounds and courtly rituals. But he remains a detached and powerless onlooker. It is only when Orfeo sees the faery falcons capture a fowl and, remembering his own love of hunting, he cheers, that he finds himself crossing the invisible threshold of the real to the otherworld. The otherworld is characterised by the beauty of its rival court, and there he wins back his wife in a reversal of the original abduction. The forest therefore again acts as a transitional space where the gateway to the otherworld has been found.

Sir Thomas Malory incorporated the established elements of romance forests into his *Morte D'Arthur*, written in the mid fifteenth century while this unchivalrous knight was serving a sentence for rape and armed assault, and published by William Caxton in 1485. It is a full reworking of Arthurian legends, incorporating the adventures of the knights of the Round Table, the quest for the Holy Grail and the romance of Tristram and Isode. The forest wears many guises and confronts those who enter it with unavoidable encounters. For Guinevere it seems a pastoral idyll where flowers are gathered on May Day, only for her to be deceived and abducted. Through Merlin it is a landscape of the supernatural, while for two of the knights, Balin and Balan, it is the landscape of their death, reinforcing the notion that the dangers of the forest can outweigh its enchantment. At various stages it is an exile for the maddened lovers Launcelot and Tristram, while it offers spiritual fulfilment to two former knights, Sir Brastias and Sir Perceval, who become hermits. The Grail quest represents a quest for spiritual fulfilment, where the most arduous path is taken as it symbolizes the difficulty of salvation. Here enchantment and trickery is the work of the Devil, but only the elect find suitable adventure in the Grail forest. For other knights of lesser moral worth, such as Gawain, the Grail forest remains barren.

Principally, however, Malory's forest is the landscape of the knight errant. Knights are men of action, epitomised by the 'Book of Sir Launcelot', which begins with the knight telling his nephew Sir Lyonell 'we must go to seek adventures', upon which 'they mounted on their horses, armed at all ryghtes, and rode into a depe foreste'.[9] It is a forest not peopled by charcoal burners and foresters, but by knights, dwarfs, hermits, damsels and white harts. Even damsels cannot lure Launcelot away from the domain where a knight must prove his worth: 'for to be a weddyd man, I think hit nat, for than I muste couche with hir and leve armys and turnamentis, batellys and adventures. And as for to sey to take my pleasaunce with peramours, that woll I refuse.'[10] As a knight, Launcelot is to a large extent defined by the forest, whose adventures are an end in themselves. He needs the forest and its challenges to uphold his chivalric status, and he needs frequent release from the social graces of the court. The latter need often leads him to disappear to the hermitage of Sir Brastias.

Although largely translated from French, Malory's own style and approach are evident, especially in his realistic portrayals of the forests and hunt. Contemporary readers would have relished such scenes as well as numerous references to real places – including Windsor and Sherwood Forests – structured around feast days such as Pentecost, Candlemas, Easter and Lady Day. By setting the stories in known places and around the Christian calendar, Malory made the world of myth seem closer to the world of the reader.

Hunting is a persistent theme in the work, allowing readers to envisage themselves in the desperate straits endured by the characters. Delight in the sport is personified by Tristram, born in the forest and described as 'the chief chacer of the worlde and the noblyst blower of an horne'. Normally a social pursuit, the rules of narrative require the protagonist to be separated from the hunting party because supernatural encounters only happen to solitary men. Early in the work, Arthur rides out hunting near his court at Caerleon after a night when he has dreamed portentously of slaying wild beasts. Here, having chased a hart until his horse collapses with exhaustion, he is suddenly alone and vulnerable as he awaits a fresh mount. It is the cue for a sequence of extraordinary events. First he hears a strange beast making a sound like thirty pairs of hounds. His instinct is to hunt it down, only to learn from King Pellinore, who has been pursuing the beast unsuccessfully for a year past, that to chase the 'questing beast' is futile. A curious amalgam of hunter and hunted, Pellinore's pointless pursuit amounts to a chase without any possibility of a kill, and yet he is unable to give it up. Then Arthur is visited twice by Merlin, disguised successively as a young boy and an old man. First the young man tells him who his real father is, even though he is seemingly too young to know Arthur's father; then the old man tells him he has sinned against God by unwittingly fathering a child by his sister.[11] Merlin is the symbol of the otherworld used throughout the narrative, and the enigmatic quality of his prophecy that Arthur is to die at the hands of treachery adds to the otherworldly tone.

Merlin presages another encounter with hunting and the otherworld later in the narrative of the Round Table. After the wedding of Arthur and Guinevere, Merlin tells the assembled knights that 'ye shall se a straunge and a mervailous adventure'. With that a white hart bounds into the hall pursued by a white brachet followed by thirty black running hounds. The hart leaps around the hall and out, and one of Arthur's knights follows the hounds in pursuit. Then a lady on a white palfrey enters the hall claiming the brachet as her own and that one of Arthur's knights has run off with it, only for another mysterious armed knight to appear and abduct the lady. It is one of the rare scenes in medieval literature where the forest and its supernatural cohorts invades the court. Arthur is not sorry to see the back of her – 'for she made such a noyse' – but Merlin decides that the matter is not closed.

A threefold quest ensues: Arthur sends Gawain to hunt the white hart, Sir Torre to bring back the white brachet, and King Pellinore to seek the lady and her abductor. In each of the three quests success is achieved only after they have slain the knights who challenge them. Gawain chases the hart across a river – another symbolic threshold to the otherworld

– and hunts it down in a castle, only to find that the hart belongs to the lord and was a gift from his lady. The lord reciprocates by slaying two of Gawain's greyhounds. Gawain retorts ironically that 'I wolde that ye had wrokyn youre angir uppon me rather than uppon a dome beste'. The supernatural brachet is also used as a device in the 'Book of Sir Launcelot', where he encounters the sinister black hound 'sekyng in maner as hit had bene in feaute [pursuit] of an hurte dere'. Launcelot does not otherwise hunt, but he follows the brachet, which is part of a scheme to entrap him by the sorceress Hallewes, and which takes him to encounters with ghostlike knights at the Chapel Perilous.

In the Quest of the Holy Grail, Sir Galahad, Bors and Perceval encounter religious magic in the forest. While they are chasing a white hart and four lions, the animals take refuge in a hermitage where a hermit is singing mass. The knights enter to hear the mass, where they see the hart transformed into a man, 'which mervayled hem'. Meanwhile the lions are changed into the forms of a man, eagle, lion and ox – emblems of the four Evangelists Matthew, Mark, Luke and John. They hear a voice say, 'in such maner entred the Sonne of God into the womb of the Maydyn Mary, whos virginité ne was perisshed'. The hermit explains to them the myth that a white hart can renew its own life and is therefore a symbol of Resurrection, 'and for that cause appered oure Lorde as a whyght harte'.[12]

The earlier *Sir Gawain and the Green Knight*, written by an unknown author in the late fourteenth century, shares some of Malory's themes, especially the use of real places as a setting that turn into otherworldly landscapes, and the importance to the narrative of hunting. The romance begins at Christmas in Arthur's court where a Green Knight enters the hall and challenges any knight to strike him a blow. The condition is that one year hence he will seek out the Green Knight in the 'green chapel' and take a reciprocal blow. Gawain takes up the challenge and decapitates the Green Knight, who simply picks up his head and rides off. Gawain then sets out in search of the green chapel, travelling across England and Wales, eventually reaching the forest of the Wirral where, when he finds a castle, he effectively crosses the threshold to an otherworld. The lord of the castle, Sir Bertilak de Hautdesert, welcomes him and tells him that the green chapel is nearby. For the next three days Gawain is a guest at the castle, but while the lord is out hunting Gawain is seduced by the châtelaine who steals into his chamber and kisses him. Gawain acknowledges this by kissing the lord on his return from the hunt, but on the third day she gives him a charm in the form of a girdle of green lace, which he conceals. In the final part Gawain enters the green chapel despite the dire warnings of the guide who takes him there. There he kneels and awaits the blow of the Green Knight, who mocks him. When the axe falls on Gawain, however, it merely grazes him. The Green Knight reveals himself as Sir Bertilak and Gawain learns that the test was contrived by his half-sister Morgan-le-Fay. Gawain has received only a slight wound for concealing the girdle of green lace and the compact is settled.

The extraordinary entry of the knight into the new year's feast at Arthur's court, imitating the role of the king's champion at coronation feasts, is a dramatic symbol of the forest challenging the court. The Green Knight and his horse have a green hue and are dressed entirely in green, the colour of the woods, signifying to the court the colour of 'fantoum and fayrye'. The knight carries a holly branch, traditionally gathered at midwinter. His conduct is that of a civilized man, dressed appropriately in a tight-fitting cloak and mantle, while his horse has green saddle, stirrups and harness, all bedecked in green gems and enamel. But set against the trappings of the court, the manner in which he picks up his severed head and departs marks him as a man from a supernatural world. Efforts to equate the Green Knight with the green man of medieval ecclesiastical carvings fail on a number of counts, not least because the term 'green man' is of recent derivation and therefore fortuitous rather than meaningful. The Green Knight is not a spirit of nature or a vegetable god. He is clearly presented as an enigmatic figure, not one familiar to the knights or to the reader from medieval art, while the combination of his greenness and his sophisticated dress creates an ambiguous image to tantalize the reader. It is as a figure of the unknown that he is able to offer a suitable challenge to a knight of the Round Table.

Descriptions of the hardships of winter suffered by Gawain are followed by his arrival at the castle of Sir Bertilak, known as Hautdesert with significant wilderness connotations, where he passes imperceptibly into the otherworld. His sojourn in the castle is structured around the symbolism of the hunt. While Sir Bertilak hunts his prey, Lady Bertilak's quarry is Sir Gawain. A sharp contrast is drawn between the devout Sir Bertilak, rising early to hear mass before riding out hunting, and the dissolute Sir Gawain lounging in bed, his idleness leading him astray to affairs of the flesh. Hunting is portrayed with a verisimilitude that would have been appreciated by an audience of courtly status. On the first day deer are hunted using the bow and stable method, where Sir Bertilak rides with the hounds and is not a member of the line of archers. Only the hinds and does are killed, and are broken in the ritual manner prescribed in the hunting manuals. The stags and bucks go free because it is 'fermisoun', the close season. The next day his hounds chase a boar to a stream where Sir Bertilak dismounts and confronts the animal in the conventional manner, except that he brandishes a sword rather than the more usual spear described in the hunting manuals. Cornering the boar in a stream was a deliberate strategy that allowed the hunter to exploit the advantage of having longer legs. On the third day he is up at dawn and out hunting the fox. The author describes the long chase of the wily and courageous beast who refuses to yield until, exhausted, he is at last brought down and torn apart by the hounds.

When, finally, Gawain is taken to the green chapel he finds it is not a chapel at all. Rather, it is nothing but an old cave overgrown with grass, and so far from holy that 'Here myght aboute mydnight The Devel his matynes telle'.[13] Yet the Green Knight turns out not to be a devilish figure and the solution to the compact is not what the reader is led to expect. Honour is saved because Gawain courageously exposes himself to the blow of the axe. The Green Knight only admonishes Gawain for concealing the gift of the green girdle, on the basis that Gawain deceived him in order to uphold the virtue of Lady Bertilak. Whether in the guise of the Green Knight or Sir Bertilak, he is a moral figure and a model knight, pious, courteous, brave, vigorous and honest. The castle of Hautdesert is an alternative court offering a standard by which Arthur's court may be judged, and the forest is a landscape of natural justice, an idea which a contemporary readership would have easily understood.

5

Outlaws

One man's rebel is another man's champion of liberty. This dichotomy
was played out in British woods throughout most of the historic period,
since woodland both sheltered fugitives and provided a den for thieves
and the ideal terrain for ambush. The Roman army discovered this in
its Scottish campaign under Agricola when, as soon as the enemy made
a tactical retreat to the woods and the legionnaries and cavalry went
in after them, 'all the brave beasts charged at us' and the enemy 'rallied
and profited by their local knowledge to ambush the first rash pursuers'.[1]
Dense woodland formed a barrier against the expansion of the Anglo-
Saxon kingdoms, for example in the south east where the Weald formed
a frontier zone that effectively hemmed in the kingdoms of Kent and
Sussex. According to Gildas, the heavily-wooded Chilterns later became
an enclave of British resistance to Saxon domination. Much later, forest
felling was an important part of the strategy of Edward I in his campaigns
in Wales, beginning in 1277. Instructions were issued to clear all woodland in difficult mountain passes to remove any cover likely to be used
in ambush. Passes in upland west Wales were ordered to be cleared to
the width of a bow shot. In 1287 over three thousand English wood-
cutters, charcoal burners and diggers were ordered into Wales to carry
out an ambitious policy of clearance.[2]

The most famous product of medieval greenwood myths was Robin
Hood, but as late as the fourteenth century he was merely one among
many popular outlaws with adventurous tales to tell. An outlaw was an
individual who for a variety of reasons could not be brought to justice,
and was therefore placed outside of the protection of the law, with no
more rights than the wild beasts of the woods. And it was the woods,
or any other uncultivated places, that provided refuge for such people
who, stripped of their dignity, had the same price on their head as a
wolf. Although these men endured hardships, the precariousness of their

existence implied by the legal definition was misleading, especially when a pardon could be had at the right price. And who would dare claim a reward for killing an outlaw without fearing retribution from his associates?

One of the best-documented cases of medieval outlawry concerns the Leicestershire family of de Folville. Their exploits began in 1326 when Sir Eustace de Folville, in league with his brothers and a band of some fifty men, settled a family score by murdering Sir Roger Bellers, a baron of the exchequer. Not everyone threw up their hands in horror at this – Henry of Knighton, the chronicler of Leicester Abbey, thought that Sir Roger had received his just desserts. However, in proceedings instituted against the brothers they could not be apprehended and so a sentence of outlawry was passed. They became outlaws and for over five years lived by robbery and extortion – even though, after the murder of Edward II in 1327 and the accession of his son Edward III, they had been pardoned. Accounts of their exploits show them to have been well organised with their band of followers, living a peripatetic life, relying on the compliance of local communities. Their final and most audacious crime was the kidnapping in 1332 of Sir Richard Willoughby, a king's justice who had previously crossed the family's path. In planning the kidnap the Folvilles drew upon the assistance of another notorious local greenwood gang led by James Coterel. The widespread lack of sympathy for Willoughby among contemporaries can be read as a lack of respect for the law brought on by the corruption of its officials – Henry of Knighton considered the kidnap reasonable revenge on a corrupt man who was said to have sold justice like selling cattle. Of the ransom of 1300 marks, the Folvilles received only 300, the remainder being distributed among their associates and followers.[3]

Outlaws could make the innocent woods fearsome places to tread. The vulnerability of strangers in a wood was described in the fourteenth century by the Minorite friar Bartholomaeus Anglicus, who typically interpreted a walk in the woods as a cautionary tale against the devious schemes of the Devil in diverting souls from their true path:

> For often in woods thieves are hid, and often in their awaits and deceits passing men come and are spoiled and robbed and often slain. And so for many and diverse ways and uncertain men often err and go out of the way. And take uncertain way and the way that is unknown before the way that is

known and often come to the place these thieves lie in wait and not without peril. Therefore are often knots made on trees and in bushes in boughs and in branches of trees in token and mark of the highway; to show the certain and sure way to wayfaring men. But often thieves in turning and meeting of ways change such knots and signs to beguile many men and bring them out of the right way by false tokens and signs.[4]

Roger Godberd, a Sherwood Forest outlaw of the 1260s, was said to have targeted priests for robbery and extortion. The most vulnerable strangers were merchants, but not all robbers were forced into crime by poverty. Sir Robert Rideware, of Rideware Parva in Staffordshire, seized a consignment of merchandise headed for Stafford market in an ambush in Cannock Wood in 1341. Rideware used two local priories as a refuge. Despite the king's bailiff recovering the booty in an armed struggle, Rideware obtained reinforcements and the assistance of his brother Sir Walter Rideware and retook it. The merchants were prevented from entering Stafford to make their complaint, and had to travel to Lichfield in order to alert the authorities. Robbery, with all its action and danger, was in some ways a parallel sport to hunting, one where knowledge of the local woods could be turned to advantage.

Whatever the reality, outlaws were easily turned into folk heroes. An early example was Hereward the Wake, a dispossessed Saxon earl in defiance of William the Conqueror. But Hereward's refuge was the marshy Isle of Ely, not the greenwood of his later counterparts. It was in the fourteenth and fifteenth centuries that woodland became firmly associated with outlaws, providing an additional layer of myth to green places. Hereward was of noble birth, as were Fulk Fitzwarin and Eustace the Monk, two of his most famous successors, a useful attribute for any greenwood hero. Here, of all places, natural leaders came to the fore, and the mythology accords with evidence that social hierarchy was maintained among criminals – the Folvilles and others did not lose any respect for their rank when they took to the woods.

Fulk Fitzwarin, of Whittington in Shropshire, was one of many unruly barons who quarrelled with King John, and in his case it led him to be put outside the law in about 1200. When he was pardoned, a year later, he was leading a band of thirty-eight men. Little more is known of his outlaw activities. The rest, including his transformation from brigand to romantic hero, is fictional and well developed in early fourteenth-century tales. Legends of Fulk see him roaming forests evading John's men, or as a guest in rival courts of Llywelyn of Wales or Philip Augustus of France. In various meetings he gets the better of the king, is able to draw upon many sympathisers, and takes refuge in the sanctuary of the church. Once he waylays the king's merchants in the Forest of Bradene and divests them of their cloth, which he uses to robe his motley band of followers. In another episode Fulk is in Windsor Forest when he hears that King John will be there hunting. So Fulk sets a trap, concealing his men ready to ambush the king once Fulk has led him away from his retinue. Disguised as a humble charcoal burner, Fulk throws himself at the feet of the king when he rides by, in ironic submission, and upon enquiry tells John that he has seen a stag and can lead the king to his lair. In a reversal of classic hunting technique, the king and three of his knights are detached from the main hunting party, driven to a predetermined location in the manner that deer were driven to a line of archers, and duly ambushed by Fulk's men. In a further reversal of roles, the king grovels to the charcoal burner for his life. Once the charcoal burner reveals himself as Fulk, John offers him forgiveness and the restoration of his rightful inheritance. The moral of the tale is simple, and the narrative archetypal. Disguises, mistaken identity and the reversal of roles describe the disorientating effect of the woods in human relations, and point to the ultimate reversal, that humble folk are more virtuous than their betters.

Legends surrounding William Wallace show him to have more in common with Robin Hood and other outlaws than with Scottish heroes like Robert the Bruce. William Wallace was a patriotic outlaw of the greenwood. The finest hour of the real William Wallace was victory over Edward I, who had claimed Scotland as a fiefdom of England, in 1297. When the Scottish aristocracy, mainly of Norman stock and holding land in England, was ready to accommodate the English king, Wallace stood out with his army of peasants for the independence of Scotland. He is also said to have slain the sheriff of Lanark in revenge for the execution by the English of his bride-to-be, who was found guilty of harbouring him. It made him a rebel and made his life suitably malleable for makeover as a greenwood hero. After his army was defeated at the battle of Falkirk in 1298, Wallace lost his pre-eminent position among the Scots but remained at large as an outlaw until he was tracked

down and executed by the English. This is what made him a martyr for
Scotland.

The William Wallace of myth grew up in fifteenth-century tales and
ballads, reaching their apogee in the late fifteenth century in the narrative
of a minstrel known as Blind Harry, and given a new lease of life in
the late twentieth century as Braveheart. In the poem of Blind Harry
he is seen waging a guerrilla war against the English, using the likes of
Shortwood Shaw, Methven Wood and the Forest of Clyde as cover, and
adopting various disguises to entrap servants of the English crown,
relying on the sympathies of local people to wrest him from trouble. It
is in the woodland haunts that Wallace is able to rally men behind him,
emphasising the association of wild nature with natural justice. Blind
Harry describes Wallace's life in the woods, its hardships and delights,
and of killing the king's venison. The greenwood gives him pleasures
superior to anything that money can buy. Like his later English counterpart, Wallace is generous to the local inhabitants, who in turn protect
him, while the spartan life makes him virtuous and wise. Many times
had Wallace given

> To pour and rych, upon a gudlye wis.
> Humyll he was, hardy, wis and free,
> As off rychess he held na propyrte.

But the romanticism is tempered by a narrative in which violence is
savoured in all its grisly detail and of the racial hatred of the hero:

> I lik bettir to se the Southren de [die]
> Than gold or land that thai can giff to me.[5]

William Wallace and Hereward the Wake were real men fighting
tyranny, but all outlaw ballads and tales had some suitable oppressor
to make their cause a just one. This covers other Scottish greenwood
outlaws including Murray of Ettrick forest, or Johnie Cock, an elusive
Border outlaw betrayed in a moment of vulnerability when he is discovered sleeping with his dogs in the woods and is hunted mercilessly
by the foresters.

A similar vein runs through the fourteenth-century *Tale of Gamelyn*.
The only written version of the story was found posthumously in the
possession of Geoffrey Chaucer, although it is not Chaucer's own work.

The hero Gamelyn is down a peg or two from the knights of medieval romance, and being of commoner stock is not privy to the world of damsels and white harts. Gamelyn's woods are real places where rain and hunger bring on more prosaic discomforts. Gamelyn is forced to take to the woods after a violent dispute with his unnamed malicious elder brother, with the sheriff in hot pursuit. Gamelyn and his loyal follower Adam the Spencer fall in with a band of outlaws, and before long Gamelyn is their king, his true integrity emerging in the greenwood where his rise to prominence reflects the natural order and hierarchy. Gamelyn eventually presents himself at the shire court where his other brother, Sir Ote, stands surety for him and Gamelyn is able to go free. When, however, Gamelyn's case is tried, the jury is packed with the elder brother's men and Sir Ote is sentenced to death. Gamelyn and his band of outlaws, however, have anticipated such a verdict. They enter the court and overthrow and bind the corrupt judge and false jurors. An alternative court is convened with the outlaws as jurors, and subsequently judge, sheriff and jurors are all hanged. The outlaws of the woods are therefore the champions of true justice and the corrupt officials are defeated. A similar moral lesson can be drawn from the tale of *Adam Bell, Clim of the Clough and William Cloudesley*, medieval in origin but known from two sixteenth-century versions. These 'yeomen of the north country' are outlaws living off the king's venison at Inglewood in Cumberland. Their triumph over false justice is a bloody affair; they make a personal appeal for pardons and delight in archery contests, all attributes in common with contemporary tales of Robin Hood.

The central theme of *Gamelyn* is the corruption of justice and of the unscrupulous greed of the wealthy, be they landowners or abbots, at the expense of the poor. The moral of all outlaw ballads is that the good win and evil is defeated. They celebrate the freedom of the individual against corrupt institutions. The individual prepared to stand up for justice will attract a loyal following or, to set it in its conservative guise, simple folk want moral leadership and are instinctively drawn to real against false leaders. They believe in social justice but do not trust the agents of its institutions to deliver it. Outlaw ballads therefore say as much about contemporary attitudes to the law as they do about greenwood idylls.

The independent spirit of the outlaws is characterized by their existence in the greenwood, where the ability to endure real hardships is a
badge of integrity. Greenwood men are not bound to one place like
other men; their peripatetic lives are more free than any other way of
life, and they enjoy the savour of unpredictability. Perhaps they convince
themselves that they live freely as men must have lived before they tilled
the soil. In their idealized form outlaws do not have property to emphasize their status and as barriers against congress with lower ranks,
nor do they dress differently to mark their status out to strangers. Unlike
other men, they live by their own efforts, share the fruits of their labour
in a spirit of comradeship and, like huntsmen, cannot be accused of the
sins of idleness or luxury. These qualities become more accentuated
when they are contrasted with officers of the law and high-ranking
churchmen, who abuse their privileges and treat justice as a commodity.

The outlaw leading a gang of men and at odds with the law's corrupt
officials is a recognizable medieval type. In taking from the rich he is
only doing what others called extortion when it was taken by real men.
The retributive violence in outlaw tales, which is so shocking to a
modern readership, would have seemed less so in a society where taking
the law into one's own hands was regarded as an ancient right. But in
order to portray justice in black and white it was necessary to set the
events of outlaw ballads safely in the distant past, which also had the
advantage that it offended no one. It is a social commonplace that the
past was more honourable than the present. It also created an important
historical perspective in which woodland landscapes were cast in contemporary culture.

Whoever the real Robin Hood was, or indeed if he ever existed, is beside
the point. His life is as nothing compared with his tales. The earliest
mention of him occurs *c.* 1377 in William Langland's *Piers Plowman*
where one of the characters, Sloth, declares his knowledge of rhymes of
Robin Hood, suggesting that they were already popular by that time.
The earliest surviving written tales of Robin Hood are *Robin Hood and
the Monk* of *c.* 1450 and *Robin Hood and the Potter* of the early sixteenth
century. The earliest printed work, *A Gest of Robyn Hode*, survives in
two versions of the early sixteenth century, one printed in Antwerp and
the other by the early English printer Wynkyn de Worde.

The character of Robin Hood in the early tales is quite different from that in the later legends. The scene is Barnsdale in South Yorkshire rather than Sherwood, there is no mention of Richard the Lionheart or his brother King John, and significantly there is no Maid Marian. There was no place for a real woman in outlaw tales, the greenwood being male territory in the same manner as the hunt. Instead Robin Hood is piously devoted to an ideal woman – the Virgin Mary – to whom the chapel founded by him at Barnsdale was dedicated, something which had more resonance to a medieval than a post-Reformation audience.

As poems they are relatively unsophisticated and draw on the popular morals of other outlaw literature. The narrative of the *Gest* is a rambling sequence of events tied together with a tenuous thread. Robin meets an ill-clad knight who has been obliged to mortgage his estates to the grasping abbot of St Mary, in order to secure a loan to bail the knight's son, who is charged with homicide. Robin lends him £400 to repay the abbot and much is made of the abbot's chagrin that the debt has been repaid and he will not be able to get his hands on the knight's property. In the final part of the poem Robin's men waylay a monk travelling in the woods who reluctantly agrees to be their guest at dinner. Revealed as the high cellarer of St Mary's Abbey, the monk pleads poverty when he is asked to make a contribution for his meal, but Little John opens his bag and finds £800. The monk is sent on his way penniless, while the outlaws have their loan repaid twofold. The attack on the monk requires some explanation to a modern audience, given Robin Hood's stated piety elsewhere in the tale. Monasteries, however, were popularly criticised for their excessive wealth and their power as landlords, and contrasted with members of mendicant orders like Friar Tuck who worked among the poor and lived humble lives.

It is always fair weather in the greenwood and the tales begin with stock praise of woody places on a sunny May morning. In this idyllic landscape the ultimate pleasure is the joy of archery. Archery is introduced in the *Gest* when Little John enters an archery contest at Nottingham disguised as Reynolde Greenlefe and proves to be a master of the art. Skill with the bow and arrow, and strength in one-to-one combat, is in direct proportion to the protagonists' real virtue. The archery contest is, in fact, a ruse used by the sheriff of Nottingham to lure Robin Hood to town. The sheriff of Nottingham is in turn lured to Robin's alternative greenwood court by the promise of good hunting. The fact that a single night sleeping rough is enough for the sheriff to long for the comfort of his bed is symbolic of his low moral status. When he is in the hands of Robin Hood the outlaw typically shows mercy, although he kills the sheriff later in the story:

> Robyn bent a full goode bowe,
> An arrowe he drowe at wyll;
> He hit so the proude sherife
> Upon the grounde he lay full still.[6]

Events reach a conclusion when the king comes to Barnsdale to hunt Robin. Disguised as a monk he enters the forest where Robin and his men find and entertain him with the characteristic generosity of green-wood men. They set up an archery contest at which, for once, Robin is bested by the monk. But the monk then reveals himself as the king and the outlaws immediately bow down before him. The king and Robin Hood return together to Nottingham in their Lincoln green and Robin enters the king's service. Here the *Gest* follows other outlaw ballads in its distrust not of the king but of the officials who operate in the king's name. The narrative ends when Robin Hood, dulled by the court, departs for the greenwood again, just as Sir Launcelot always chooses the adventure of the forest:

> Robyn slewe a full grete harte;
> His horne than gan he blow,
> That all the outlawes of that forest
> That horne coud they knowe.[7]

Robin Hood's devotion to the Virgin Mary comes to his rescue in another tale, *Robin Hood and Guy of Gisborne*, in which Guy is hunting the outlaw, and in combat Robin is wounded. Calling upon the Virgin, Robin is reinvigorated and is able to slay Guy. Subsequently, in one of the most gruesome scenes in the Robin Hood tales, Robin mutilates the head of Guy so that no one may recognise him. Robin then dresses in Guy's clothes and delivers the dead man to the sheriff claiming him to be Robin Hood. When Robin eventually makes himself known, the sheriff and his men realize that they are ambushed and try to flee, but the sheriff is slain by an arrow fired by Little John.

In none of the tales does Robin Hood take from the rich and give to the poor. In fact he is socially conservative in his respect for the church and the king. His justice is rough and ready, and retributive, very much in the spirit of the times. Nor in the tales is he a man of noble birth. His identification with Robert, earl of Huntingdon, was the invention of Andrew Munday in 1598 and prompted claims that an epitaph had been inscribed on his grave. A grave slab in the church-yard at Kirklees in Yorkshire is said to have commemorated Roberd Hude, although it was illegible by the eighteenth century. The setting of Robin Hood's life in the late twelfth-century heyday of Forest Law was introduced in 1521 by the Scots historian John Major. It was in the Tudor period that Robin Hood legends gathered pace, exactly in parallel with his growing popularity in English culture at the expense of the other outlaws of myth.

During the fifteenth century Robin Hood became an increasingly familiar figure at parochial summer festivities. Robin Hood plays were performed at many such events, and remind us that the *Gest* and other known tales were not the only versions of the stories. A surviving fragment of a Robin Hood play of *c.* 1475 is a variation on the story of Robin and Guy of Gisborne. Performed locally, however, there was plenty of opportunity for players to introduce episodes and innuendo relevant to local people and events. One of the earliest performances of a Robin Hood play is recorded at Exeter in 1427, indicating not so much the rise in popularity of Robin Hood but of summer gatherings at May Day, Whitsun and Midsummer. Robin Hood plays were performed at many market towns in southern England and to a lesser extent in the midlands, but ironically they were absent from the north of the England, the landscape in which they are set. Nevertheless they show clearly that Robin Hood had become a national institution by the fifteenth century, as do the many other undated associations of topographical features throughout England – Robin Hood's Butts, for example, became a popular name for groups of prehistoric round barrows. He even found favour in Scotland in the first half of the sixteenth century where he was also a familiar figure at summer festivities.

The purpose of staging Robin Hood plays was to raise money for the parish, but because it required a large cast of costumed characters they tended not to be performed by smaller parishes. Any Robin Hood play

'A Lyttel Geste of Robyn Hode', by Thomas Bewick, from Joseph Ritson, *Robin Hood* (1795).

must have been liberally spiced with violence and other action likely to raise excitement among the audience. What followed a performance was not always what the players bargained for and the parish did not always see the money that had been raised. In 1498 the corporation of Wells saw none of the money raised by the Robin Hood players. In the same year a serious riot followed a Robin Hood play at Willenhall in Staffordshire at which there were fatalities. The plays were banned in Exeter in the early sixteenth century on the basis that they promoted boisterous discontent.[8]

If a parish did not have the resources to stage a play, it might still be able to afford a costumed Robin Hood to preside over the summer games. The crowning of a 'mock king' was a feature of these games, at which a Robin Hood dressed in green was the perfect symbol of summer. Robin Hood may have appeared at the head of a parade, or might just have been a character mingling and raising money. Although his popularity had a peasant origin, Robin Hood was also able to amuse the royal court. In a highly staged event on May Day 1515, at Shooters Hill near London, Henry VIII and Catherine of Aragon witnessed a Robin

Hood extravaganza. They were greeted by two hundred men of the royal guard, dressed in Lincoln green, firing a volley of arrows in salute. Robin Hood, and his retinue of Little John, Friar Tuck, Maid Marian and Lady May, led the royal couple into the symbolic greenwood – woods with a specially constructed bower decorated with aromatic herbs – where they feasted on venison. It was perhaps the apogee of the festive culture of late medieval England that has been characterised as Merry England.[9] The greenwood was an integral component of Merry England, but in addition to outlaws and adventurous knights there was another dimension that influenced cultural associations of the greenwood. Woods were places of adventure, danger and natural justice, but they were also idyllic places of love and play.

6

Lovers

Hunting and adventure characterize the woodlands as a predominantly male domain, and a place where the Devil could test the mettle of the vulnerable. But there is a softer, less aggressive tradition of pastoral literature that shares much of the contrast between nature and the court. Some of the most memorable early writing in praise of nature comes not from sophisticated French romance but from Celtic Britain and Ireland, where the descriptive writing has the vividness of lived experience. In Ireland at least, the origin of this idyllic pastoral literature is religious, be it Christian or pagan, but it came to be much more than that. In a well-known ninth-century poem, probably written in Leinster, the 'scribe in the woods' was a monk:

> In a grey mantle the cuckoo's beautiful chant
> Sings to me from the tops of the bushes
> Truly, may the Lord protect me –
> I write well under the green wood.[1]

Paradise is a woodland filled with birdsong. This woodland literature concentrated upon early May, welcoming the beginning of summer when 'the harp of the wood plays melody, its music brings perfect peace', and when 'the vigour of men flourishes'.[2] In this landscape the woods are a benign place of common pleasures. Simple pleasures, too, as in the work of an anonymous tenth-century Irish author, written in the form of a dialogue between Marban the hermit and his brother Guaire, king of Connaught. Marban describes a plentiful and self-contained world of humility and simplicity that suggests the proper way to live in harmony with the world's creatures:

I have a hut in the woods, none knows it but my Lord; an ash tree this side, a hazel on the other, a great tree on a mound encloses it. Two heathery door posts for support, and a lintel of honeysuckle; around its close the wood

sheds its nuts upon fat swine. The size of my hut, small yet not small, a place
of familiar paths, the she-bird in its dress of blackbird colour sings a melodious
strain from its gable.

This is a place where the spring water is clear and fresh, the fox is not
a pest, where there are plenty of swine and deer to feed on, while the
summer provides abundant apples, strawberries, sloes, pignuts, mar-
joram and watercress. Many of the trees, like the hazel, ash and yew,
surrounding the hermitage have otherworld associations while in the
'great tree on a mound' the hermitage has its own guardian tree. It is
a God-given place and offers a life of peace and fruitfulness that is
normally associated with kings. He has his own musicians in the birds,
the wind in the trees and the swarming bees, where a king would have
to pay for such entertainment. In the end, Guaire declares his envy of
Marban, who is as rich as any king could ever hope to be.[3]

The pleasure taken in trees for their own sake was not of course an
exclusively Celtic phenomenon. Pliny wrote that in imperial Roman
society less reverence was paid to ivory and gold images than to the
forests and to forest silence. Irish literature is similarly reverential.
Suibhne (or Sweeney) was a king in north-eastern Ireland who in 637
attacked St Ronan as he was building a church on his territory. Ronan
cursed him and Suibhne was turned into a bird and fled. He lived for
many years as a wild man before his conversion, but even afterwards
preferred birdsong to church bells and the majesty of the woods to the
ceremony of the mass. A passage from *Suibhne the Wild Man of the
Forest*, written in the twelfth century, hails the forest trees:

> Oak, bushy, leafy, you are high above trees; hazel bush, little
>   branchy one, coffer of hazel nuts ...
> Holly, little shelterer, door against the winds; ash tree, baneful,
>   weapon in the hand of a warrior.
> Birch, smooth, blessed, proud, melodious, lovely is each entangled
>   branch at the top of your crest.[4]

It is not always summer, however, and 'dismal is this life, without a
soft bed' for the wild man 'enduring the shower, stepping along deer
paths, traversing greenswards on a morning of raw frost'.[5] But at least
these were natural hardships, not ones created by human or supernatural
agencies. This strain of writing is full of longing and establishes that for

a person with adequate sensitivity the woodlands were an emotional rather than an intellectual or a magical experience. As such they became the special domain of lovers in medieval literature, nowhere better represented than in the work of Dafydd ap Gwilym.

The literary career of Dafydd ap Gwilym was confined to the middle years of the fourteenth century and, unlike his Celtic predecessors, Dafydd was a bard rather than a monk. His themes are universal themes – the praise of women and nature – and his influences widespread across Romance literature, including Provencal lyrics. The love theme is developed in the idealized setting of the woods, but as often as not the woodland, with its animals and birds, is the real subject. 'To May and January' praises nature in early summer and reinvigorates the author emotionally after the long winter, which leads inevitably to the matter of his love for Morfydd. The May and greenwood is especially associated with lovers, giving a clue to the ensuing nostalgia that images and memories of the greenwood would later inspire:

> A thick shade, clothing the highways, has draped every place in its green web; when the battle with the frost is over, and it comes like a close-leafed canopy over the meadow hedges, the paths of May will be green in the place of April, and the birds will celebrate for me their twittering service. There will come on the highest crest of oak trees the songs of young birds, and the cuckoo on the heights in every domain, and the warbling bird and the glad long day, and white haze after the wind covering the midst of the valley, and bright sky in the gay afternoon, and lovely trees, and grey gossamer, and many birds in the woods, and green leaves on the tree branches; and there will be memories, Morfydd, my golden girl, and a manifold awakening of love. How unlike the black wrathful month which rebukes everyone for loving; which brings dismal rain and short days, and wind to strip the trees ...[6]

In a fuller passage by Dafydd ap Gwilym, the birch, a native and common Welsh tree, is developed as the lovers' meeting place. He eschews the stylised images of the greenwood of romance literature for the freshness of his own experience:

> The happy birch wood is a good place to wait for my day-bright girl; a place of quick paths, green tracks of lovely colour, with a veil of shining leaves on the fine boughs; a sheltered place for my gold-clad lady, a lawful place for the thrush on the tree, a lovely place on the hillside, a place of green treetops,

a place for two in spite of the cuckold's wrath; a concealing veil for a girl and her lover, full of fame is the greenwood; a place where the slender gentle girl, my love, will come to the leafy house made by God the Father. I have found for the building a kind of warden, the nightingale of glorious song under the greenwood, in his fine tawny dress in the leafy grove; a symbol of woodland delight, a forester always in the copse guarding the tree tops on the skirt of the slope. I shall make us a new room in the grove, fine and free, with a green top-storey of birches of lovely hue, and a summer-house and a fine bed, a parlour of the bright green trees, a glorious domain on the fringe of the green meadow. An enclosure of birches shall be maintained, with corner seats in the greenwood; a chapel of the lovely branches would not displease me, of the leaves of the green hazels, the mantles of May. The fine trees shall be a solace, a soot-free house for us today.[7]

As a special place for lovers the woodland suspends the normal rules of the world and is immune from all influence of society. As Tristan and Iseult, and Aeneas and Dido found out, it is a refuge from the world and its slanders, an earthly paradise from which a return to the real world can only be a descent. In such a place no one is anyone, social graces can be cast aside and there is no deference. Romance can flourish in a pure form, its naturalness symbolized by contemporary authors in the planting of trees and entwined boughs. In the words of Dafydd ap Gwilym again:

It was delightful for us a while, my girl, to pass our lives under the same birch grove; to dally in the secluded wood – the more delightful; together to lie hidden, together to range the seashore, together to linger at the woodland's edge, together to plant birch trees (oh happy labour!), together to entwine the shapely plumage of the boughs, together with my slender girl to tell of love, together to look out on the lonely field. A blameless art it is for my girl to walk the wood together with her lover, to keep countenance, to smile together, to laugh together lip to lip, together to lay us down by the grove, together to shun the crowd, together to lament our lot, together to pass time pleasantly, together to drink mead, together to make love, together to lie, together to maintain our true stealthy passion.[8]

Such intimacy was rare in medieval life, during which time activities whether religious or secular were nearly always communal. Nevertheless love was one of the principal sub-plots of the communal May festival that marked the beginning of summer in the medieval period. The

festival had a much earlier vintage as the Celtic festival of Beltane, which
has encouraged writers since James Frazer to conceive it as the remnant
of a prehistoric tradition. In fact there was no unbroken tradition in
England, while in Celtic Britain and Ireland Beltane continued in a
sporadic and reduced form as a fire festival, where purification by fire
protected animals from supernatural forces. May festivals enjoyed a
revival in England from at least the middle of the thirteenth century
when Bishop Grosseteste of Lincoln complained to his archdeacons
about priests joining in May games. These festivities had a distinctly
medieval character and their revival should be explained in social rather
than religious terms. The practice was sufficiently established by the
fourteenth century for it to be an effective literary device used by
Chaucer, and later by Malory and others. In 'The Knight's Tale', for
example, the heroine Emelie picks flowers on May Day morning to
make a garland for her hair. Meanwhile the hero Arcite observes May
Day by riding from the court into the woods:

> By adventure his wey he gan to holde
> To maken hym a gerland of the greves,
> Were it of wodebynde or hawethorn leves,
> And loude he song ayeyn the sonne shene:
> 'May, with alle thy floures and thy grene,
> Welcome be thou, faire, fresshe May.' [9]

Apart from their social significance in celebrating the life of the
community, May festivities also suspended the routine of everyday life,
allowing people to dress themselves and their homes in the guise of the
greenwood. Festivities included the appearance of May Queens and
figures dressed as Robin Hood, Maid Marian and Little John, as well
as St George. May ales and May games were organized on a parochial
basis and were an important source of parish revenue. Furthermore they
were not confined to the beginning of May, as they could be held at
any time during the early summer months from May to July. Nor were
they confined to rural parishes, as they were held regularly in Oxford,
Salisbury and York and less commonly in other towns, including Bristol
and London.

It was the custom for parishioners to go out to the nearest woods on
the morning of the festival to gather flowers and greenery with which

to deck their homes and streets, although greenery was never taken inside the house. This was known as bringing in the May and could be an elaborate affair, as in Exeter where in the 1440s the city council provided a platform for setting up an arbour. At St Andrews University it had been the custom for tutors and students to bring in the May disguised as monarchs, something which was condemned in 1432. The blossoming hawthorn was the most common form of greenery collected, from which it derived its alternative name of May tree. The tree was commonly associated with love, while in May it was claimed, in the words of a fourteenth-century lyric, that 'the hawthorn blows the sweetest of every kind of tree'. Elsewhere other species were favoured, such as the birch in Wales and the sycamore in Cornwall, while other forms of blossom were also popular.[10]

Dawn expeditions were community affairs and centred upon the young. They specifically allowed young people their own space within the structure of a ritualized event, within which they could pursue their own affairs. In the late sixteenth century John Stow recalled Londoners returning with maypoles, and of May games during daytime, followed towards evening with plays and bonfires. At the beginning of summer able-bodied Londoners would habitually 'walk into the sweet meadows and green woods, there to rejoice their spirits with the beauty and savour of sweet flowers, and with the harmony of birds'.[11]

The most famous contemporary description of May customs has none of the innocence implied by Stow's account. What may have started as a group activity ended with individuals pairing off. Philip Stubbes wrote his account of sexual promiscuity in his *Anatomie of Abuses*, published in 1583, which is an illuminating account of contemporary society if the author's admonitions are filtered out:

> all the young men and maids, old men and wives, run gadding over night to the woods, groves, hills and mountains, where they spend all the night in pleasant pastimes; and in the morning they return, bringing with them birch and branches of trees, to deck their assemblies withall … the chiefest jewel they bring from thence is their May-pole, which they bring home with great veneration, as thus. They have twenty or forty yoke of oxen, every ox having a sweet nose-gay of flowers placed on the tip of his horns, and these oxen draw home this May-pole (this stinking idol, rather), which is covered all over with flowers and herbs, bound round about with strings, from the top

to the bottom, and sometimes painted with variable colours, with two or three hundred men, women and children following it with great devotion. And thus being reared up, with handkerchiefs and flags hovering on the top, they strew the ground round about, bind green boughs about it, set up summer halls, bowers and arbours hard by it. And then fall they to dance about it ... I have heard it credibly reported (and that *viva voce*) by men of great gravity and reputation, that of forty, threescore, or a hundred maids going to the wood over night, there have scarcely the third part of them returned undefiled.[12]

The custom of dancing around a maypole had already been established by this time, and is well attested in late medieval and Renaissance literature, but the origin of the custom is unknown. If it was a native British practice established before the Roman Conquest, it is not found in Irish tradition, an island untouched by the Roman Empire. This has encouraged the argument that it is in fact of medieval origin.[13] It was clearly not a Celtic invention, as maypole dancing was at one time very widespread across Europe – James Frazer recounted similar customs from Scandinavia to the Mediterranean. One of the earliest accounts of a maypole in Britain was written in the mid fourteenth century, a lament to 'a birch tree cut down and set up in Llanidloes for a maypole'. In it the bard Gruffydd ap Adda ap Dafydd decries the cutting down of the tree and the rape of its leafy branches: 'you who were the majestic sceptre of the wood where you were reared, a green veil, are now turned traitress to the grove', and 'was it not barbarous, my birch, to make you wither yonder, a bare pole by the pillory' at a crossroads in the village.[14] The tree and perhaps also the dancing were rough and ready affairs and quite different from the stilted courtesy that stemmed from the nineteenth-century revival of the custom. For example, the intertwining coloured braids attached to the top of the pole, so familiar from English school dancing in the later twentieth century, is a comparatively late addition to the tradition and has a Mediterranean origin – its first known appearance in Britain being at a performance of J. T. Haines's drama *Richard Plantagenet* at the Victoria Theatre in London in 1836.

What, if anything, did the maypole signify? One theory was advanced by Sigmund Freud, but has an older vintage in the work of Thomas Hobbes, who suggested that the tree symbolised the god Priapus and that the maypole was a phallic symbol. There is no evidence to back this up and so long-lived a symbol may have meant different things at different times. The maypole can, however, be drawn into the rites of spring along with fire festivals and the greening of towns and churches. Dancing was by its nature communal, but so was the effort of erecting a maypole and dressing it with garlands and flags. It was the secular side of a society that practised a traditional religion swept away by the Reformation. It was in this context that the more hard-line Protestant reformers saw the maypole as idolatrous. A permanent pole set up in Cornhill in London, which had been mentioned in the fourteenth century by Chaucer, was destroyed and burned during the reign of Edward VI. A new pole brought into Fenchurch parish in London was also destroyed at this time.[15]

The arch-Protestant Philip Stubbes was not slow to point out that to all intents and purposes people were dancing around not a phallic symbol but a tree. The practice seemed so primitive that it has long been deemed to be the earliest form of religion. There does not need to be any pagan religious symbolism in this, however, and likewise there is no reason to equate it with primitive practice. May Day is the first day of summer. While there may not have been continuity between May festivities and the earlier festival of Beltane, their purpose was similar.

The reverse is the beginning of November, Samhain in the Celtic year and All Saints followed by All Souls Day in the Christian calendar, when Christians prayed for the souls of the dead. At this dangerous time the souls of the dead were reputed to be at large. Beltane and May Day celebrated the survival of those difficult times and the renewed fertility of the Earth. As a secular celebration it locked society into the natural rhythm of the year, and connected individuals with their neighbours and their native surroundings. May festivities answered a basic need for communal celebration at a time when the weather was clement enough to allow an outside gathering. As such the maypole is a descendant of a prehistoric Celtic festival, but not of a prehistoric religion. The maypole is one of the most potent symbols of the image of Merry England and its resurrection in the nineteenth century brought with it a new message: to provide reassurance that the relation between nature and society remained a harmonious one.

The decline of May festivals and games began in the latter half of the sixteenth century, led initially by disapproving radical Protestants but subsequently reinforced by the fears of social disorder that had come to be associated with parish gatherings. In any case they were not rigid institutions, but reflected fickle popular taste. For example, Robin Hood had been a popular figure at May festivities in the first two decades of the sixteenth century but his popularity was waning by the third. Nevertheless the May celebrations remained a fertile symbol of English life for a generation of writers that included Shakespeare, Edmund Spenser and Robert Herrick, all of whom drew on these traditions.

Shakespeare drew upon the indigenous greenwood and the literary romance form, above all in two of his plays. *A Midsummer Night's Dream* was written in 1594–95. It is a complicated interweaving of separate plots that see the main characters leave Athens for exile in its neighbouring woods. Hermia and her lover Lysander escape from the city to avoid the authority of Theseus, duke of Athens, who has been prevailed upon by Hermia's father to force her to marry Demetrius. Helena, in love with but spurned by Demetrius, betrays the whereabouts of Hermia; and Demetrius, followed by Helena, heads off in pursuit. Once in the wood the fairies meddle in the affairs of the four young lovers and chaos ensues. Oberon, king of the fairies, gives his lieutenant, Puck, a love-juice to smear on Demetrius's eyes to make him fall in love with Helena, but Puck mistakenly applies it to Lysander, who then leaves Hermia for Helena. Oberon then tries to rescue the situation by himself applying the love-juice to Demetrius, with a consequence that both men are now in love with Helena and are jealous of her affections, while Helena and Hermia at first think a trick is being played and then quarrel. The trouble is sorted out when Oberon orders Puck to apply a new magic-juice to Lysander to undo his previous mistake and restore him to Hermia. Once this is achieved, the now suitably paired lovers return to Athens and marry. In another plot, a quarrel takes place between Oberon, king of the Fairies, and his wife Titania. In revenge Oberon applies the same love-juice to Titania, which causes his wife to fall in love with the first creature she sees when she wakes up. Thanks to the mischievous Puck, that person is Bottom, one of a group of Athenian workmen rehearsing a play, who has been transformed by Puck into a man with the head of an ass.

In the play the action begins and ends by day in Athens, which stands for reason, while in between the events take place at night in the woods, which stands for irrationality, dreams and absurdity. Shakespeare presents the woodlands as the natural haunt of lovers, as he had done in his earlier play *The Two Gentlemen of Verona*, and as he was to do later in *As You Like It*. This was partly literary convention, although he could never have described a lovers' meeting place as 'the wood, where often you and I, upon faint primrose-beds, were wont to lie' without having experienced English woods for himself. He inverts the greenwood idyll, however, in presenting the disorientating aspect of the woods at night. Romantic allusions in nature are turned on their head as Titania comically says to the man with the head of an ass:

> Sleep thou, and I will wind thee in my arms ...
> So doth the woodbine [and] the sweet honeysuckle
> Gently entwist; the female ivy so
> Enrings the barky fingers of the elm.[16]

In general, however, the atmosphere of the woods is exotic and magical, partly because it is the domain of otherworldly fairies. The love-juice used by Puck is drawn from the purple 'love-in-idleness' flower (now known as the pansy), where Cupid's arrow fell. In a famous passage, Oberon describes the bank upon which Titania sleeps:

> I know a bank where the wild thyme blows,
> Where oxlips and the nodding violet grows,
> Quite over-canopied with luscious woodbine,
> With sweet musk roses, and with eglantine;
> There sleeps Titania, sometime of the night,
> Lull'd in these flowers, with dances and delight.[17]

These Athenian woods teeming with English flowers are quite different from the forest in *As You Like it*, which is much more recognisable as the greenwood of Robin Hood and his merry men. *As You Like It*, a rewriting of Thomas Lodge's 1590 romance *Rosalynde*, itself a variation on the tale of *Gamelyn*, was first performed in 1599. The play uses the greenwood to contrast culture and nature, and is in that sense familiar from medieval romance, except that now the forest is more benign and the court more dangerous. The play concerns a duke who has taken refuge in the Forest of Arden after being usurped by his younger brother Frederick. Their respective daughters, Rosalind and Celia, quarrel with Frederick and also take to the forest 'in content to liberty, and not to

banishment'. There they encounter Orlando and Oliver, brothers es-
tranged from their father and also wandering the woods. The play
centres upon the love between Rosalind and Orlando.

It is appropriate that the greenwood is introduced by a voice from
the court, albeit only Duke Frederick's champion wrestler. Of the exiled
duke, 'they say he is already in the Forest of Arden, and a many merry
men with him: and there they live like the old Robin Hood of England ...
and fleet the time carelessly as they did in the golden world'.[18] If that
was the case then one wonders why the duke ever wanted to return to
the court. Although Duke Senior maintains a court in the forest, the
social hierarchy of conventional society is maintained throughout. The
courtiers dress as foresters to distinguish themselves from the peasants,
but the duke's alternative court is never a commune and as such seeks
to equate an idea of social justice with the natural world. The usurpation
by Duke Frederick is therefore not only bad but unnatural.

Ironically Duke Senior's women-free alternative court can hardly have
offered a natural, let alone idyllic, life, but the duke himself describes
it in precisely those terms, recalling the male camaraderie of the hunt:

> Now my co-mates, and brothers in exile
> Hath not old custom made this life more sweet
> Than that of painted pomp? Are not these woods
> More free from peril than the envious Court?

Even the adverse conditions of winter can be borne as the wind and
the cold

> feelingly persuade me what I am:
> Sweet are the uses of adversity
> Which like the toad, ugly and venomous,
> Wears yet a precious jewel in his head:
> And this our life exempt from public haunt,
> Finds tongues in trees, books in the running brooks
> Sermons in stone, and good in every thing.[19]

Meanwhile Rosalind and Celia are unable to go about the forest as
their true selves and put on men's clothes instead, with all potential for
comic misidentification pursued. All of these characters are different
people when they enter the forest, the locus of metamorphosis. The
same device is used for the resolution of the play. As Duke Frederick

enters the forest in search of his elder brother, he meets an 'old religious man' who persuades him to give up his worldly crown and to take up the contemplative life in the woods, thereby allowing the exiles to return to the court where the 'natural' order is reclaimed. Each of the characters is somehow transformed by the forest and by using the seasons, beginning in winter and ending summer, the play is an affirmation of the renewal of life.

The setting of the play is the Forest of Arden (which is nearly Eden), a real place for sure but not one that Shakespeare needs to portray in its own right. Rosalind and Celia live in a 'sheep-cote, fenced about with olive trees'. 'An old oak, whose bows were moss'd with age' provides a lair for a 'green and gilded snake' and a lioness, both of which have literary precedents rather than a basis in natural history. Shakespeare subverts the idyll by frequent references to winter hardships and the poverty of its native people. In his description of the hunt Shakespeare has one of the minor characters, Jaques, sympathize with the 'poor sequester'd stag' and exposes the essential cruelty of the sport. The duke and his men are cast as usurpers and tyrants 'to fright the animals and to kill them up in their assign'd and native dwelling place'.[20] It sums up the ambiguity inherent in the attitude to nature. If the greenwood is idyllic, why leave it? Ultimately the play confirms humans as social beings and the court as their proper domain. The Forest of Arden is their holiday world that allows them to step aside from their true selves and temporarily to suspend the normal rules of social intercourse. Ironically the only man to find a lasting peace in the woods is the usurper Frederick, but only if he renounces the social world and lives an unnatural life of withdrawal.

In *Macbeth*, Shakespeare has another famous wood, Birnam:

> Macbeth shall never vanquish'd be, until
> Great Birnam Wood to high Dunsinane Hill
> Shall come against him.[21]

Macbeth is convinced that no man can defeat him, for 'who can impress the forest, bid the tree unfix his earth-bound root?' The trees are here emblems of natural justice that will confront Macbeth's debased nature, and it is no coincidence that Macbeth's dealings with the witches have taken place on the treeless heath. The climax of the play starts with the soldiers of the opposing army using boughs cut from Birnam Wood as camouflage as they advance on Macbeth's stronghold. It is, despite being one of the dramatist's darkest tragedies, a morally satisfactory conclusion. It equates the natural world with natural justice in a manner more profound than the world of the greenwood outlaw.

Two poets, Spenser and Herrick, who were near contemporaries of Shakespeare, wrote works that mark the culmination of a medieval sense of the greenwood. *The Faerie Queene* is Edmund Spenser's unfinished Arthurian romance where the forest is an allegory of the snares of the wicked world that confront a succession of knights in their quest for virtue. The poem is firmly in the romance tradition. In his earlier poem *The Shepheardes Calendar*, completed in 1579, May is a dialogue between two ministers, a Protestant and a Catholic. It begins with one of the most evocative descriptions of gathering in the May, but this is subsequently dismissed as lustful and wanton merriment:

> Youth's folks now flocken in everywhere
> To gather May baskets and smelling brere
> And home they hasten the posts to dight
> And all the Kirk pillars ere daylight,
> With hawthorn buds and sweet eglantine,
> And garlands of roses and sops of wine.
>
> ... to the greene Wood they speeden hem all,
> To fetchen home May with their musicall:
> And home they bringen in a royall throne,
> Crowned as king: and his Queene attone
> Was lady Flora.[22]

There follows an exchange of views on the virtues of the simple life and of simple pleasures and finally the Protestant tells a story of the kid goat who strayed into a wood. Like a Catholic *exemplum* turned on its head, the kid is tricked and consumed by the fox, the moral of which is to be vigilant not against the machinations of the Devil but of the Roman Catholic.

Robert Herrick's famous May Day love poem 'Corinnna's Going a Maying', written in the 1630s, has none of the improprieties suggested by Elizabethan Protestants, nor is it likely to have had any from a poet who was also the vicar of Dean Prior on the edge of Dartmoor. Herrick was an outsider fascinated by the customs of his parishioners, but never seems to have assimilated himself into the country life. He described his return to London in 1647 as a relief from 'the dull confines of the drooping west', although he was to return to Devon after the Restoration. Herrick's personal detachment from his subject matter is itself the mark of a declining practice, while the poem's innocuous tone suggests a note of nostalgia for the passing of the culture of communal festivity.

> There's not a budding Boy, or Girle this day
> But is got up, and gone to bring in May.
>   A deale of Youth ere this, is come
>   Back, and with White-thorn laden home.
>   Some have dispatcht their cakes and creame,
>   Before that we have left to dreame:
> And some have wept, and woo'd, and plighted Troth,
> And chose their Priest, ere we can cast off sloth:
>   Many a green-gown has been given;
>   Many a kisse, both odde and even;
>   Many a glance, too, has been sent
>   From out the eye, Loves Firmament;
> Many a jest told of the Keyes betraying
> This night, and Locks pickt, yet w'are not a Maying.
>
> Come, let us go while we are in our prime,
> And take the harmless Folly of the time.[23]

In the long view Spenser and Herrick were marking a process of social change that would profoundly influence the manner in which the natural world was experienced. The gathering of the May was rooted in native communal life but Herrick himself was detached from it, while Spenser introduced characters into the supernatural world like Pan and nymphs imported from the classical world. So did Shakespeare in *A Midsummer Night's Dream*, where many classical references are made to gods and nymphs such as Venus and Cupid, Apollo, Neptune and Aurora, in a play that assumes a sophisticated audience but at the same time draws upon the rustic simplicity of native woods.

The same classical sophistication is apparent in one of the most vivid spectacles of late Elizabethan architecture, Hardwick Hall in Derbyshire, built by Robert Smythson in 1590–97. In its great chamber is a carved and painted frieze by Abraham Smith depicting Diana the huntress.

Based on engravings by the Flemish artist Martin de Vos, it is an allegory in which Diana is a flattering allusion to Elizabeth I. A landscape of stylised trees is roamed by unicorns, monkeys and elephants instead of native fairies, and is peopled by classical figures in place of Arthurian knights. Traditional culture would eventually be left to the labouring classes, becoming quite distinct from the polite culture of the privileged classes, who assimilated in the Renaissance a fresh wave of Mediterranean and classical influence. No longer communal and traditional, the response to natural places like woodlands would become detached and personal.

7

Patriots

Nemorensis Rex – King of the Grove – is how the restored Charles II was hailed by John Evelyn, one of his loyal subjects, on his return to London in 1660, but it was a triumph that nearly never was. The Stuart dynasty had survived not by the skin of its teeth but by the branches of an oak tree in which the young Charles, shortly after his coronation in Scotland, had concealed himself from Cromwell's forces after defeat at the battle of Worcester in 1651. The oak tree, at Boscobel in Worcestershire, fostered a new and decisive link between oak trees, kingship and the national well-being. According to John Evelyn,

> The loyal Tree its willing boughs inclin'd,
> Well to receive the climbing Royal Guest,
> (In Trees more pity than in men we find)
> And in thick leaves into an arbour press'd.
>
> A rugged Seat of Wood became a Throne,
> Th' obsequious Boughs his Canopy of State,
> With bowing Tops the Tree their King did own,
> And silently ador'd him as he sate.[1]

A tribute to the success of the new cult of kingship is that the Boscobel oak became a shrine, with ultimately fatal consequences. So many patriots tore off branches for souvenirs that the original tree was dead by the end of the nineteenth century.

The cult of kingship was part of a political strategy suited to a nation of Protestant patriots with increasingly imperial ambitions. It was begun by the institution by Charles II of a royal day to commemorate the Restoration.[2] The date, 29 May, was the anniversary of his formal entry into London as well as his birthday. Initially 'Restoration Day' was marked by bell ringing and bonfires and survived as a low-key festival after the accession of James II, followed by William and Mary. Its revival, and the close association it subsequently gained with oak trees, occurred after the accession of George I in 1714, marking the beginning of the Hanoverian dynasty and a long period of Whig political supremacy. Restoration Day became a rallying point for the supporters of the exiled Stuarts and marginalized Tories. In 1715 the church bells of Norwich continued to ring all day while the streets, as in Bristol and Manchester, were decked with flowers and greenery. People wore sprigs of oak as a badge of their patriotism. Those that did not display the leaf were liable to attract suspicion and in Oxford attacks were made on suspected Whigs and nonconformists. The Oxford Whigs were intimidated sufficiently to wear sprigs of oak the next year. In the ensuing years Restoration Day metamorphosed into Royal Oak Day when oak sprigs were worn and parishes were decked in greenery. Royal Oak Day effectively superseded May Day as an early summer parish festival, its political element demonstrating how popular culture could be reinvented to suit contemporary society.

As a political gesture, Royal Oak Day exposed political divisions within the nation. The government, for example, banned the sporting of leaves in London from 1717, and a similar move was instituted in Manchester in 1747 following the Jacobite rebellion of 1745. Walsall in 1750 saw its celebrations descend into a riot during which an effigy of George II was used for shooting practice. In Newcastle upon Tyne in the 1720s the Whigs responded to Tory taunts by wearing sprigs of plane tree leaves. The tension subsided when festivities became gradually focused on a more distant and therefore by now innocuous villain, namely the Commonwealth. But the festival could still reflect a disunited kingdom. For example, in Lyme Regis nonconformists defiantly displayed nettles instead of oak leaves on their doors.

The success of Royal Oak Day was in large part due to the fact that it was a public holiday, but this was discontinued after 1859, which prompted the rhyme:

> Twenty-ninth of May,
> Royal Oak Day,
> If you don't give us a holiday
> We'll all run away.

The loss of the public holiday precipitated the demise of the festival. It survived in a few isolated places into the twentieth century for specific local reasons, while oak leaves continued to be displayed in military parades, fulfilling the forces' role in the vanguard of defence but in the guard's van of culture. Some parishes, such as St Neot in Cornwall, still dress their church with oak boughs. The survival of such customs is owed to a certain malleability of meaning, as it can hardly still be claimed to be a thanksgiving for the survival of the church from the threat of Puritan destroyers. On the contrary, it is an opportunity for pageantry that says more about the continuity of the parish community through the twentieth century than it does about the disputes of the seventeenth. A more organized festival has survived at Great Wishford, near Grovely Forest in Wiltshire. Here the festival was a local custom transmuted from a Rogationtide ceremony held to assert commoners' rights to gather wood from Grovely Forest. The festival recalls the medieval May festival and may of course have been influenced by accounts of it. The young disappear to the woods in the early hours and return with branches to deck the houses, forming a procession through the streets, and hoisting branches on the church tower like a flag. A procession to Salisbury follows, where the parishioners dance on the cathedral green.[3]

In the nineteenth century the festival acquired its alternative name of Oak Apple Day, named after the curious crab-apple-like galls formed on oak twigs in May by wasp larvae, which have a variety of localized names such as yak bobs and shig-shags. The last widespread observance of the day was among schoolchildren, who wore sprigs of oak and were allowed to inflict petty punishments on those who did not, a licence for playground bullying that is no longer tolerated.

John Evelyn (1620–1706) was one of the multitude who flocked the streets of London to welcome the returning king, accounts of which bear a striking resemblance to Christ's entry into Jerusalem. He noted in his diary the flower-strewn roads, the chiming of bells and the banners, and that 'such a restauration was never seene … in any history … nor so joyfull a day, and so bright, ever seene … in this nation'. Evelyn was a staunch royalist who had served in the exiled king's embassy in Paris and had married the ambassador's daughter. His loyalty was rewarded when he was appointed one of the founding fellows of the other and more illustrious institution founded by Charles, the Royal Society. The society was the perfect forum for a man of general intelligence whose published work ranged from the history of engraving to architecture and forestry. Evelyn found himself on commissions for regulating the Mint and the regulation of London hackney coaches, and in 1662 was one of a group of fellows consulted by the crown commissioners on the problem of supplying timber to the Royal Navy shipyards.

Evelyn produced a digest from the contributions of the other fellows, who included the governor of Connecticut, and presented a 'Discourse Concerning Forest Trees' to the Royal Society in 1662. Nearly two years elapsed before the first edition of his *Sylva*, the only best-selling title to have been written on the subject of forestry, was published. Evelyn was quick to associate the husbandry of forests with the king and the rightful order, and by the same token to associate the degradation of the forests with the Commonwealth. His opening address to the king praised the monarch's lead in tree planting as an example for his subjects to follow: 'Having (like another Cyrus) by your own Royal example, exceeded all your predecessors in the Plantations which you have already made, and now design beyond (I dare affirm it) all the Monarchs of this Nation since the Conquest.' The point was that 'by cultivating our decaying Woods, [we] contribute to your power, as to our greatest wealth and safety', because 'there is nothing which seems more fatally to threaten a weakening, if not a dissolution of the strength of this famous and flourishing nation, then the sensible and notorious decay of her wooden-walls'.4

Evelyn did not blame the obvious causes, such as the increase of merchant shipbuilding, or the use of charcoal in the iron and glass industries of the Weald, for the diminution of the nation's trees. Instead he picked on the disproportionate grubbing out of woodlands to create arable land by profiteering Commonwealth sequestrators depriving landowners of their rightful inheritance. Woods and forests were a national asset 'which our more prudent ancestors left standing, for the ornament, and service of their Country'. Indeed Evelyn was careful to cultivate the sense of duty and pride in landowners whom he readily conceded had of late paid little attention to silviculture, a 'sordid and vulgar' pursuit for men of nobility. He reminded them that the planting of trees had been the tradition of great men since classical antiquity, 'esteeming it the greatest accession of honour to dignifie their lasting names with such rural marks'. In the light of Commonwealth upheavals,

SYLVA,

Or A DISCOURSE Of

FOREST-TREES,

AND THE

Propagation of Timber

In His MAJESTIES Dominions.

By *J. E.* Esq;

As it was Deliver'd in the *ROYAL SOCIETY* the xv[th] of
October, CIƆIƆCLXII. upon Occasion of certain *Quæries*
Propounded to that *Illustrious Assembly,* by the *Honorable* the Principal
Officers, and *Commissioners* of the *Navy.*

To which is annexed
POMONA Or, An *Appendix* concerning *Fruit-Trees* in relation to *CIDER*;
The *Making* and several ways of *Ordering* it.

Published by express Order *of the* ROYAL SOCIETY.

ALSO
KALENDARIVM HORTENSE; Or, *Gard'ners Almanac*;
Directing *what* he is to do *Monethly* throughout the *Year.*

───────*Tibi res antiquæ laudis & artis*
Ingredior, tantos ausus recludere fonteis. Virg.

NVLLIVS IN VERBA

LONDON, Printed by *Jo. Martyn,* and *Ja. Allestry,* Printers to the *Royal*
Society, and are to be sold at their Shop at the *Bell* in S. *Paul's* Church-yard,
MDCLXIV.

Title page of John Evelyn's *Sylva* (1664).

it also symbolised the continuity of the natural social order. Planting trees, therefore, 'is what every ... owner of land may contribute to, and with infinite delight, who are touched with that laudable ambition of imitating their most illustrious ancestors'.[5]

Evelyn was not the first author to mythologise the association between kings and woods. John Manwood's *A Treatise and Discourse of the Lawes of the Forrest* was written in 1598, more than half a millennium after William the Conqueror had brought Forest Law to England. As an apologist for the laws, Manwood described a period of forest degradation under Saxon kings whose expanding civilization encroached upon its native woods, cutting off the wildwood as islands of green threatened by the ever rising tide of arable and pasture. According to this view, by placing forests off limits the Norman kings were heroically trying to halt the legacy of decline bequeathed by their predecessors. The irony of his work is that by the end of the sixteenth century the legal authority of the laws had lapsed, leaving its author to reconstruct the merits of the old regime in idealized terms.

Evelyn's historical perspective was also a case of manipulative hindsight. By focusing on the degradation brought about by the Commonwealth, he gave a misleading impression that Charles I had a real claim to have been a sovereign of the greenwood. Anthony van Dyck's portrait of Charles showed a warrior king on horseback beneath a large spreading oak, perhaps symbolising the realm and most certainly placing him in the tradition of hunting kings that had characterized William the Conqueror and his successors. In reality, however, Charles had been a seller of woodland for profit, notoriously the crown forests of Dean, which were purchased by the Catholic Sir John Winter. By the 1630s the Catholic infiltration of the royal household and affairs had become a touchy subject. The Forest of Dean was said to produce the best oaks in England, and it had been alleged that in the wreckage of the flagship of the Spanish Armada a letter had been recovered, in King Philip's hand, ordering the destruction of Dean's trees. Evelyn himself did not fail to mention this 'fact'.[6] Winter, a parvenu and not from the old landholding stock with whom Evelyn sought to ingratiate himself, was removed from his office of forest warden in 1642 as soon as the king's authority collapsed. Not every act of the Parliamentarians, therefore, was antipathetic to the link between the greenwood and national security. But Evelyn was able to carry the day with a few choice examples of the felling of trees constituting an attack on the king, including the Commonwealth Council of State's plan to fell 'the Royal Walk of elms in St James' Park' and sell the resulting timber.

Sylva was an immediate literary success and earned its author more plaudits in his lifetime than the diaries for which Evelyn posthumously became famous. In truth it was not an original work, having drawn on the work of previous authors like Thomas Tusser and Gervase Markham. The most significant influence, however, was the pamphlet *The Commons Complaint*, written in 1611 by Arthur Standish, who followed it with another pamphlet in 1613, *New Directions for the Planting of Wood*, which advocated a policy of a General Plantation whereby forty out of every thousand acres should be set aside for planting trees. Evelyn's great contribution, or good fortune, was his timing. Its message was simple, direct and tailor-made for the heady years of the Restoration. Four editions of the work were published in Evelyn's lifetime and in 1678 he boasted that some two million trees had been planted in England as a direct result of his exhortations.

The manifesto for planting trees appears at the beginning of the book. In the following pages, patriotic notions are soon subsumed by the hard facts of utilitarian planting. The bulk of his text is a detailed character-isation of species, with recommendations of where they should be planted and to what use they can best be put. Tree species should be selected according to their suitability for 'Building, Utensils, Ornament and Fuel', a policy that favoured hardwoods such as oak, beech and elm, but disfavoured other native species like hornbeam and lime. For example, ash and hazel had many uses in tools, spears, poles and palisades; elm leaves were excellent cattle fodder; and box was especially suitable for combs and mathematical instruments. Advice was mixed with super-stitious claims, for example that oil from box trees cured venereal disease, and that a tree is best felled when the moon is on the wane in order to retain its moisture. A tree felled on the winter solstice, if it coincided with the last day of a waning moon, would yield immortal wood.[7] The treatise closes with an account of cider making, which seems oddly out of place now but made sense in contemporary society. The fashion for brewing beer with hops had begun to overtake ale as a staple drink, but Evelyn wanted to promote cider as a native and patriotic alternative.

Evelyn's plantations comprised rigid rows of trees, homogeneous woods where every tree was of the same age and the same species. They had little in the way of living communities, although well-spaced oaks could provide grazing for deer and cattle, while chestnuts provided 'a lusty and masculine food for Rustics'.[8] Gone is any notion of community festivities in the woods; if a wooded plantation had an amenity value it was largely to flatter and delight the landowner. Underneath all this pandering to the landed classes, Evelyn was nevertheless a lover of trees for their own sake, if perhaps not of woodlands as places. Trees were primarily for planting and felling, but some trees had an almost sacred value and were never recommended for felling. Evelyn contributed to the growing cult of the individual tree. Plenty of them were described, the older the better, like the Shire Oak whose canopy stretched over the border between Yorkshire, Derbyshire and Nottinghamshire, Chaucer's Oak in Berkshire said to have been planted by the poet himself, and the yew tree at Brabourne in Kent, nearly fifty-nine feet in circumference.

Much of the panic surrounding the reserves of timber for the navy was misplaced. If the Spanish king really did order the Forest of Dean to be razed to the ground his intelligence was at fault. The Forest of Dean, like the New Forest, was not exploited as a source of timber for the Royal Navy until the seventeenth century. It has been argued that the complaints emanating from naval dockyards boiled down to shipbuilders working on a tight budget struggling to meet the price of good timber, in contrast to which merchant yards never complained of a shortage of timber and built considerably more vessels.[9] Evelyn also exaggerated the degree to which Wealden ironmasters were responsible for depleting the nation's woods. Charcoal was a renewable resource derived from well-managed woodlands and did not require the felling of timber trees.

A mixed picture was presented half a century later by Daniel Defoe as a result of his tour of Britain. In Nottinghamshire he found that Sherwood Forest

does not add to the fruitfulness of the county, for 'tis now, as it were, given up to waste; even the woods which formerly made so famous for thieves, are wasted; and if there was such a man as Robin Hood, a famous out-law and deer-stealer, that so many years harboured here, he would hardly find shelter for one week, if he was now to have been there.

In Hampshire, within a radius of ten miles of the shipyards at Southampton, 'I saw the gentlemens estates ... so overgrown with wood, and their woods so full of large full grown timber, that it seem'd as if they wanted sale for it'. Later, 'as I rode through New Forest, I could see the antient oaks of many hundred years standing, perishing with their wither'd tops advanc'd up in the air, and grown white with age, and that could never yet get the favour to be cut down, and made serviceable to their country'.[10]

Nevertheless woodland, and the oak tree in particular, became inextricably associated with the spirit of a patriotic nation. And in the succession of wars that characterised much of the eighteenth century, Britain's wooden walls were its mythical bastion against Catholic Europe. Alexander Pope's poem *Windsor Forest* was drafted in 1704 but rewritten in 1713 in the wake of the peace of Utrecht that ended the war of the Spanish Succession. The poem also discoursed on national politics, praising the Stuart dynasty against the Whig duke of Marlborough, whose victory at the battle of Blenheim in 1704 had made him a national hero. Windsor was a forest that Alexander Pope (1688–1744) knew personally from childhood, but in the poem it is an imaginative place that draws upon a range of national myths, moving beyond the immediate topical context of victory over Louis XIV to include the destiny of a civilization.

'Thy forests, Windsor! and thy green retreats' are compared with 'the Groves of Eden, vanish'd now so long', and contrasted with the exotic species of India. For

> Let India boast her plants, nor envy we
> The weeping amber or the balmy tree,
> While by our oaks the precious loads are born,
> And realms commanded which those trees adorn.[11]

The forests are considered through time, whereby the peace and plenty of the present reign of Queen Anne are contrasted with the despotism under the Norman yoke, although presented in generalised terms and having been transferred from the New Forest to Windsor. In the upside-down world of the Norman despot 'the subject starv'd, the beast was fed' when the king made 'his trembling slaves the royal game'.[12] The death of William Rufus was punishment for the Norman hubris, but what a difference from that world to the contemporary woodland ways of Pope's own time, when the woods yielded pheasants, partridges and woodcocks, a fertile ground for a civilization worthy of it. Happy, thought Pope, is the man who enjoys the humble pleasures of the forest, 'who gathers health from herbs the forest yields', which preludes praise for the literary and royal associations of the forests. This is not praise of nature but of culture. Through the medium of the River Thames the narrative progresses beyond Windsor Castle to the city and port of London, continuing to construct a vision of peace and trade. London is a celestial city of a golden future in Stuart and Tory colours, and contrasts with Windsor Forest, which stands for Arcadia. The two are linked in Pope's vision of the future:

> Thy Trees, fair Windsor! now shall leave their woods,
> And half thy forests rush into my floods,
> Bear Britain's thunder, and her Cross display,
> To the bright regions of the rising day.[13]

In Pope's time the druid revival in Britain was growing. Evelyn's friend John Aubrey had shifted the focus of druid rites away from the groves described by classical authors and towards the megalithic remains that were being discovered and recognized in the British countryside, of which Stonehenge and Avebury were the most celebrated. But the druids lived on as oak men. Evelyn entered into the spirit in a later edition of *Sylva*:

> Our British Druids not with vain intent
> Or without Providence did the Oak frequent,
> That Albion did that tree so much advance
> Nor superstition was, nor ignorance
> Those priest divining even then bespoke
> The Mighty Triumph of the Royal Oak.[14]

By the mid eighteenth century William Stukeley had established himself as the leading authority on ancient druidry, and in a self-portrait portrayed himself as an archdruid with a sprig of oak in his hair. James Wheeler's *The Modern Druid* of 1743 made a more explicit association

William Stukeley, self-portrait as a druid with oak sprig, from *Abury* (1743).

between the oak men and Britannia ruling the waves. The frontispiece depicts an oak tree beneath the motto *Britannia Decus et Tutamen* (the glory and protection of Britain). Beneath the tree is a seated Britannia holding a branch of oak, while in the background is a fleet of naval vessels, the fruit of the acorn-laden oak tree. From it grew a mystical notion that, like its people, British oaks were hardier than their softer European counterparts, and consequently produced sturdier ships. Britannia was nonetheless haunted by the nightmare of its oak woods becoming depleted, despite the fact that oak was not the only tree crucial to building a formidable navy. The tall straight conifers that were vital for building masts never attracted the same cult following, but they did benefit from the patriotic planting of trees.

In *Windsor Forest* Pope had been right to associate British prosperity with the strength of what other authors regularly described as its 'wooden walls'. As a mercantile nation, shipbuilding was vital to British trade and to the defence of its interests, so there was a logic in the patriotic associations of tree planting. Throughout the eighteenth and early nineteenth century there were alternating bouts of triumphalism and panic around Britain's most precious natural resource, none of it particularly measured.

One of the longest-running campaigns was begun in 1757, after the outbreak of the Seven Years War, by the Royal Society for the Encouragement of Arts, and continued until 1835. It awarded gold and silver medals to tree-planting landowners. Although throughout the eighteenth century timber had been an attractive long-term investment, the institution of awards produced some enthusiastic greenwood patriots, the most illustrious of whom were in Celtic Britain. The agricultural improver and idealist Colonel Thomas Johnes planted some five million trees, oak, beech, birch, alder, ash, rowan and elm but with a predominance of larch, on his Hafod estate on the bare uplands of the Ystwyth Valley in Ceredigion, to where he moved from Croft Castle in Herefordshire in the 1780s. It turned a portion of Wales into a new Caledonian forest, and fittingly his chief forester, John Greenshields, was a Scotsman. Meanwhile successive dukes of Atholl planted fourteen million larches in Perthshire between 1740 and 1830. Even so a parliamentary inquiry held near the end of the Seven Years War to investigate the national oak shortage produced one of the landmarks of sylvan literature. Roger

Fisher, a Liverpool shipwright, testified to the committee and published his report in 1763 as *Heart of Oak: The British Bulwark*. Fisher's assessment was pessimistic and blamed the destruction of woodlands on landowners with short-term interests, while history had shown, or so he argued, that empires rise and fall on the strength of their reserves of naval timber.

Fisher's message was an exhortation to plant more trees in the national interest. The same motive prompted Alexander Hunter in 1776 to publish a new edition of *Sylva*. The date was again significant, coinciding as it did with the outbreak of the American War of Independence. Mast timber for British naval vessels had traditionally been purchased from the American colonies, the alternative to which was to use composite sections held together by iron bands, or to exploit home-grown stocks. Loss of access to the best materials would place the Royal Navy at a disadvantage to the French with their well-ordered and considerably larger timber reserves. In reality, inferior timber was the bane of the naval shipyards, where poor quality or poorly seasoned timber, some of it imported from Scandinavia, invited fungi to eat their way through ships' hulls. In 1782 the hundred-gun *Royal George* suffered the ultimate humiliation of sinking in Portsmouth Harbour when the bottom fell out. As Nelson was to discover, the best timber was procured not by chopping down native trees but by capturing French ships.

Trafalgar was the last great naval battle fought with timber-hulled vessels. In its aftermath William Pontney recalled the 'last order of the Patriot and Hero, the immortal NELSON', that England expects every man to do his duty, and 'let it be especially and perpetually sounded in the ears of British Timber owners'. Memorial columns were erected among trees in Sherwood Forest, while new plantations were named after the late admiral. None of this triumphalism was the least concerned with any personal or communal association with wooded places.

As an economic investment, land for forestry had to compete with other uses, particularly for wheat. The final decade of the eighteenth century saw rampant inflation and a mushrooming price for wheat that encouraged landowners to grub up their trees for arable. After all, why should a field of wheat be less patriotic than a grove of oaks? At a time when Britain was a net importer of grain, the exhortations to plant trees did not go unchallenged. A House of Commons committee was told in

1791 that the preservation of oak in 'maritime mortmain' was a waste of land use, and that 'for Royal Navies, Countries yet barbarous are the right and only proper nurseries'.

Events superseded the patriotic and social significance of woodlands. After Trafalgar, Britain was never threatened by a sea power that could only be repelled by a wooden-hulled navy, while social tensions in the countryside were to be overshadowed by the politics of the industrial town. The association of trees and nationhood was a largely mystical one. As a young man, John Ruskin evoked merry England in a woody setting. The English woods still echoed with 'our memories of forest freedom, of our wood-rangers, and yeoman with the "doublets of the Lincoln Green"; with our pride of ancient archers, whose art was fostered in such long and breezeless glades; with the thoughts of the merry chases of our kingly companies'.[15] For a man of Ruskin's stature there is some naïve and wishful thinking behind this passage, but perhaps its author recognized that national myth-making had little to do with intellectual rigour, and romantic myths are better than chauvinist ones. But it shows that patriotism is a moulding of the past to suit the present.

By the mid nineteenth century it was possible to direct sylvan patriotism at the only class of people who could perhaps still really believe in Merry England: children. Captain Marryat – even his preference for rank rather than forename is indicative of his concern for the hierarchy of things – was a retired naval officer who enjoyed a second career as a writer of adventure stories. *The Children of the New Forest* was his last and most successful novel, first published in 1847, without which his name would be forgotten. As a historical romance it was hardly an innovative subject, and it shared with other historical novels the placing of the villains safely in the past tense where they can no longer hit back. There were few villains in the woods by the nineteenth century.

Set during the Commonwealth, the story concerns the orphaned Beverley family, two boys and two girls, whose ancestral seat of Arnwood has been burned down by Commonwealth forces and whose property is in the hands of the sequestrators. Presumed to have perished in the fire, the Beverley family are sheltered by an old faithful forest ranger, Jacob Armitage, and live with him in his cottage pretending to be his grandchildren. After he dies peacefully in his bed, they are forced to fend for themselves. They eke out what soon becomes a comfortable existence in a cottage in the forest, piously saying their prayers and pacifying nature. The elder brother Edward proves his worthiness by his skill as a huntsman, upstaging the other local men by taking a hart royal with twenty-five teeth on its antlers. His younger brother Humphrey pacifies nature by establishing a farm and taming the wild cattle, goats and pigs of the New Forest. They even take in a Spanish gypsy boy after capturing him in an animal trap – indeed throughout the story he shares many of the characteristics and intelligence of a farm dog. The girls, meanwhile, remain exactly where nice girls should be – tending the home.

The story draws on an established tradition of greenwood literature, and in doing so acknowledges that such literature had become a part of the national heritage. As in *As You Like It*, the protagonists must pretend to be peasants to go unnoticed, but their role reversal is not comic. The most obvious parallel is with the later tales of Robin Hood and other outlaws, of nobility forced to take to the greenwood and live beyond the law by the usurpation of natural justice. This usurpation is characterized by the new Intendent of the Forest, imposed from London and ignorant of all things arboreal. Its larger scheme is to present the Commonwealth as the natural order turned on its head, which is only restored at the end of the novel when the brothers join Charles II in front of the multitudes on the streets of London hailing their new king. Like all Victorian children's tales it has a clear didactic intent. It affirms conventional social attitudes and hierarchies, over and above which is its loyalty to the monarchy. It also preaches the simple virtues of loyalty, honesty, fortitude, endeavour and piety.

These were themes that Rudyard Kipling would later regard as wasted assets whose neglect threatened the wellbeing of the nation. Kipling settled in England after his purchase of Batemans in East Sussex in 1902. Here was the inspiration that saw the creation of *Puck of Pook's Hill*, *Rewards and Fairies* and other children's literature, written in a period before the First World War that saw him take a strong anti-liberal, staunchly right-wing stance. His children's books were also written partly for the instruction and entertainment of his own children. Kipling was no scholar and drew some of his material for the historical books from the extreme right-wing views of C. R. L. Fletcher's *Introductory History of England*. Kipling admitted that his purpose was to instil an understanding of English heritage among children and their parents, and to awaken a sense of urgency at a time when it was being under-mined by liberal and socialist politicians, something which Kipling regarded as a deviation from the true legacy of English history.[16]

The woods were no longer the raw material for building a fleet to establish an empire. By now, trees had become one of the mystical elements that made England England:

> Of all the trees that grow so fair,
> Old England to adorn,
> Greater are none beneath the Sun,
>   Than Oak and Ash and Thorn.
> Sing Oak and Ash and Thorn, good Sirs,
>   (All of a Midsummer morn)!
> Surely we sing no little thing,
>   In Oak and Ash and Thorn!
>
> Oak of the Clay lived many a day,
>   Or ever Aeneas began;
> Ash of the loam was a lady at home,
>   When Brut was an outlaw man;
> Thorn of the Down saw New Troy Town
>   (From which was London born);
> Witness hereby the ancientry
>   Of Oak and Ash and Thorn!
>
>   . . .
>
> Oh, do not tell the priest our plight,
>   Or he would call it a sin;
> But – we have been out in the woods all night,
> A-conjuring Summer in!
> And we bring you news by word of mouth –
>   Good news for cattle and corn –
> Now is the Sun come up from the South,
> With Oak and Ash and Thorn!
>
> Sing Oak and Ash and Thorn, good Sirs
>   (All of a Midsummer morn)!
> England shall bide till judgement Tide,
>   By Oak and Ash and Thorn![17]

Kipling's patriotism had essentially rural roots in a civilization that was trying to come to terms with increasing urbanization and the changes consequent upon it. In this he resembled Robert Baden-Powell, who had become a celebrity commanding the British forces at the siege of Mafeking in 1900. Returning to Britain after the Boer War, Baden-Powell was concerned that the pale listless youth of the nation would grow up into the recruits unfit for service that he had encountered in South Africa. *Scouting for Boys* was published in 1908 and a year later the new movement had attracted 130,000 members. Health, character and manliness were requisites of both the citizen and the soldier, according to Baden-Powell, whose movement took boys out of the grey towns and into the green woods. Ideals of international brotherhood were checked by the outbreak of war in 1914, however, when the movement was accused of militarism. Scouting was not specifically about woodlands, but it is the woodland habitats with which their camps are most associated. The association with woods and with Kipling was strengthened when the wolf cubs were founded in 1916. Baden-Powell specifically wanted to inspire boys through association with Kipling's *Jungle Books* (1894–95), whose main character Mowgli was brought up by wolves, themselves led by the 'great grey lone wolf', Akela, to become the master of the jungle.[18]

Kipling's mystical nationalism draws English trees into the realm of conservative politics, Anglicanism and imperialism and is a reminder that trees do not wear any political colours themselves, but can be adapted to suit any political persuasion. Other political causes also invoked trees as shrines. For example, Kett's Oak in Norfolk commemorates Robert Kett who, in 1549, led an uprising against the enclosure policies of church and state, while the Martyrs' Tree at Tolpuddle in Dorset is the sycamore under which in 1834 agricultural labourers congregated in their ill-fated effort to form a trade union. The mystical association of trees with Englishness has a long ancestry. Such sentiments were implicit in the theories of Richard Payne Knight, for whom 'native woods' were 'creation's boast and pride'. Ruskin identified a particularly English form of woodland, with 'sunny glade, and various foliage, and dewy sward' quite distinct from the black forests of other nations. It has also persisted beyond Kipling. One of its most conspicuous recent uses has been the use of an oak branch as the symbol of the National

Trust. The Trust adopted the motif, designed by Joseph Armitage, in 1935, in preference to an alternative lion motif designed by Eric Gill.[19] The timing of the Trust's adoption of acorn and oak leaf coincided with its appropriation as a national symbol in Germany, a rival nation with its own ancient forest heritage.

8

Altdeutsche Wälder

Germany was one of the nations that Kipling thought would profit from England's weakening moral fibre. A gesture of emerging German power had been made by Bismarck in 1895 when he presented a young oak to the retired British Prime Minister Gladstone, a notorious feller of trees on his Hawarden estate in North Wales. Kipling might have recognized an affinity between Britain and Germany, in contrast to the United States of America, a nation he criticized for seldom attempting 'to put back anything it has taken from Nature's shelves'.[1] In fact forest attitudes in Britain and Germany both followed the current of political change, where nationalism was only one response to changing social and environmental conditions. The forest had been an important component in German national identity from the Renaissance – and long before it achieved single nation status in 1871. But as a cultural symbol it owed much of its resonance to a man who had never visited the German forest and had little sympathy with its people. Tacitus provided subsequent generations with the most authoritative account of ancient Germany. He also documented the German triumph over the Roman imperial army, a notable victory that had been won in the depths of the forest. In the process Tacitus offered the forest as a symbol of invincibility to a people that needed one.

Tacitus was writing for a Roman audience and did not set out to laud the natives, a fact glossed over by later German nationalists. To classical authors like Strabo and Julius Caesar the dense Hercynian Forest covered a vast land mass from the Cevennes to the Carpathians, a measureless mass of trees, although by the middle ages the term was confined to the forests of Bohemia. Shrouded by its unremitting foliage, Germany was portrayed as the inverse of the sunlit Roman Empire and, however squalid it seemed to a Roman readership, Germans wore their rugged credentials with pride. Tacitus wrote of a robust and virile people living in wooden huts and worshipping in temples among the trees, in contrast to the marbled decadence of Rome. Its terrain 'either bristles with woods or festers with swamps' and was hardly attractive to anyone reared on Mediterranean sun, 'for who would leave Asia, Africa or Italy to visit Germany, with its unlovely scenery, its bitter climate, its general dreariness to sense and eye?' 2 These landscapes were the antithesis of the civilized Roman countryside. They were inhabited by men hardened to discomfort, for whom hunting was a necessity rather than a sport, and who drank barbarian ale instead of civilized wine. Other writers offered similar far-fetched accounts. Pomponius Mela described the Germans as a hardy and robust people who needed war as an outlet for their natural ferocity. German males went about naked until puberty, after which time they dressed themselves in garments made of tree bark. These innate characteristics marked out the Germans as a distinct and powerful race. After all, it was Germany's woodland warriors who shook off the most formidable military power the west had ever known.

Tacitus flattered the Germans by writing two lengthy accounts of them, the first and most detailed in the *Germania* and the second in his later, work *The Annals*. In the former its general characteristics and people were described, including passages that would echo nastily centuries later such as: 'the peoples of Germany have never been tainted by intermarriage with other peoples, and stand out as a nation peculiar, pure and unique of its kind'.3 The latter chronicles the Roman offensive east of the Rhine during the years of imperialist ambition under the Emperors Augustus (31 BC–AD 14) and Tiberius (AD 14–37).

When Rome moved on Germany it intended to enlarge its empire by taking the region between the rivers Rhine and Elbe, amounting to a considerable proportion of modern Germany. Germany was one of the most richly endowed parts of Europe in terms of forest. From the Black Forest in the south west, a band of forest confronted western invaders across the Rhine, at a time when the densest population in Germany lived not there but on the coast and northern plains. The initial campaigns were successful, but a series of revolts elsewhere in the empire took attention and men away from German conquests. The German offensive, still occupying the attention of over three legions, was commanded by Quintilius Varus. Varus was ill-prepared for campaign duties after having spent most of his career in the more agreeable surroundings of North Africa and the Levant, and arrogantly dismissed the Germans as little better than the wild beasts of the woods. His incompetence shouldered a greater portion of the blame for what happened in 9 AD than any German military nous. In one of the bloodiest slaughters suffered by the Romans, Varus, his legions and six auxiliary regiments were ambushed in the Teutoburger Wald in northern Westphalia by Arminius (known in Germany as Hermann), the chief of the Cherusci tribe. The army had been marching to its winter quarters, when it found itself caught between inhospitable swamp and impenetrable forest. Here was an ideal terrain for the German warriors, and a nightmare for a Roman army whose ordered formations were little use away from open country. In disarray, the Romans were ignominiously destroyed and the unstoppable Roman military machine was temporarily halted.

The succession of Tiberius as emperor saw a renewed campaign, led by his nephew Germanicus and recounted in the *Annals*. The slaughter of Varus and his men still rankled. In the midst of the campaign Germanicus visited the woods where Varus and his men had perished and found the battleground untouched since that day. Survivors told how the German warriors had insulted the Roman standards, and Germanicus could see for himself that they had had so little respect for the fallen enemy that men had been left unburied:

> The scene lived up to its horrible associations ... On the open ground were whitening bones, scattered where men had fled, heaped up where they had stood and fought back. Fragments of spears and of horses' limbs lay there – also human heads, fastened to tree trunks. In groves nearby were the out-landish altars at which the Germans had massacred the Roman generals and senior company commanders.[4]

Germanicus settled a few scores. His first act, after crossing the Rhine with twenty-six auxiliary battalions and six cavalry regiments, was to launch a surprise attack on the Marsi tribe at its most vulnerable moment – during a religious festival. The carnage was total: 'No pity was shown to age or sex. Religious as well as secular centres were utterly destroyed – among them the temple of Tanfana, the most revered holy place of those tribes.'[5]

In the long run control of Germany's forests proved too costly and the idea of conquest was in due course abandoned. Rome could not even claim the head of Arminius, who was eventually to perish by the treachery of his own side. For Rome's pampered citizens, the legacy of Varus was a glimpse of the horrors that lay beyond the boundary of its civilization. The significance of the German experience is demonstrated by the special attention that Tacitus devotes to it. The *Germania* was written in 98, just at the time when Rome's expansionist tendencies were giving way to a policy of fixed imperial boundaries. It asked a timely political question: what would Rome gain by mastering an unruly barbaric people and their inhospitable terrain?

Tacitus was little read by medieval scholars. A manuscript copy of *Germania* was probably held at the German of monastery of Fulda in Hessen, where a reference was made to it in 852, but the manuscript appears to have gathered dust over the next six centuries. The text was rediscovered not by Germans but by Italian Renaissance scholars. It was tracked down in 1425 by Poggio Bracciolini and a manuscript copy of it returned to Italy three decades later, after which it was first issued in printed form in Venice in 1470. Italy's apparent cultural imperialism prompted a German response. The *Germania* was reclaimed by Konrad Celtis (1459–1508) of the university of Ingolstadt, who was concerned to persuade Germany to explore its own identity, particularly in relation to its great forested landscapes. At the end of the fifteenth century Celtis could cite Tacitus as evidence that Germany was in essence distinct from Latin Europe and added momentum to the argument that its future did not lie under the papal yoke. Just as in England, the pope's claim to dominion over foreign territory was attracting unease. In an oration delivered at the university in 1492 Celtis made his point but overstated his case: 'to such an extent are we corrupted by Italian sensuality and by fierce cruelty in extracting filthy lucre that it would have been far more holy and reverent for us to practise that rude and rustic life of old'.[6] Celtis extolled the virtues of the German woods while a later scholar, Ulrich von Hutten, was to invoke Arminius as the father of the nation.

In medieval Germany, however, woods had been savage places personified by the mythical wild man. The idea of the wild man was of Greek origin, and is found first in the work of Herodotus, where his habits were a contrast to civilized values. The figure was taken up by

Roman authors such as Pliny the Elder, and after the conversion to Christianity became one of those mythical creatures demonized as being in league with the Devil. As one of the bogeymen of Christendom, the wild man was at the height of his popularity in the high middle ages. Gradually his repulsive image softened, however, as artists such as Albrecht Altdorfer (*c.* 1480–1538) began to portray him more sympathetically with wreaths of oak sparing his modesty. Wild men were rehabilitated as virtuous men on a par with hermits and anchorites, noble savages who demonstrated the simple virtue of native woodlanders against the pomp and circumstance of Rome.

A strong sense of national identity was not rewarded with the establishment of a German nation. As Germany remained a scatter of independent states national aspirations waned, to the extent that by the mid eighteenth century Frederick the Great, king of Prussia and a German hero, spoke and wrote in French. In 1773 the *Sturm und Drang* group of writers issued a manifesto, *Blätter von Deutscher Art und Kunst* ('On the German Way of Life and German Art'), that attacked the wholesale conquest of Germany by French classical culture. German culture, however, was soon in the ascendant. The end of the eighteenth and the early nineteenth century was a period of high achievement that encompassed the careers of Goethe, Schiller, Mozart, Beethoven and Kant. Romantics were at the forefront of attitudes and directions in German culture that remained influential well into the twentieth century. One of these directions was a growing self-awareness and national assertiveness.

Johann Gottfried Herder set in train a revision in attitudes to vernacular culture. His *Kritische Wälder* ('Critical Forests') was published in 1769 and advocated an approach to native culture whereby the vernacular would challenge the classical as the received order. In fact there was already growing interest in a romantic anticlassical past in Germany that ran parallel to similar movements in Britain, where it was characterized by William Stukeley's druidism, the druid revival in Wales and the popularity of Macpherson's fake poems of Ossian in Scotland. In Germany this movement saw the resurrection of Arminius and the re-establishment of the forest as the soul of the nation, even though the ancient forests were by now much diminished and large-scale replanting was mainly of coniferous trees to replace the ancient oaks and beeches.

Friedrich Gottlieb Klopstock wrote a trilogy of patriotic plays on the life of Arminius, beginning in 1769 with *Hermanns Schlacht*, in which he rejected the Latin inventions of court and city in favour of the natural Germanic tendency for village life, while he had native druids proclaiming the oak trees of Germany as the dwelling place of the gods and the embodiment of the Fatherland. Under the influence of Klopstock, a group of students from the university of Göttingen formed a *Hainbund*, or 'Grove League', in 1772 and spent the night in what purported to be an ancient oak grove, where they swore fraternity with their hands linked by oak garlands, a familiar kind of student ritual that Englishmen like William Stukeley had also indulged in as a young man.

In contemporary German art woodland became a natural subject for landscape painters at a time when it was not so in the English landscape schools. In fact the idea of the forest as art had earlier coincided with the national self-awareness of the Renaissance scholars. Albrecht Altdorfer had been one of the first painters to adopt the landscape as a subject in its own right. The breakthrough was a profound one. Altdorfer presented pictures that at first glance seemed to lack a subject. If humans or animals were included they were a token presence, not a central theme or part of a narrative. There is no story in a landscape picture, in contrast to Altdorfer's other and more numerous allegorical scenes in woodland settings. Regular themes of earth and heaven, civilization and wilderness were usually tackled through the medium of satyrs and wild men, where nature was normally the setting and not the subject. If woodland was the subject there would be a town or a church spire glimpsed in the distance as its foil. Moreover, these early landscapes, like *A Landscape with Woodcutter* of *c.* 1522, are small enough to hold in the hand and were created for private consumption. They emerged independently of any Italian and Netherlandish prototypes and in doing so stand for German artistic independence.

Altdorfer's *tour de force* is his painting of *St George and the Dragon* of *c.* 1510. It is an enclosed landscape where the protagonists are dwarfed by oaks and evergreens, which are the real heroes and are portrayed with a close attention to detail. The trees are not a wasteland to be avoided but are benign and beautiful, and the picture perhaps has something of the sacred devotional image about it. The forest seems more the province of the saint than the lair of the monster, a place of heroism not of evil, and therefore expresses the independent spirit of German religion against the Roman Church and its representative, Boniface, who famously took an axe to the forest. But the picture is not overtly nationalist. St George and the dragon look curiously stilted and conventional, so much so that it is difficult to make a case that George is Arminius and the dragon the defeated Roman legions.

Eighteenth-century German artists like Karl Wilhelm Kolbe (1757–1835), nicknamed 'Eichen-Kolbe' (Oak Kolbe), and Pascha-Weitsch (1723–1803), were more self-consciously German. They stalked the woods with their sketchbooks and cast them as a German paradise. When Napoleon's army crossed the Rhine in 1806 it inflicted a crushing defeat on Prussia's army at Jena and began a period of humiliation that was avenged only by the German War of Liberation in 1813–14. The most celebrated image of victory over France is that of the huntsman by Caspar David Friedrich (1774–1840). It pictures a French *chasseur*, or it might well be a Roman legionary, in a clearing facing a dark coniferous forest that dwarfs the onlooker like a mighty fortress. Contemporary critics noted that the raven on a tree stump represented the fallen German warriors in the war with Napoleon, while the forest itself appears precipitous and impregnable.

If the forest embodied the German character, it also embodied German origins. Interest in the antiquity of German culture led scholars to investigate its folklore, songs and legends, and the roots (and branches) of its language. Where Herder led, others followed. Between 1782 and 1787 Johann Karl August Musäus published *Volksmärchen der Deutschen* ('Popular Fairy Tales of the Germans'), a collection of tales suggested by national folklore. His work, however, was eclipsed by the *Kinder und Hausmärchen* of the Grimm brothers, published between 1812 and 1815, which has enjoyed as much popularity in the English-speaking world as in the German. Jacob Grimm (1785–1863) and his brother Wilhelm (1786–1859) were prolific scholars in the fields of ethnography and philology. Apart from the tales, their other major collaboration was a dictionary of the German language (completed after their deaths).

The Grimms' scholarly interests had been nurtured at the university of Marburg, where they studied law under the tutelage of Friedrich Karl von Savigny. Savigny was the single most important influence on the Grimms' approach to history, which was distinctly social rather than to do with personalities. In order to understand a society, it was not the purpose of a historian to describe great events and great people. Instead, emphasis was placed upon the language and customs of the common people, the *Volk*. The Grimm brothers concentrated their efforts upon language and folklore because it was these shared linguistic and historical ties that bound communities together. Modern literature, due to the influence of the Renaissance, was unable to express the essence of the people, whose natural form of expression was in tales and legends. The Grimms sought therefore to recover and reinstate the vernacular, what was termed *Naturpoesie*, as the authentic German culture.

Symbolically, the most important repository of German culture was the forest. The irony in this is that Germany's forested reserves had been depleted since the seventeenth century; but, as in England, as trees dwindled in numbers on the ground so they loomed larger in the imagination. In 1813 the Grimms published a journal, *Altdeutsche Wälder* (Old German Forests), a miscellany of forest lore from tales to the folklore of plants, that linked the genesis of German culture with the forests. In the forests the Grimms thought they had found the essential elements of German law, language and customs, as well as profound truths about the origins of European civilization. Forest heritage offered pride and perhaps a spirit of unity when the individual principalities were politically separate and some were occupied by France. Forests were needed because they made Germans feel German.

The forest in a Grimm fairy tale has a certain resemblance to the forests of medieval romance. Outside the normal social environment, the forest is not so much enchanted as the place where magical trans-formations occur. This is where the protagonists find themselves isolated and vulnerable to the tricks of witches and fairies. Hansel is transformed into a fawn and is hunted by a king, while a woodman and his wife have a son, the diminutive Tom Thumb, who can steer a horse and cart and is swallowed by a cow which is eaten by a wolf. As in medieval romance, the forest is where the protagonists are sorely tested. In 'The Twelve Brothers', for example, a father tells his wife that if their thirteenth child is a girl he will have the boys put to death so as to concentrate his legacy on to the daughter. On hearing of this, the boys flee to the woods, being forced to take up a forest existence when they learn that their mother has in fact given birth to a girl. They live in a hut where the forest provides their refuge but also tests their loyalty to each other. Eventually the daughter finds out about her lost brothers and goes off in search of them. Although she is quickly and successfully united with her brothers, a further twist occurs when she plucks twelve white lilies from the garden and inadvertently casts a spell on them. The boys are transformed into ravens and an old woman tells the girl that they can only be restored to their human form if she remains mute for seven years. Again sibling loyalty is tested to the limit. But the daughter manages to remain mute, marries and does not answer back the mischievous slurs of her stepmother-in-law, even when her husband succumbs to malicious rumour and has his wife tied to a stake. Fortunately the seven years expires at this moment and twelve ravens fly and land near her, and are restored to human form just in time to stamp out the flames licking at her feet. The moral of the story is in its affirmation of family values that are challenged in the forest.

Measureless and mysterious, the forest is also where supernatural interventions allow natural justice to prevail over social injustice. This is the case in 'The Three Dwarfs in the Forest', another typical Grimm tale. A widowed man and woman wed and bring their respective daughters into the new household. The woman is jealous of her stepdaughter and cruelly sends her out in the middle of winter, wearing only a paper dress, in search of strawberries. The stepdaughter obeys because she has been taught to obey her parents. Given only a piece of dry bread to eat, the jealous wife assumes she has seen the last of her. The girl enters a wood where she sees a cottage with three dwarfs in it. When they let her in she shares her bread with them and tells them of her plight, then they give her a broom and ask her to sweep the snow away from the back door, which uncovers a bed of perfect strawberries. The dwarfs also want to reward her for sharing her bread with them. The first says that as every day goes by he will make her more beautiful; the second decides that every time she opens her mouth to speak a gold coin will drop out; and the third says that she will marry a king. So far so good: the forest is the place for enchantment where, isolated and vulnerable, she had been tested and then rewarded. The daughter then returns home with the strawberries, looking more beautiful than ever before, and with so many gold coins falling from her mouth that the family are soon knee-deep in them.

Her step-sister then ventures into the forest, but in her case her mother gives her a warm fur dress, some bread and butter and cake. She enters the same wood, sees the same cottage, and goes in uninvited to eat her cake, refusing to share it with the dwarfs on account of there being so little of it. Having refused to sweep snow from the path, and finding that no strawberries or riches are forthcoming, she leaves. The dwarfs, meanwhile, consider her fate. One says that she will become uglier by the day; the second that every time she opens her mouth a toad will fall out; and the third that she will come to an unhappy end. The story then continues back in the real world. The first daughter meets and marries a king, and bears a son, but the step-sister usurps her, throws her into a river and impersonates her. But the ugly sister is found out and, with her scheming mother, is thrown into a river inside a barrel of nails. The first daughter survives her ordeal and is restored to her rightful place in the family.

The moral of the tale is straightforward enough. The dwarfs offer traditional hospitality – even Tacitus remarked that in a German home the door was always open – and the first girl reciprocates by sharing her food, while the second breaks the social code by her selfishness. The tale highlights the shared values of the community, which are tested beyond the normal boundary of society in the forest. The role of the forest is to act as the ultimate moral arbiter. The forest belongs to no one and pays no heed to rank, only to personal qualities. But these tales are also always about family values, and in particular about blood ties: that love is better than money is the moral of Tom Thumb, and that the loyalty of the sister to her twelve brothers, and of Grettel to Hansel, will be justly rewarded. The villain in the family is usually the wicked step-mother. Punishment is severe, such as death in a vat of boiling oil or in a barrel of nails thrown into a river. From this rich corpus of moral tales the Grimms claimed that the forest folk possessed a traditional system of natural justice, an innate sense of right and wrong, of community and family values, that would provide the solid foundation of a German nation and was the reverse of urban Enlightenment intellects of the Latin nations.

In fact, the Grimms were as much engaged in myth-making as many of their contemporaries.[7] Although they presented the tales as faithful transcripts of what that they heard from common folk, in reality the tales were infused with the brothers' creative embellishments, moral attitudes and patriotic sympathies. But myth-making is an important component in building national consciousness and here the Grimms can be seen in the context of a drift to nationalism over a much longer timespan. Among the more strident mid nineteenth-century nationalist voices was Wilhelm Heinrich Riehl, who published *Die Naturgeschichte des Deutschen Volkes* ('The Natural History of the German People') in three volumes between 1851 and 1855. According to Riehl, the forest was the foundation of the German way of life:

> In the opinion of the German people the forest is the only great possession yet to be completely given away. In contrast to the field, the meadow and the garden, every person has a certain right to the forest, even if it only consists in being able to walk around it when the person so desires. In the right or privilege to collect wood and foliage, to shelter animals and in the distribution of the so-called *Losholz* from communal forests and the like, there is a type of communist heritage that is rooted in history. Where is there anything else that has been preserved like this other than with the forest? This is the root of genuine German social conditions.[8]

Riehl described a village without a forest as like a town with no civic buildings or galleries. Moreover, the forest dwellers rooted in their locality were the antithesis of the wandering Jews who had colonized the cities. Riehl's prejudices, dressed up as social science, represent a nascent mood of racism in Germany that ran parallel with an unprecedented interest in nature conservation. Riehl was a campaigner against deforestation and of maintaining traditional rights, similar to English common woodland rights of cutting firewood and grazing, arguing that a basic provision of ancient German law was to allow universal access to forest, pasture and water. This at least he shared with Karl Marx, one of whose earliest political writings was a defence of customary forest rights. Written in 1842, it protested against a measure of the Sixth Rhine Province Assembly that guaranteed the interests of landowners and criminalized the gathering of wood. Marx saw nothing unnatural in the poor gathering up the dead wood that living trees had cast off, and treated customary rights as inalienable and as environmental good sense. Romantics like Riehl agreed, since customary rights expressed those same communal values that were extolled by the Grimms as one of the defining national characteristics.

As the area of the German forest declined, and as more of it was planted with conifers to suit commercial interests, so the importance of memorializing the site in the Teutoburger Wald where Arminius defeated the Romans became more urgent. The site eventually chosen, near Detmold, became the place of official commemoration, but the exact location is still disputed, a necessary component of the myth. The sculptor Joseph Ernst von Brandel spent nearly forty years on his uninspired gesture of German heroism, the Hermannsdenkmal, which placed the warrior with his sword brandished aloft on top of a German-Romanesque style rotunda. All of the German principalities and states contributed something to the project but by the time it was opened, in 1875, things had changed. The Second Reich was already four years old, Germany had liberated itself from the latest incarnation of Latin empire building, Napoleon III's French army in 1870, and Kaiser Wilhelm I was being hailed as the latest incarnation of Arminius. National destiny was at last on course.

Revival of interest in the forests also spawned a back-to-nature movement similar to those movements elsewhere in Europe that rejected urban industrial society. Opportunities for mystical communication with nature were taken up principally by the young, in Germany in the form of the Hermannskinder. They had something in common with like-minded movements and men elsewhere, such as the Woodcraft Folk in Britain, or the extraordinary American Joseph Knowles, who in 1913 stripped himself naked and strode fearless into the woods of Maine to live 'as Adam lived', emerging hale, hearty and triumphant two months later.[9]

In Germany these impulses were steered into groups controlled by aggressive nationalists expressing their Teutonic destiny. In 1925 50,000 young German men in warrior costumes marched through the woods to the Hermannsdenkmal, in a celebration organised by Jungdeutschenordnen (Order of Young Germans) and Stahlhelm (Steel Helmet). This tendency became further emphasised by the Third Reich, which liked to associate German distinctiveness with its forests, and watched approvingly as a number of scholarly works celebrated the national forest character, such as *Der Wald in der Deutscher Kultur* ('The Forest in German Culture') by Karl Rebel (1934), and *Deutscher Wald, Deutsches Volk* ('German Forest, German Folk') by Julius Kober (1935). Forestry was allotted generous resources by the Reich and it has often been remarked that the most ecologically conscious of twentieth-century

European regimes was at the same time its most repugnant. In 1939 Hitler introduced the Order of the Knight's Cross for military valour. It had three levels, 'with oak leaves', 'with oak leaves and swords', and 'with diamonds'. An additional higher level, the only recipient of which was the Stuka pilot Colonel Hans Rudel, was 'with golden leaves'.[10]

Tacitus continued to haunt the German consciousness even in wartime, as is shown by German efforts to acquire the only surviving early manuscript copy of the *Germania*. The manuscript from which the first printed version had been derived had been in Italy since the mid fifteenth century and passed through many owners. By the 1930s it was the property of the anti-fascist Count Balleani and German nationalists were determined to reclaim it. Alfred Rosenberg, the Nazi ideologue, had argued for its reclamation from the 1920s. A request to Mussolini made in 1936 for its return to Germany was initially accepted, until Italian opposition forced him to change his mind. The issue became more urgent in 1943 with the Allied invasion of Italy. A detachment of SS was sent to rescue the manuscript from the Palazzo Balleani at Fontedamo. They arrived too late to arrest the count and failed to track down the manuscript – they could have found it had they bothered to search one of the count's other palazzi.[11]

The post-war reconstruction of German culture made forests a difficult issue. Did the association drawn between German character and German forest taint the forest, or was the forest capable of rehabilitation as the victim of a corrupt ideology that could just as easily have been turned into a more responsible and creative movement? Joseph Beuys (1921–1986) was one artist who challenged Germany to confront its past. In the early 1970s he staged a successful demonstration against the felling of a wood near Düsseldorf, for the building of country-club tennis courts, by painting crosses and rings on the trees in an attempt to reinvent the myth of the German forest. A later campaign to plant seven thousand trees in German cities, bringing the forest to the city as an act of redemption, was completed posthumously by his son.

One of Beuys's chief disciples is Anselm Kiefer (1945–). Kiefer's contribution to German culture has been to force it to recognize that the defeat of the Third Reich did not allow the slate to be wiped clean. Taking up landscape painting, in itself a challenge to the American-dominated modern movement, he produced a series of works intended to discomfort a nation trying to forget its immediate past. Kiefer provocatively painted a blood-stained, snow-bound grove where the name of Varus is painted, along with names of other Germans who had helped to promote the myth of Arminius in German origin, among them the philosopher Martin Heidegger. Kiefer could argue that he confronted German myths that might otherwise have been left for neo-Nazis to appropriate as their own.

Like other western nations, Germany has also had to rethink its relation to the forest in terms of technological civilization, not merely in those of national origin. The German Greens are the most successful of all the ecological political parties in Europe, partly because of the potency of German nature myths. Heidegger exorcized his Nazi associations by retreating to the Black Forest, living like a hermit and addressing neighbouring villagers in ancient German dialect. But he was able to shake off neither the past nor the present. His answer to technological materialism was to postulate a proper relationship with the natural world, a search that led him back to the German myth of rootedness and all its ambiguity.

In the end nationalism is, however, no answer. Heidegger's rehabilitation arguably came about through his environmentalism, his criticism of the anthropocentric view of the world, and his influence on the Norwegian philosopher Arne Naas and the 'deep ecology' movement. Humans have always sought to justify doing whatever they like with the natural world. Heidegger understood that the response to this malaise, which affects everyone, cannot be confined to any national self-interest and can only be tackled as a citizen of the world.

9

Big Trees

A continent more prodigiously endowed with forests than North America can scarcely be imagined. It has been estimated that at one time 45 per cent of its land mass was covered in forest, of which the vast majority lay to the east of the Mississippi, continuing all the way to the Atlantic coast. Coming from Europe and its already denuded native woodlands, early settlers were confronted by a wall of trees, leading them to conclude that the continent was 'almost universal forest'. Most of it could be turned to a practical use, as American species were variants of familiar European species. In his *Description of New England* of 1616, John Smith described oak, elm, ash, beech, walnut, pine, cedar, cypress, spruce, alder, birch, maple, hawthorn and more. The immeasurably vast endowment of wood provided ideal building material that contributed to a distinct New England architectural character, but had consequences in the profligate waste of timber. In fact it has been suggested that the American word 'lumber' was adopted instead of the English 'timber' because trees were so prolific that they 'lumbered the landscape'.

America was, in fact, not the wilderness it may at first have seemed. It has been calculated that, before the arrival of Columbus, North America had a greater population than western Europe.[1] By the time the first settlers arrived on the continent large tracts of the eastern forests had been partially cleared for agriculture and altered to a more open, park-like woodland suitable for hunting. This allowed small villages to be constructed at the centre of a network of fields, but with easy access to woodland for gathering firewood, and for hunting expeditions. The openness of the forest was an ongoing manipulation of the woods that early settlers recognized and remarked upon. Writing in 1637 the New Englander Thomas Morton explained in his *New English Canaan*:

The Salvages are accustomed to set fire to the Country in all places where they come, and to burne it twize in the yeare, viz: as the Spring and the fall of the leafe. The reason that moves them to do so, is because it would other wise be so overgrowne with underweedes that it would all be coppice wood, and the people would not be able in any wise to passe through the Country out of a beaten path.[2]

Early settlers, landing on the Atlantic coast between Maine and Florida, gradually moved inland and transformed the landscape into agricultural land. Amerindians were forced out by design, disease or as an indirect consequence of the settlers' activities. Large-scale clearance by the white man inhibited the indigenous style of living, with its characteristic small clearings and access to the forests, encouraging a Indian retreat westward. The best Indian farmland was appropriated by the settlers, to the extent that two centuries later it was forgotten that Indians had ever had fields of corn, potatoes, tomatoes and tobacco. Dutch settlements in the lower Hudson valley, for example, had taken advantage of abandoned Indian fields, which they found fertile ground for growing oats and wheat to brew beer. Elsewhere tobacco provided an important cash crop for hard-up settlers. The disappearance of the Indians disrupted the managed equilibrium of the forests, however, which subsequently grew thicker than they had been before. But the loss was cultural as well as ecological. As James Fenimore Cooper pointed out, the area of New York state alone saw the disappearance of the Cayuga, Mohawk, Oneida, Onondago, Seneca and Tuscarora tribes, and with it a whole forest way of life.

American attitudes to the forest were initially those imported by the pioneers from Europe. European culture had set the forest as the antithesis of civilization, which in America had some additional reson-ance because the forests were the habitat of dangerous wild animals, notably bears and wolves. In this context to fell trees was to slay the haunt of demons and civilize the landscape. Alexis de Tocqueville noted as late as 1831 that the pioneering Americans were 'insensible to the wonders of inanimate nature, and they may be said not to perceive the mighty forests that surround them till they fall beneath the hatchet'. The pioneer in the Michigan forests 'only prizes the works of man. He will gladly send you off to see a road, a bridge, or a fine village. But that one should appreciate great trees and the beauties of solitude, that possibility completely passes him by.'[3]

The felling of timber became an act of heroic conquest, and the woodsman and pioneer became symbols of the New World. But the first Americans were also shaped by the environment they worked in. Hacking their way through the forests, pioneers were simple folk living sober, hardy, self-reliant, frugal, hard-working and God-fearing lives. Their ambitions were the honest and humble personal ambitions upon which American society was based and stood in stark contrast to old world decadence and corruption. Even Henry Thoreau, no chauvinist, could remark that 'Adam in Paradise was not so favourably situated on the whole as is the backwoodsman of America'.[4] As a potent national symbol, however, the backwoodsman only gained popularity once he had become distant from the actuality of people's lives. It is certainly true that relentless hardship can make people humbler, and more spiritual, but for sober one could equally read dreary, for self-reliant lonely, for frugal poor. The pioneer had in theory to be master of all trades – lumberjack, carpenter, farmer – but the reality did not always live up to the myth. Abandoned Indian land was seized upon readily, while many pioneers simply felled the trees and then sold the land to more permanent farmers, allowing them to move on to fresh ground for further clearance.

The backwoodsman is a romantic myth of urban America, and specifically of post-colonial America redefining its origins. Previously, pioneers were regarded as almost as savage as the wilderness they worked in. In the late eighteenth century Hector St John Crèvecoeur, a 'gentleman farmer', could still describe the woodsmen as social 'off-casts' in his essay *What is an American?* Such men 'appear to be no better than carnivorous men of a superior rank ... there, remote from the power of example and check of shame, many families exhibit the most hideous part of our society'.[5] Taming the wilderness was a dirty business. Progress meant replacing the forest with fertile farmland, allowing civilization to move in.

America had proclaimed its independence in 1776 with a unique political constitution and had simultaneously created national icons in George Washington and Thomas Jefferson. It then set about establishing its political and economic independence, but nation building needed a cultural foundation to define what made Americans distinctly American. The conquest of nature was part of this emerging national psyche.

Nature is what America possessed in abundance and would provide the basis of American self-image among the leading nations of the world. Even so, early champions of American nature bristle with the inferiority of provincials in the presence of sophisticated Europeans. So Abigail Adams, in 1784 wife of the American ambassador to Paris, remarked that, for all the manufacturing and artistic superiority of Europe, 'do you know that European birds have not half the melody of ours? Nor is their fruit half so sweet, nor their flowers half so fragrant'. Alexander Wilson, a Scottish-born ornithologist, pointed out that if a small country like Britain could inspire so many poets, then how many might sing the praises of the infinitely more vast America.[6]

Appreciation of nature became an act of patriotism in America. It was also morally and socially desirable. As an editorial in the art journal *Crayon* put it in the mid 1850s, 'the enjoyment of beauty is dependent on, and in ratio with, the moral excellence of the individual'.[7] And appreciation of nature inevitably led to the forests. 'For variety, the American forest is unrivalled', wrote the artist Thomas Cole in his *Essay on American Scenery*, first published in 1836. Richly endowed with commingled oak, elm, birch, beech, plane, pine and hemlock, the autumn splendour of American autumn 'surpasses all the world in gorgeousness'. Cole singled out the American hemlock as 'the sublime of trees, which rises from the gloom of the forest like a dark and ivy mantled tower'. Thomas Cole and others countered criticism that American scenery lacked historical association by pointing out that, while European landscapes were 'the great theatre of human events', American nature was characterized by its natural grandeur – 'the most distinctive, and perhaps the most impressive, characteristic of American scenery is its wildness'.[8]

The logical conclusion to this was that America still bore the imprint of God's creation. The French author Chateaubriand remarked on visiting America that 'there is nothing old in America except the woods', which had become the equivalent of Europe's ancient monuments, and that 'the soul delights to busy and lose itself amidst the boundless forests'.[9] There was European grandeur – in the Alps for example – but the landscape of the Old World was characterized by the accretions of age, while in America the landscape could be appreciated in its pristine state. Even so, it was a mistake to think of the American landscape as

timeless. As Thomas Cole put it: 'the great struggle for freedom has
sanctified many a spot, and many a mountain stream and rock has its
legend'. The difference was that 'American associations are not so much
of the past as of the present and future'.[10] This absence of historical
association was a great boon to America, lacking as it did the negative
social imprint acquired by English woods in the eighteenth century. If
the continent had no history, then it lacked the dimension of linear
time – only the circular time of the seasons. The arrival of the settlers
marked the beginning of linear time in America.

Direct association between forest groves and the founding instincts
of the American people was made explicit by the popular poet William
Cullen Bryant (1794–1878). He saw in the forest a distillation of two of
the most important aspects of American national identity – a sense of
freedom and of the proper reverence for holiness. In 'Forest Hymn'
(1825) the forest was the primordial church:

> The groves were God's first temples. Ere man learned
> To hew the shaft and lay the architrave
> And spread the roof above them – ere he framed
> The lofty vault, to gather and roll back
> The sound of anthems; in the darkling wood
> Amidst its cool and silence, he knelt down,
> And offered to the Mightiest solemn thanks
> And supplication.

The use of the word 'grove' indicates the religious inspiration that
Americans would find in nature, a theme pioneered in the transcend-
entalist writings of Ralph Waldo Emerson, and how they convinced
themselves that the forests were coeval with the creation of the world.
Many New England revival meetings were conducted in open-air groves
in the nineteenth century, bringing with them a greater religious authority than any purpose-built chapel could hope to command.

In James Kirke Paulding's 1818 novel *The Backwoodsman* the protagonist goes west to the woods rather than east to Europe, a move adopted
with great success by James Fenimore Cooper in his *Leatherstocking
Tales* published between 1823 and 1841. As a setting for adventure stories
it was a wonderful new place to contrast with popular novels of the old
world such as Walter Scott's historical romance *Ivanhoe* of 1819, set in

Merry England at the time of Robin Hood and Richard the Lionheart. Cooper (1789–1851) had, as an infant, moved with his family to the frontier settlement of Cooperstown, New York, founded by his father. His early initiation into the ways of the woods, and his reverence for them, was exploited later in his career as a novelist. Cooper is a classic example of the truism that writers write best out of their own experience. His first novel was an attempt to transplant Jane Austen across the Atlantic and failed. Only when he wrote about his own American backwoods did he succeed in creating a convincing American literature.

Although he was the child of frontier settlers, Cooper never portrayed the forest as an impediment to be pacified and conquered. His chief protagonist and mouthpiece, Natty Bumppo, is a European who has adopted the woodland ways against the axe of the white settler. His exposure to the woods has made him an expert in woodcraft and has also taught him innate common and moral sense. Against the exploitative and sacrilegious world of farmstead and town, Natty prefers 'the honesty of the woods', a place where the hand of God is far more likely to be encountered than in the town. In his early novels Cooper was not against the advance of civilization *per se*, only its needless destruction and lack of respect for the wilderness. For the urban readership that turned his novels into bestsellers, it provided a self-serving emotional release to a society with a voracious appetite for cleared land.

Cooper did not challenge his readers directly, who could always comfort themselves with the thought that the most shameful despoilers lambasted by Cooper were other people. For example, *The Last of the Mohicans* (1826), a historical novel set in the Seven Years War, presented the greatest threat to American wilderness as the 'cold and selfish' policies of Britain and France. Here the opposing forces plod through the forest, in contrast to the Indians who seem to melt away into the darkness of the woods and skip along forest tracks barely discernible to the white man.

The corresponding artistic figure who kick-started the national soul-searching in the second quarter of the nineteenth century was the English-born artist Thomas Cole (1801–1848). An insider in the American art establishment from early in his career, the outward and inward life of Cole stands for much of the emigrant European's experience of nineteenth-century America. Born in Lancashire, he emigrated with his family in 1818 and settled in the upper Ohio Valley, whose wild forests made a lifelong impression on him. Trained as a calico painter, Cole undertook a variety of jobs in commercial art, but his preoccupation with finding a distinctly American art was inspired by visits to the Pennsylvania Academy of Art, then at the forefront of debates concerning a national style. Determined to make his name as a painter, he headed for New York in 1825, taking with him the sketches he had made on a tour up the Hudson river, flowing for some three hundred miles from the Adirondack Mountains to the Bay of New York, and including the artistically fertile scenery of the Catskill Mountains. Cole visited the Catskills a year after its first hotel had opened and was attracting the American elite in their search for the grandeur of nature. The resulting paintings sold well, partly because he had found in John Trumball, President of the American Academy, someone who liked his work and could introduce him to the city's well-healed clients, art collectors following the similar European fashion that equated a man's status with the sophistication of his taste. Their existence also reminds us that there was already a market for paintings of American scenery, and artists like Thomas Birch and Thomas Doughty to service it.

European stylistic conventions were difficult for American artists like Thomas Cole to unlearn. The creation of a distinctly national art was to be achieved on terms already set by Europe, to whose sophistication America at that time deferred. American scenery was such that the techniques of landscape painters such as Salvator Rosa (1615–1673) and Claude Lorrain (1600–1682) could be applied to unexplored places to give a fresh impetus to landscape painting and produce a body of work that could never have been produced by an artist in Rome or Paris. In 1831 Cole went to Italy, where he stayed for a year and lived in a studio that tradition held once belonged to Claude. Claude remained a revered painter to Cole long after he had established his own reputation. Cole was also familiar with English theories of the Picturesque, but recognised that the scale of American forests called for something altogether more epic than the compressed scenery of England. Cole's originality was largely the product of his subject matter. A wilderness landscape had to eschew the pastoral style of European art whose formula required a landscape to be peopled with rustics, and whose scenery bore the imprint of civilization, whether in the form of classical or medieval ruins, or a church spire. Where human figures appear in Cole's work, like the dwindling indigenous Americans of the eastern forests, they are diminutive and dwarfed by the wilderness.

Cole wrote in his journal in 1835 of the privileges enjoyed by the painter of American scenery, where all nature was new to art, where its 'virgin forests, lakes and waterfalls feast the eye with new delights ... preserved untouched from the time of creation for his heaven-favoured pencil'.[11] In effect Cole and his compatriots appropriated these landscapes for themselves, bringing nature under the dominion of art, representing another kind of conquest. Cole's 1826 painting of the Kaaterskill Waterfall is shrouded by forest trees, but this was not quite the untouched landscape that so heaven-favoured the American artist. Cole eliminated all traces of contemporary tourism, such as the steps and handrails for negotiating the precipitous terrain, and the wooden tower for viewing the waterfall, because he was attempting to portray the wilderness as it might have appeared before white settlement. The painting includes a solitary Indian brave on the rocks overlooking the falls. This last Mohican was emblematic of a disappearing wilderness, but Cole was not mourning the Indian's disappearance. Indigenous Americans could be removed from the American forests without disturbing the idea that the landscape was in its primeval state. American wilderness myths were blind to the presence of indigenous Americans in the landscape and of their impact upon it. This entailed the belief, which Cole subscribed to like most of his contemporaries, that these native people were untutored savages incapable of altering their natural environment, which was tantamount to saying that they remained at the mercy of the seasons and were therefore incapable of organizing their future. The forests were believed to have been in a state of equilibrium with nature when the settlers began their heroic transformation. In fact indigenous Americans were remembered best in romanticized fiction of Cooper and others when they were already safely out of harm's way.

The attitude of Europeans to Amerindians had been ruthless and hypocritical even before President Andrew Jackson legalized ethnic cleansing in the 1830 Indian Relocation Act. To the discoverers of the New World, Indians were Noble Savages. Arthur Barlowe, who travelled to Virginia in 1584 with Sir Walter Raleigh, said that he found the people

1 *Landscape with the Finding of Moses,* by Claude Lorrain (1600-82). The landscape of the Nile has been Europeanized and, instead of being discovered in bul-
rushes, Moses is found beneath the shade of a tree.

2 *Charles I*, by Anthony van Dyck (1599-1641). Charles had himself glorified as a warrior king under the shade of an oak tree, the spirit of the nation.

3 *Portrait of the Artist with his Wife and Daughter,* by Thomas Gainsborough (1727-1788), in a woodland setting. It was said of Gainsborough that 'nature was his teacher and the woods of Suffolk his academy'.

4 *Cornard Wood*, detail, by Thomas Gainsborough (1727-1788). Gainsborough described this important early work as 'an early instance how strong my inclination stood for landskip'.

5 *The Cenotaph to Reynolds' Memory, Coleorton,* by John Constable (1776-1837). The memorial to the great British painter was set up in a lime grove at Coleorton, Leicestershire. Constable added busts of Michelangelo and Raphael.

6 *The Menin Road,* by Paul Nash (1889-1946). Commissioned by the Imperial War Museum and painted in 1918-19, Nash shows a wood shattered by heavy artillery, standing for a devastated civilization.

7 Green Man bench end in Crowcombe church, Somerset, carved in 1534. The Green Man has mermen coming out of his ears, representing the demons in his head.

'most gentle, loving and faithfull, void of all guile, and treason, and such as lived after the manner of the golden age'. In the nineteenth century the classic Indian portraits by Charles Bird King and George Catlin are similarly respectful. New England puritans initially thought them innocent and ripe for conversion, although their resistance to Christianity would later brand them sinful. When the British army used Indians as auxiliaries against the colonists they were accused of employing savages. Yet Americans stressed their independent identity by dressing as Mohawks to tip tea chests into Boston harbour. The demonization of Indians gathered pace in the 1830s when they became the enemy of the white man and suffered the humiliation of his vengeance. Uncivilized and treacherous, few people considered that the Indians made any more impact on their natural environment than did the wild bear.

The quickening pace of forest clearance in the first half of the nineteenth century was unsettling to romantics. Economic development continued to override all other attitudes to the forests. As late as 1830 President Andrew Jackson could ask:

> What good man would prefer a country covered with forests and ranged by a few thousand savages to our extensive Republic, studded with cities, towns, and prosperous farms, embellished with all the improvements which art can devise or industry execute ... and filled with all the blessings of liberty, civilization, and religion? [12]

Thomas Cole documented the reality behind the rhetoric in the valley of Catskill Creek, a tributary of the Hudson. In two paintings, of 1837 and 1843, viewed from the same vantage point, Cole contrasted the green canopy over the landscape of the earlier painting with a similar view denuded of much of its wilderness vegetation in the later. The causes were many, but all ultimately in the name of commerce. The Canajoharie and Catskill Railroad had seen the felling of large numbers of trees, and Cole even remarked that this included felling an 'ancient grove of cedar, that shadowed the Indian burying ground'. Tree clearance for the railroad was small fry. Even the stripping of bark for the tanning industry was dwarfed by the insatiable advance of the lumberjack:

> The ravages of the axe are daily increasing – the most noble scenes are made desolate, and often with a wantonness and barbarism scarcely credible

in a civilized nation. The wayside is becoming shadeless, and another generation will behold spots, now rife with beauty, desecrated by what is called improvement.[13]

Cole's inner life was one of escape to nature from encroaching industrialization, while at the same time fully recognizing that its progress was inevitable. As a young man he had left industrial Lancashire for the American frontier, while as an adult he saw the same forces creeping upon him from the east – from which he fled through the medium of painting. Cole was a man of conservative instinct. As society began to change at an ever-increasing pace, so he looked for permanence in nature. To that extent his romantic impulses had a pronounced English ancestry. Gradual encroachment upon the pristine landscape of the eastern states transformed this old world response into a distinctly American frontier mentality, one of the consequences of which was that the powerful myth of primordial wilderness was gradually edged westwards. For, as Cole had argued, if progress 'makes us fear that the bright and tender flowers of the imagination shall all be crushed beneath its iron tramp, it would be well to cultivate the oasis that yet remains ... and thus preserve the germs of a future yet fairer system'. It was an early rallying cry to conservationists, and expressed reservations that had also been rehearsed by Cooper.

Cole expressed a much darker vision in his series of five paintings entitled 'The Course of Empire' (1834–36). These allegorical works, commissioned by the grocery millionaire Luman Reed for an almighty $5000, ruminated on the rise and fall of civilizations, a cycle that America was at the beginning of but would inevitably see to the end. Uplifted by nature, Cole was among the first people to articulate American nature as a spiritual resource to be cherished, not merely territory to be exploited. He introduced into America the notion of wild landscape as an object of aesthetic appreciation, noble sentiments that elevated a society founded upon its exploitation. But Cole was far from a simple man of the woods. His work as an artist implicitly accepted the necessity of civilization, which he wanted to be a part of. Trips to Europe, and specifically his year living in Rome, saw him wrestling with the two conflicting impulses whose only solution was to divide his time: communion with nature and comradeship with his fellow beings. In his journal he wrote that 'the sublime scenes of nature are too severe for a lone man to look upon and be happy', a feeling reiterated in his poem 'The Spirit of the Wilderness' a year later.[14] The competing claims of wilderness and civilization have preoccupied many subsequent generations of Americans.

Cole had been the founder and leading light of the Hudson River School of painters, a term first used, and not flatteringly, in 1879. His more conservative successors continued to depict the Hudson Valley as the epitome of American scenery, a genre that would come to look increasingly provincial against emerging French Impressionism. Cole's mantle was taken by Frederick Edwin Church (1826–1900) whose most famous woodland painting was a patriotic work entitled *Hooker and Company Journeying Through the Wilderness from Plymouth to Hartford in 1636*. It depicts a small party of Puritans making their way through the virgin New England woods to establish a new colony. Starr moved on from this unsophisticated patriotism to explore the vastness of America from the Andes to Canada. Other artists, notably Albert Bierstadt (1830–1902), ventured west to the sierras, the Rockies and the land of big trees in search of new territories to conquer in the name of art.

Unlike the trees of the East Coast of America, the Californian giant redwood and its cousin the coast redwood are like no species found in the Old World. Long after their discovery they were considered to be the biggest and oldest living creatures on the planet. Since the perfection of accurate tree-ring dating in the 1950s the accolade of the oldest tree has been taken by the bristlecone pine, the oldest of which are above four thousand years old, while the Australian peppermint gum tree claims to be the world's tallest. Redwoods are certainly mighty beasts. One coast redwood was measured at over 367 feet while the famous giant redwood, nicknamed General Sherman, was measured at 272 feet in 1931 and is now the largest tree in America. The species was discovered by disappointed gold diggers in 1852 in the western foothills of the Sierra Nevada near Mariposa. A specimen was stripped of its bark in 1854 and displayed in New York as a hollow but otherwise genuine botanical marvel, to a sceptical response. The English and French discussed the matter more seriously and more competitively – the English wanted to name it *Wellingtonia gigantea*. However, the generic term *Sequoia* had been ascribed to the coastal redwood and was named after a half-blood Alabama Cherokee Indian. The adoption of *Sequoia gigantea* for the giant redwood by the Harvard Botanical Garden saved the pride of the American forests from being named after an English hero.[15]

As had happened in the eastern states, the contribution of the Ahwahneechee Indians to the landscape of the big trees was not recognized and they were quickly ousted. The western forests were classified as an Edenic wilderness in contrast to the now pacified wilderness of the east and soon attracted tourists, or pilgrims as they preferred to be known. Hotels were put up and lumberjacks moved in – it was said that felling a giant redwood could take five men three weeks. But most people left in awe not with lumber. Paintings by Albert Bierstadt, and photographs by Eadweard Muybridge and Carleton Watkins, helped to promote the Californian forested wilderness to the eastern states as a place of veneration (and helped to establish photography as an artistic medium). The red columns were temple-like and added to the reverence of the forest wilderness, which is as Bierstadt portrayed them, even including an indigenous Indian family dwarfed by the grandeur, like fairies in a European pine forest. The Unitarian preacher Thomas Starr King declared the redwood groves to be standing 'as the Creator fashioned it, unprofaned except by fire'. Perhaps some of the trees were sending up their first shoots just as the Star of Bethlehem rose in the East.

The answer to the relentless advance of the lumberjack was not simply to rue the dwindling forests in well-chosen words or in paintings, but to do something practical to save them. The possibility of preserving areas of the nation's wilderness developed parallel with the nationalistic associations of wilderness. The lamentations of artists like Thomas Cole and the bird painter John James Audubon had drawn attention to the plight of the forests, but it was George Catlin, the painter of native Americans, who in the 1830s first advocated a national park to safeguard a portion of the wilderness, including the native Americans and the buffalo, before it yielded to improvement: 'What a beautiful and thrilling specimen for America to preserve and hold up to the view of her refined citizens and the world, in future ages! A nation's park, containing man and beast, in all the wild[ness] and freshness of their nature's beauty!' [16]

Henry David Thoreau argued that 'in wildness is the preservation of the world', and specifically that humanity needed forests 'for inspiration and our own true recreation'. In 1859 he advocated that in his home state of Massachusetts each township should have a primitive forest of between five hundred and a thousand acres, for just such inspirational purposes. Thoreau had realized that a balance needed to be struck between nature and civilization, the same compromise being sought by Samuel Hammond, an Albany lawyer and a vocal advocate of preservation. Hammond was equally attracted by civilization and the wild. Although he criticized the utilitarian approach to nature, he did not suggest that progress should be halted, only confined to certain areas. This would leave wild places for the nourishment of the soul.

The wilderness pressure group needed a popular voice behind its political momentum. This it found in the Scottish-born John Muir, one of the best-known popular journalists and authors on America's natural inheritance. Drawn to the wilderness first as a boy settling with his pioneer family in Wisconsin, then by inclination at the University of Wisconsin, and finally by compulsion after being temporarily blinded in an accident, Muir was a gifted communicator who infected readers with his enthusiasm. Human beings had spent their primitive years in the woods, giving them a taste for adventure and freedom not satisfied by the urban existence. Therefore 'going to the woods is going home', and 'the clearest way into the Universe is through a forest wilderness'. Constructing himself as a kind of John the Baptist, Muir could inspire with the simplicity of his message: Nature, the terrestrial manifestation of God, was a 'window opening into heaven', the primitive forests were 'God's first temples', while its trees were 'psalm-singing'. In such places 'nature's peace will flow into you as the sunshine into the trees'. Muir, who was instrumental in the establishment of the Yellowstone National Park in 1872, was equally adamant in his exhortations to preserve forests, and for them to be taken into public ownership.[17]

Preservation had practical as well as philosophical motives. Until the 1870s American forests seemed endless, but once settlers moved into the final timber frontier, represented by the forested parts of the Rocky Mountains and Pacific Coast, the end was in sight. Americans needed to rethink their approach to forestry if they were to avert a catastrophe, which in turn posed the difficult problem of modifying the strong pioneering mentality and the rationale of progress. The federal government was urged to take a leading role in introducing measures that would regulate the cutting and sale of timber in such a way that would allow natural regrowth. Early legislation, like the 1878 Free Timber Act, attempted to restrict the places where timber could be harvested but was largely unsuccessful, as it was open to abuse and difficult to police. Congress appointed a forestry agent in 1876 who produced *Reports upon Forestry* between 1877 and 1884 and was given a brief to study European forestry practices, and by 1886 forestry was a branch of the federal Department of Agriculture. The aim was now to manage trees as a renewable resource, although this could only be implemented on publicly owned land.

As for private landowners and lumbermen, the inclination to preserve came from economic pressure. Overproduction and the slump in prices in the 1880s brought it home to many lumbermen that their business was not a licence to print money and that the future lay in better forestry practice. To this end, the American Forestry Association had already been set up after a congress in Chicago in 1875 to promote forestry education in agricultural colleges and better economic and technical management of forests. The lumber interest did not facilitate preservation of wilderness directly, but it eased the passage of preservation into the debate about forests.

A different and highly effective practical approach to preservation was taken by George Perkins Marsh (1801–1882), whose ground-breaking *Man and Nature: Physical Geography as Modified by Human Action* was first published in 1864. The book challenged many of the assumptions about progress and, although not a devotee of wilderness himself, Marsh provided a strong intellectual basis for the wilderness lobby. He challenged the dictum of Genesis 1:28 that man had been given the Earth to dominate and subdue, arguing that by excessively altering the Earth a natural equilibrium was being disrupted. Man, he argued, disturbed the in-built balances in nature, which could only be restored when he withdrew, and was the only creature on Earth to whom this applied. 'I am not aware of any evidence that wild animals have ever destroyed the smallest forest, extirpated any organic species, or modified its natural character ... which nature has not, of herself, repaired.'[18] He singled out forest clearance as the most dangerous example of how God's creation had been abused. The felling of trees in the headwaters of so many rivers had caused drought, erosion and climatic changes, because the forests acted like a sponge drawing in rainfall and releasing water

at a regular outflow into rivers. The decline of Mediterranean civilizations was blamed by Marsh on excessive felling that disrupted a balanced
environment and was a salutary lesson to Americans. Preservation and
planting were therefore economically as well as ethically desirable. With
this in mind Marsh advocated a forest preserve in the Adirondack
Mountains, in northern New York State, which would serve many
purposes. A large and easily accessible region of American soil should
be retained in its primitive condition, 'at once a museum for the
instruction of the student, a garden for the recreation of the lover of
nature, and an asylum where indigenous tree, and humble plant that
loves the shade ... may dwell and perpetuate their kind'.[19]

The heavily forested Adirondack Mountains soon became the focus
of the conservation lobby in the east. They had escaped large-scale
clearance for agriculture largely because there was more favourable land
further west. As the economic development of the eastern seaboard
continued apace, the Adirondacks became a favourite holiday destination. William H. Murray, a Congregationalist pastor, wrote a popular
account of the district for city dwellers, praising the delights of its
hunting and fishing and advocating its preservation. Murray's principal
argument was that the forests were necessary refreshment for jaded city
minds, and that he always returned from his stays with 'elasticity in his
step, fire in his eye, depth and clearness in his reinvigorated voice'. The
sporting magazine *Forest and Stream*, founded in 1873 and also active
in promoting a national park in the Adirondacks, saw the watershed
argument as the trump card in favour of preservation.

Ironically the first national park was declared in 1864 during the
Civil War, the most divisive years in American history. The Yosemite
district in the western Sierra Nevada, including California's now famous redwood groves, was the first of the national parks designated,
so as to prevent them becoming private property, and for the physical
and mental reinvigoration of all the people. Almost immediately a
campaign began for the Adirondacks to be similarly designated, which
succeeded in 1885 when 715,000 acres became a forest preserve to be
'kept forever as wild forest lands'. Other voices, including the *New
York Times*, had also joined the preservationist cause and in 1872 the
newly created New York State Park Commission produced its first
report.

It did not intend to create 'an expensive and exclusive park' for recreation, however, but intended to retain the forests as a measure of political economy. Without a regular and constant flow of water the state's canals and rivers would be dry, impeding the passage of grain and other produce from west to east. In the early 1880s the issue became more urgent when the levels of the River Hudson and Erie Canal declined. The worrying situation was blamed by apprehensive New Yorkers on the timber and mining interests in the Adirondacks, which in turn led to the involvement of the New York Chamber of Commerce with claims that the internal commerce of the state was being placed in jeopardy. It was this, and not cultural arguments, that won the day in 1885. Wilderness preservation was by this means established in conjunction with industry and commerce and was never placed in opposition to it. Although the fact of its preservation vindicated Thoreau and Samuel Hammond, the spirit of the legislation came from the utilitarian arguments of Marsh.

The cause of further forest protection took its greatest leap forward in 1891 when the Forest Reserve Act was passed by Congress. One of its provisions allowed the President to set apart publicly owned forested land as public reservations. Presidents Benjamin Harrison and Grover Cleveland created over 47,000,000 acres of public forest reserves over the next decade, but it was only a qualified triumph for the wilderness lobby. Unfortunately the manner in which the reserves were to be managed was vague, and there was no adequate means of enforcement. These issues were resolved in the 1897 Forest Management Act, but not everyone was pleased. A bitter dispute developed as to whether the legislation was intended to preserve wilderness or if it was a regime for best managing forests as a sustainable economic resource. It could hardly be both, as a managed wilderness is a contradiction in terms. It opened the door to a new breed of conservation-minded foresters, the chief of whom was Gifford Pinchot, chief of the Forestry Division of the Department of Agriculture, a Yale graduate with a training in forestry acquired in France and Germany. Pinchot firmly believed that forests should be at the service of civilization rather than be allowed to exist for their own sake, whether or not they have any utilitarian use. Even purists like John Muir conceded at one point that it was impossible to stop at preservation, but it raised a dilemma in conservation strategy

Chestnut oak (*Quercus prinus*), native to north-east America, drawn by Pierre-Joseph Redouté from André Michaux, *Histoire des chênes de l'Amerique* (1801).

that has never been fully resolved. It also exposed a delusion that had existed all along. Conservationists did not recognize that the forests cleared by pioneer settlers had already been subtly altered by native Indians and so forest reserves could never represent what the world was like before human interference.

America's national parks were the equivalent of Europe's national monuments and a product of its nineteenth-century nation building. Even the US Department of Agriculture could ask, in its annual report for 1860:

> What monument erected by human skill could be compared to forests of gigantic trees, like those of Maine, Mississippi, and California, which have outlived the empire of Rome with all its grandeur and architecture, and may yet live after all modern nations have become lost in the history of the past? [20]

The early culture of the forests was imported by European settlers, whose successors created a new, distinctly American forest culture, and in the form of conservation policy exported it back to Europe and beyond, influencing forest practice in India, Australia, South Africa and Japan by the turn of the century. America's other major contribution to woodland culture has been to overturn the association of forests with barbarism. Germany had previously identified this as a Latin prejudice but German and American national identity otherwise chose different forest paths. By creating national wilderness parks it sought a compromise between the need for civilization and the wild.

Forests and nationhood in America, Germany and Britain all demonstrate the need equate the qualities of its people with the innate qualities of the natural environment. It also shows that the manner in which we view nature is often the legacy of deliberate political construction. Ironically, in each case this self-identification has been accompanied by blindness to the large-scale and often needless destruction of the natural resource. Nevertheless, there are positive aspects to the relationship and important lessons. Societies need to see themselves in relation to the natural world. The example of nationalism also shows that it is very hard or impossible to view the woods and forests for their own sake exterior to human interests. Nature cannot exist for us outside of its particular human context, and a tree is never far from being a political issue.

10

Patrician Trees

In contrast to eighteenth- and early nineteenth-century America, where the fate of the woodlands was in the hands of rough and ready backwoodsmen, in Britain the fate of woodlands was increasingly controlled by a small economic and social elite. But patriotism did not top the agenda, for which reason British landowners usually fell far short of the high aspirations that John Evelyn had tried to set for them. Their contribution to the woodland heritage lay elsewhere. Plantations, many of which would now be regarded as natural woodlands, were moves away from the woods of communal celebration and towards the private domain. In this respect many of the woodlands that originated in the eighteenth century spoke more of social privilege than they did of aesthetic appreciation or even of economic investment. Tree planters had their own agenda in maintaining and expressing their position within society, and by the end of the eighteenth century the political establishment felt itself threatened as much from within as from across the English Channel. Patriotism was an impulse, but the country estate was a self-contained world in miniature. This is what the estate woodlands of the eighteenth and early nineteenth century represent.

Country estates had been a phenomenon growing in importance from the sixteenth century, when the holdings of the medieval aristocracy were augmented by the sale of monastic holdings after the dissolution of the monasteries between 1536 and 1539. The growing confidence and importance of the landed aristocracy had followed the Glorious Revolution in 1688 and the establishment of a constitutional monarchy. This was expressed in the development of the country house, a movement spearheaded by the building of Blenheim Palace for the duke of Marlborough to celebrate his famous victory at the battle of Blenheim in 1704. The house, designed by Sir John Vanbrugh, was commissioned by Queen Anne but was far more palatial than the monarchy could have allowed itself at that time. It marked a shift in the balance of power in Britain away from the monarch and into the hands of a new landed elite. The country estate became the ultimate symbol of social success and, although its social structure was largely hereditary, it could nevertheless be entered by people whose wealth was derived from trade and industry. Where a landed family had no heir, it was often new money that stepped in to replace it.

The rise of the country estate also coincided with another profound change in rural culture: deer hunting, the sport of kings, was overtaken by fox hunting, the sport of the aristocracy. No longer stalking the woods for his prey, the huntsman, now on a swift horse, was to be seen on extensive chases over open country. The eighteenth century saw the formation of what have become the famous English hunts such as the Quorn, Pytchley, Raby, Holderness, Bilsdale and Brocklesby, with permanent packs of hounds and hunt masters who enjoyed considerable celebrity for their prowess. Fox hunting became part of the repertoire of the country squire, with all the social consequences that went with it, and land use on an estate was modified to accommodate new demands. Foxes need cover to breed undisturbed, and enough of it to ensure the continuation of the species. In areas where there was sufficient woodland, these could be used, but elsewhere coverts were planted, although they were usually a scrub of gorse and blackthorn with only a sparse planting of trees. Before hunting, the foxes' earths were blocked to prevent them going to ground in the ensuing chase, in what became a sport conducted in a very controlled landscape.

As the wilderness was no longer a testing ground for manliness, woods took on a fresh set of meanings. The planting of trees was a symbol of stability, in family and broader social terms. Slow growing, a landowner needed confidence that he or his descendants would live to reap their rewards, and for this reason England became a nation of planters but Ireland did not. One of its best-known exponents, the Earl of Carlisle, commemorated his tree-planting in an inscription on a monument erected at Castle Howard in Yorkshire in 1731:

> If to perfection these PLANTATIONS rise,
> If they agreeably my heirs surprise,
> This faithful pillar will their age declare

As long as Time these Characters shall spare.
Here then, with Kind Remembrance read his Name,
Who for POSTERITY performed the same.

The Holnicote estate of the Acland family in west Somerset has two
very different kinds of private woodland. Horner Wood, at the foot of
Exmoor and acquired by the Aclands in 1745, is an ancient wood but
was personalized when its tracks were given family names – Granny's
Ride, Tucker's Path, Lord Enrington's Path – symbolizing the privatizing
spirit of the times. Sir Thomas Dyke Acland inherited Holnicote in 1808.
Although the family's principal residence was at Killerton in Devon, Sir
Thomas had spent his formative years at Holnicote and retained a great
affection for the place. Here he established a new plantation to celebrate
the birth of each of his children, ten in all between 1809 and 1827. The
woods above the estate village of Selworthy comprise oak, chestnut,
Scots pine, silver fir and ilex. They conceal a network of paths which,
in its nineteenth-century heyday, totalled some forty miles, a private
retreat maintained by an army of tenants.

A plantation was a monument to its founder and naturalized the
family in its country seat. Venerable old trees were better still. Such
trees were an important asset to estate owners and could be transposed
in pictorial form to town houses. The lure of sophisticated metropolitan
pleasures over rustic simplicity meant living a double life, and opened a
market for topographical painters offering views of country estates that
could be hung in town houses to remind owners of their estates and of
course to impress their friends. Family portraits were painted with their
property in the background, but their social position could be more
subtly portrayed by the use of trees. In Johann Zoffany's portrait of the
Drummond family of c. 1769, and in numerous of the Suffolk gentry
who sat for Thomas Gainsborough, like the Gravenor family, John
Plampin or the newly-wed Mr and Mrs Andrews, the sitters are framed
by an oak tree, assuring society that their owners had roots in the shires.
The oak was a long-lived patriarchal tree with an air of permanence
and instilled notions of longevity that great families liked to associate
themselves with – Edmund Burke described the aristocracy as 'the great
oaks which shade a country'.

The cult of the oak was also to a certain extent the cult of the individual tree, a trend perhaps best represented by Jacob George Strutt's illustrated volume *Sylva Britannica* of 1822, dedicated to the duke of Bedford and subscribed to by the gentry and aristocracy. In Strutt's idealized world old trees symbolized the social order and the labourer cherished the beloved ancient tree as much as the landowner. As he passes it 'he recalls ... the sports of his infancy round its venerable trunk, and regards it at once as his chronicler and landmark'.[1] His loyalty to the tree is akin to his loyalty to his employer.

For all their love of ancient oaks, landowners were less keen on planting new ones. The least patriotic aspect of eighteenth- and nineteenth- century planting was in the selection of species. Trees were not chosen for their fitness for naval timber, but for their amenity value and their rate of growth. For all their sturdiness, oaks are one of the slowest species on Earth. New species offered variety and in some cases, like the now naturalised rhododendron, colour. The landscape gardener Humphry Repton argued that conifers complemented classical buildings while round-headed deciduous trees were best suited to the Gothic style. In practice, though, his planting was more pragmatic. At Welbeck Abbey in Nottinghamshire, seat of the Portland family, the felling of ancient but dying oak trees was praised as a patriotic donation of timber to the Royal Navy. A new campaign of forest planting there, continuing over twenty-five years into the early nineteenth century and covering over two thousand acres, included oak, beech and birch but also larch, Spanish chestnut, Weymouth pine, Virginian tulip tree and a cedar of Lebanon planted on the highest hill. From the sixteenth to the early nineteenth centuries over one thousand new species were imported into Britain, some of which, like the cypress, laburnum and juniper, were ornamental. Spruce, silver fir and larch were especially suited to thin soils and had economic value. Others species, like the holm oak, a native of the Mediterranean, the horse chestnut and sycamore, have become so familiar that the native landscape can scarcely be imagined without them.

The importation of species was closely associated with the growth of landscape gardens. While the eighteenth century saw the contemplation of landscape become an important interest to cultivated minds, it is a reminder that it had a large element of artifice. The movement was influenced by writers like Joseph Addison and Alexander Pope who advocated a larger vision of gardening that, in Addison's words, would allow a man to make a landscape of his own possessions. The landscape garden was symbolized by the invention of the ha-ha, the sunken ditch that allowed a smooth visual transition from garden to landscape or, as Horace Walpole declared, made all of nature into a garden. The land-scape garden is widely regarded as one of the most important English contributions to European culture and the creation of woodlands was an integral part of the movement. One of its earliest practitioners, Stephen Switzer, even described the practice as 'forest gardening'.

The landscape garden could claim a distinctly English pedigree with its origin in the medieval deer park. It was also partly a reaction against the formal geometry of French-inspired gardens, whose circles and straight lines were rejected as a cold artifice, but it is misleading to think of the landscape garden as 'natural' in a way that would be understood in the twenty-first century. Nevertheless, to a contemporary audience its harmony with the surrounding landscape, contrasting with the French style, symbolized the harmony of the English constitution. This may have been chauvinism but it was hardly patriotism. One of the earliest of such landscapes was the work of successive designers Charles Bridgeman, William Kent and Capability Brown at Stowe in Bucking-hamshire. Stowe's owners, the Temple family, had become one of the most powerful aristocratic families in the nation. They had risen through their opposition to Charles I and later to James II and played a significant part in the Glorious Revolution of 1688. Sir Richard Temple had been a distinguished soldier under the duke of Marlborough and was made Viscount Cobham in 1718. Stowe symbolized the Whig authority of the Georgian period, and emphasized that this was the new ruling class. It has a Gothic temple designed by James Gibbs 'to the liberty of our ancestors', but its chief gesture of Englishness is the Temple of British Worthies, built against a wooded backdrop. The Temple has a con-spicuous absence of priests, celebrating as it does Britain's hard-won Protestant identity – Drake, Raleigh and William III – and the cultural achievements of an increasing self-confident nation – Shakespeare, Milton, Francis Bacon and Isaac Newton.

The leading exponents of the landscape style were busy men and had a lasting impact on the English countryside. William Kent (1674–1748) enjoyed an undistinguished career as a painter until he met

Lord Burlington while he was studying in Rome and was taken under his wing. Lord Burlington had pioneered the Palladian style in Britain and employed Kent to design the garden at his suburban retreat at Chiswick. Kent established himself as an architect as well as gardener and was an early professional in the art of landscape design. But the profession is perhaps best represented by Lancelot 'Capability' Brown (1715–1783) and the equally prolific Humphry Repton (1752–1818). Brown worked on nearly two hundred country estates from the late 1740s and enjoyed a national reputation, whereas other designers like William Emes (1730–1804) enjoyed only regional reputations. These professionals can be contrasted with landowners such as the Price family of Foxley and Richard Payne Knight (1750–1824) of Downton, both in Herefordshire, and the poet William Shenstone (1714–1763), who inherited an estate at the Leasowes in Worcestershire when he was twenty-one. All of these men could claim the higher moral ground of being amateurs.

Trees were a vital component in the composition of a landscape, whether in the gestural form of an avenue, or as full-blown plantations. Stephen Switzer designed Paston in Surrey with winding tree-lined walks recalling sylvan groves, a two-dimensional recreation of the forest. In 1734 William Kent began work on a garden at Holkham in Norfolk for Thomas Coke, later the earl of Leicester. Here radiating paths were laid out through a wood on the south side of the house, just as they were through the plantations at Dunham Massey Hall in Cheshire. A dense plantation of trees, however ordered it was in reality, was an element of wilderness to counterpoint a formal garden, as in the woodland walks at Castle Howard. In Capability Brown's beechwood at Clandon Park in Surrey its role was acknowledged in its name 'The Wilderness'. At the Leasowes, between 1745 and 1763, William Shenstone created winding paths through similar narrow belts of trees and wooded valleys, one of which was known as Virgil's Grove, while a structure formed out of old tree roots bore a tablet that celebrated the paradisal conceit of the walk through the garden:

> And tread with awe these favour'd bowers,
> Nor wound the shrubs, nor bruise the flowers;
> So may your path with sweets abound
> So may your couch with rest be crown'd!

But harm betide the wayward swain,
Who dares our hallow'd haunts profane! [2]

The landscape garden was a refuge from the real world, and according to Shenstone the role of the landscape designer was in 'pleasing the imagination by scenes of grandeur, beauty or variety'. Latin inscriptions nailed to trees and alcoves invoked classical associations, while urns dedicated in memory of Shenstone's friends invoked melancholy. Woodland provided a place of reflection easily understood by his contemporaries. James Thomson amplified the concept when he described woods as

the haunts of meditation, these
The scenes where ancient bards the inspiring breath
Ecstatic felt, and, from this world retired,
Conversed with angels and immortal forms. [3]

Landscape gardens presupposed that nature was a prototype that could be perfected by human agency. But there could be no such thing as a purely natural landscape. Idealized landscapes imposed anthropocentric notions that were usually associated with classical civilization. In the eighteenth century gentlemen received a classical education and were even more familiar with Virgil than they were with the classical ruins they visited on the Grand Tour. The acme of the classical Arcadia is arguably the celebrated park at Stourhead in Wiltshire, laid out by the banker Henry Hoare II in the 1740s. Its park, lying a considerable distance from the house, is peppered with temples, many of them designed by the architect Henry Flitcroft. The whole scheme is planned with vistas to delight and surprise, in the service of which thickly wooded walks had a narrative role in shielding views until the walker had reached a contrived vantage point. Some of Flitcroft's designs, like the mini Pantheon and the Temple of Apollo based on the temple at Baalbek, were reproductions which, like the inscription 'Procul, o procul este, profani' (Be gone all you who are uninitiated), were designed for sophisticated tastes only, and placed Stourhead firmly within classical civilization. Meanwhile the rustic cottage known as the 'Convent in the Wood', complete with fancy-dress prioress, provided an amusing rustic counterpoint that served to emphasize the main theme. The near-contemporary Halswell Park, Somerset, had a similar range of temples in a park developed by Sir Charles Kemys-Tynte, a friend of Hoare's, which included plantations of chestnuts and firs. A 'Robin Hood's House' was built there in 1765 whose Gothic exterior was detailed with appliqué bark to the eaves and two hollow tree trunks framing the door.

With the arbitrary use of classical or Gothic, deciduous or coniferous, the eighteenth-century landscape garden eschewed the idea of a sense of place. Not only did its chief exponents adopt the same strategy to landscapes in the otherwise contrasting east and west England, they followed fixed aesthetic rules. These rules had largely been influenced by the experience of Englishmen on the Grand Tour, by poets such as James Thomson, and by contemporary art. Three artists – Claude Lorrain, Nicolas Poussin (1594–1665) and Salvator Rosa – were especially influential. Englishmen were great collectors of these paintings, a fashion that spawned native imitators like George Lambert (*c.* 1700–1765) and John Wootton (*c.* 1682–1764). Even painters like Richard Wilson (1713/14–1782), whose subject matter was recognizably Welsh, set his Gallic landscapes under Italian skies. An Englishman recognized in a Claude painting not so much the Roman countryside as the familiar context of the *Aeneid.* Such paintings were part of the taste for all things classical.

A Claude painting of the Roman *campagna* was formulaic, arranging its stock of elements into a preconceived structure. The viewer looked from a high vantage point over an extensive landscape and a distant horizon. The foreground was shaded by trees and contrasted with the lighter green of the middle distance and blue background, set against a golden sun. The image was framed by a dense mass of trees to one side, and perhaps a rock or building to the other side. Ironically James Thomson's description of landscape worked in a similar way, taking a high vantage point as the appropriate place for contemplation of the scene. That Thomson and Claude came to similar solutions in their portrayal of landscape highlights the orthodoxy with which natural landscape was viewed by a contemporary audience, however artificial it now seems. Taste in the eighteenth century was less a matter of personal expression than of appreciating set values. Social accomplishment could be achieved only by the ability to perceive a landscape in the 'correct' manner. Jane Austen poked fun at it in *Northanger Abbey* (1818) when the heroine Catherine Morland feels out of her depth as her friends Henry and Eleanor Tilney begin a conversation about landscape: 'They were viewing the country with the eyes of persons accustomed to drawing; and decided on its capability of being formed into pictures, with all the eagerness of real taste. Here Catherine was quite lost. She knew nothing of drawing – nothing of taste.' It occurs to her that her inability to appreciate the qualities they spoke of is a limitation of her own sensibility. As she is eager to learn, Henry Tilney begins to instruct her in aesthetic rules, describing the importance of light and shade, perspective and so on, so that when they reached their destination of Beechen Cliff 'she voluntarily rejected the whole city of Bath, as unworthy to make part of a landscape'.[4]

The rules of painting were similar to the rules of landscape gardening. In the landscape style established by Capability Brown clumps and copses were more favoured than dense, dark woods. Here the emphasis was on the exclusive enjoyment of the panorama and the vista – the view from a distance. It was hardly a place where people tripped over fallen branches or ventured away from strategically planned drives. The fashion for belvederes, and of siting houses where they offered fine views of surrounding countryside, placed the viewer in the position of the painter, so that the landscape could be appreciated in pictorial fashion. In this respect landscape parks were partly suggested by pictorial images of the Italian countryside and therefore intended to mould Cumbria and Umbria in the same image. Stourhead is said to have been partly based on Claude's painting of a *Coast View of Delos with Aeneas*, which itself refers to a passage from Virgil.

The aesthetic of classical allusion never quite escaped its social context. Idealized landscapes with classical temples and woodlands haunted by nymphs and dryads were part of the gentry claim to be the heirs of classical civilization, at the same time imbuing the existing order with an ancient authority. Gardeners like Brown and Repton made a show of ancient trees in order to suggest an ancient lineage for their clients. The job of the gardener was to display the owner's property to the best advantage. If a park was too small for its owner's self-importance, Humphry Repton used belts of trees to screen off boundaries and hint at a thickly forested vastness beyond the naked eye.

A more subtle social grading could be distinguished by the end of the eighteenth century as owners of country estates could be categorized as old and new money. A country estate had strong associative powers

of longevity and rootedness, the kind of associations that new landowners were attracted to. For those in the know, however, a self-made
man could be distinguished from an aristocrat by his taste in trees. In
his early career Humphry Repton had worked for a number of aristocratic families, but as the commissions dried up in the nervous 1790s
he came more and more to rely upon the parvenus who could still
afford the luxury of his services. Repton displayed a tradesman's snob-
bery. At one time the choice of whether to plant coniferous or deciduous
trees had been a matter of aesthetics. It later became a symbol of
breeding. Commissioned in 1813 to work on Lord Uxbridge's estate at
Beaudesert in Staffordshire, he recommended that belts of fir trees be
cut down and replaced by deciduous trees more worthy of his ancestral
rank. Repton did not lose an opportunity to link modern affluence with
ignorance. Of one client he wrote:

> How could I hope to suggest an idea to this man who shewed me what he
> called 'the largest acorn he had ever seen!' at the same time producing the
> cone of a stone pine that grew near an oak and had fallen among the acorns!
> (fit emblem of him I thought who had fallen among Gentlemen but could
> not be mistaken for one).[5]

Repton's prejudices deepened with time and in his *Fragments on the
Theory and Practice of Landscape Gardening* of 1816 improvement came
to be regarded as little more than a machine for profit. He illustrated
this by two views and descriptions of a recently improved estate which
he had visited a decade previously, and where he had met an old labourer
who confirmed his worst fears. The hereditary owner had sold the estate
to 'a very rich man' who had ushered in changes on purely economic
grounds:

> By cutting down the timber and getting an act to enclose the common, he
> had doubled all the rents. The old mossy and ivy-covered pale was replaced
> by a new and lofty close paling; not to confine the deer, but to exclude
> mankind, and to protect a miserable narrow belt of firs and Lombardy
> poplars: the bench was gone, the ladder-stile was changed to a caution about
> man-traps and spring-guns, and a notice that the footpath was stopped by
> order of the commissioners. As I read the board, the old man said 'It is very
> true, and I am forced to walk a mile further round every night after a hard
> day's work'.[6]

IMPROVEMENTS

'Improvements', from Humphry Repton, *Fragments on the Theory and Practice of Landscape Gardening.*

But how did the country estate and the landscape garden interact with other classes? In the first half of the eighteenth century it became fashionable for a country house to stand within its own grounds and in lofty isolation from any community. If cottages or even whole villages stood in the way they could be removed and rebuilt in a less conspicuous location. Eight villages were relocated to accommodate the designs of William Kent and Capability Brown at Stowe. William Mason, in *The English Garden* published in 1772, marked a move away from this style when he advised landscapers to incorporate all aspects of the working countryside. In this view sylvan glades became part of an all-embracing rustic tableau. An image of a timeless and contented countryside, however artificially contrived, asserted the morality and naturalness of the existing order.

Throughout the eighteenth century landowners in fact tightened their control over the landscape. Legislation was sought to limit the customary rights of forest communities to harvest underwood, in effect turning communal woodlands into private domains. The Black Act of 1723 restricted woodland access, in particular where estate tenants could be forbidden from felling trees for timber. Access to the woods could be carefully controlled on an estate and could be turned to the owner's advantage to help cement the social hierarchy. At the well-wooded Sheringham estate in Norfolk in 1812, Humphry Repton recommended that the poor be admitted to the estate woods on perhaps one day a month under the watchful eye of the keeper, to collect dead wood. It would, he argued, prevent the unauthorized lopping of trees for firewood. Likewise the organization of coursing matches would reduce illegal poaching.[7] Social unrest made landowners twitchy, and in the dangerous times of the 1790s made them think harder about their relationship with the lower orders. Landscape gardens where the cottages had been swept away left the gentry looking aloof and vulnerable, but a park that integrated the cottages pictorially cemented the community. During the same period the ironmaster and landowner Richard Reynolds laid out woodland walks for his workmen at the Coalbrookdale ironworks in Shropshire. Known as Sabbath Walks, they led to a Doric Temple and a Rotunda. Although these people already had access to the woodlands, their purpose was a moral and practical one: to keep the workmen out of the public houses on their day off in a broader strategy to engender workplace discipline.

Sir Uvedale Price (1747–1829), to whom the art of improving an estate consisted essentially 'in the arrangement and management of trees', was acutely aware of the social management required of the estate improver. In the *Annals of Agriculture* of 1786 he advocated laws to restrict the right of wanton tenants and woodmen to crop oak and elm for firewood, a practice that affected the economic and pictorial value of estates. But in 1797, not long after the French landing in Wales, he published *Thoughts on the Defence of Property* that took a more subtle line. Social stability rested upon recognizing the importance of the local community, and that community sense should be integrated into planned improvements. Price argued that his family's tolerance of villagers, allowing them to walk through the estate, had been repaid with respect and loyalty, and that such a tactic would be a better weapon against democratic aspirations than an armed militia.

Changing social attitudes paralleled changing aesthetic approaches to the idealized landscape. The Picturesque movement of the late eighteenth century saw trees and people as essential elements of the landscape, well represented in the work of one its main influences, Thomas Gainsborough. In later life Gainsborough claimed that one of his earlier woodland landscapes – known variously as *Cornard Wood* and *Gainsborough Forest* – was begun as a child and was the means by which his father got him apprenticed to an artist in London. All of his woodland paintings, however stylized, betray a familiarity with real woodlands where the bare dead branches are intermixed with the greenery. His interest in woodland was innate, but his art was shaped by the market. Gainsborough assimilated the lessons of Claude and the French painter Antoine Watteau (1684–1721), but he was also influenced by Dutch 'landskips', a popular if not highly regarded art form.

Woodland was not a popular subject with eighteenth-century landscape painters. The ideal landscapes of Claude were all prospects. The painter was looking at a landscape while the painter of woodland needed to be *in* a landscape. But woodland did have one advantage as a subject: its lack of a specific geography. A sense of place is antithetical to a landscape ideal with strict compositional rules. Gainsborough must have experienced a sharp contrast between the flat Suffolk landscapes and the undulating and woody landscapes of the west of England, but a sense of place did not become a subject in its own right. In his native

Suffolk Gainsborough had made a living as a painter of the local gentry
and their property, but it was his move to Bath in 1759 and the visits
to estates in western Britain that derived from it that turned him into
a serious landscape painter. His acquaintance with Uvedale Tomkyns
Price led him to visit to his estate at Foxley in Herefordshire, famous
for its beech woods. Here began Gainsborough's friendship with Tomkyns Price's grandson, Sir Uvedale Price, the theorist of the Picturesque.

Gainsborough probably influenced Price's *Essays on the Picturesque*,
published between 1794 and 1798. At Foxley, the character of which was
described as 'fine trees forming a woody amphitheatre around the
mansion', he drew one of his earlier mature landscapes, a highly finished
sketch of a beech tree.[8] Gainsborough did not throw off the rules of
genre art entirely, as the distant church tower provides a prospect in
the prescribed manner, as well as introducing a moral tone to the picture.
But its focus on a single tree was to become a characteristic of the
Picturesque movement. It drew the eye to the foreground and the
closeness of nature, not the distant horizon. The finished sketch was
used by him to paint a more recognizably genre scene by adding a
woodcutter and a mounted peasant. A landscape painting, as opposed
to a drawing from nature, was not finished until it had been humanized
with contented rustics. These were not, therefore, images of nature but
highly politicized images that paralleled the fashion for incorporating
cottages on estates. They left no room for the complaints of the oppressed rural poor, living as they were the kind of simple life that men
of means dreamed about. Many of Gainsborough's important woodland
paintings were commissioned or purchased by landowners to meet their
preconceptions of a sylvan Arcadia on their own estates, paintings like
Peasants Returning from Market through a Wood, painted for Lord
Shelburne and hung at Bowood in Wiltshire. None of these paintings
can be regarded as representing a specific place. Even when he painted
for exhibition at the newly-formed Royal Academy, Gainsborough's
images remained imbued with stereotypes. His *Wooded Landscape with
Cattle* was described approvingly by the Reverend Henry Bate as 'representing a woodland scene, a sequestered cottage, cattle, peasants and
their children before the cottage, a woodman and his dog ... returning
from labour; the whole heightened by a water and sky that would have
done honour to the most brilliant Claude Lorrain'.[9] Gainsborough's

woodland pictures therefore are a long way from studies of nature or topography as later artists like Constable would have understood them.

Toward the end of his life Gainsborough chose grander historical and mythological settings for his paintings on the basis that great art is made from great subjects, which surely went against the grain of his own instincts. In *Diana and Actaeon* of *c.* 1785 a well-known tale from Ovid was imported into an English woodland setting as an appropriate classical subject for educated tastes. An earlier painting, *The Mall* of 1783, is ostensibly a painting of St James's Park in London and shows a bustling town scene. The painting has been praised for its painterly qualities as an Anglicised recreation of the French rococo style where the lessons of Watteau have been well learned. The scene is of ladies promenading, in the midst of which is a solitary male figure, perhaps the artist, but it is the setting that is important and takes it beyond a mere genre painting. Far from being a townscape, the ladies walk in a sylvan glade that serves to turn them into goddesses parading in an English woodland paradise.

The Picturesque movement owed much to Gainsborough and Salvator Rosa, whose landscape work was characterized by the drama and rough-ness of nature. An aspect of eighteenth-century primitivism, it was a reaction against an increasingly scientific and rationalist (and one could also add commercial) civilization. Its leading exponent, William Gilpin (1724–1804), was not a gardener but a commentator upon scenery. As its name suggests, the Picturesque was a pictorial approach that conti-nued to treat nature as a commodity that could be improved upon. Gilpin focused upon individual objects within the landscape – typically things like a blasted tree – and framed his views around it. Woods that in a Claude painting were on the fringe were now moved centre stage. Nature was rugged and asymmetrical and there was a distinction be-tween wild and cultivated nature. The theory was enacted in the country house setting by two notable planters, Sir Uvedale Price and Richard Payne Knight, both of whom were noted authors.

The landscapes of Price and his near neighbour Knight contrasted with the rigid order of Capability Brown, where the humbler trees were cut down and where conifers were fashionable. Brown was criticized for disrupting the organic growth of woodlands in order to impose a new structure that favoured fast-growing trees. In his later work Humphry

Repton modified his tendency to impose a preconceived order on the landscape by attempting to harmonize or improve upon the *genius loci*. Thus at Luscombe, in Devon, the terrain demanded a house in the castellated style, designed by John Nash and built in 1800, for which Repton planted a thickly wooded backdrop. Repton's later preference for deciduous trees chimed well with Price's opinion. To Uvedale Price an avenue of oaks was a 'grand Gothic aisle' while the canopy of its leaves was the vaulted roof. Knight too disliked conifers and exhorted his readers to grow elm and oak to 'banish the fir's unsocial shade'. But as society needed to be ordered, so did nature. The Picturesque style never claimed to be unadulterated nature.

At Downton in Herefordshire Richard Payne Knight shared many of Price's concerns. He was a connoisseur of landscape who could boast a large number of Claude Lorrain's pictures in his collection. Woodland walks were created along River Teme in order to appreciate the drama of the natural gorge, in keeping with a love of wildness and untamed natural forces that was best expressed in his poem *The Landscape*, first published in 1794. Originally he had intended the poem to accompany Price's *Essay on the Picturesque*, which he had encouraged Price to publish. In it Knight mocked improvers like Capability Brown by using two contrasting illustrations of a country house by Thomas Hearne. The Brown-style landscape is all mown lawn and neatly trimmed trees, in the midst of which a Palladian mansion sits coolly isolated in both time and space. This is contrasted with an unimproved landscape viewed from the edge of an 'ancient forest', which immediately gives it a dimension that Brown's landscape lacked. The house is an older Elizabethan pile, the unkempt trees grow out of a rampant undergrowth of ferns and thorns. Nature is allowed to express itself. Elsewhere Knight suggests that it has an innate hierarchy that paralleled the social hierarchy:

> Some [trees], tow'ring upwards, spread their arms in state;
> And others, bending low, appear'd to wait:
> While scatter'd thorns, brows'd by the goat and deer,
> Rose all around, and let no lines appear.[10]

Knight also had a radical political streak, remaining in sympathy with the aims of the French Revolution. The undressing of a Brownian landscape, allowing a forest to regenerate naturally and for a release of primordial nature, resembled the liberation of the oppressed. Political revolution was expressed in the terms of chaos leading to eventual better order by analogy with nature:

> So when rebellion breaks the despot's chain,
> First wasteful ruin marks the rabble's reign;
> Till tir'd their fury, and their vengeance spent,
> One common int'rest bids their hearts relent;
> Then temp'rate order from confusion springs,
> And, fann'd by freedom, genius spreads its wings.[11]

Jacobin sympathies were spotted by Horace Walpole and others, who were as horrified by Knight's view of nature as they were by his politics. To leave nature to its own devices was the road to ruin. Knight retreated from the association between the Picturesque landscape and radical politics in the second edition of the poem. But he remained a Whig and a believer in free trade, understandably so because the wealth that sustained Downton was not derived from the fruits of rural labour. The Knights were prominent midland ironmasters and had amassed their fortune in trade. Richard Payne Knight made a healthy profit from coppices that supplied charcoal to the family's ironworks, and in 1815 he extended his grounds at Downton by cancelling the lease of nearby Bringewood Furnace and Forge and converting their reservoirs to lakes with waterfalls. A bachelor, Knight also followed another trend of spending more time in his London house than he did on his country estate. But rural life meant one thing to men like Knight, who could escape to the metropolis when they got bored of rustic simplicity, and something quite different to those rural dwellers whose whole lives were fixed there.

11

Plebeian Underwood

The rise to prominence of the country estate, and the gradual privatization of the countryside that went with it, inevitably had consequences for the common use of woodlands. The decisive event in the erosion of traditional rights is usually attributed to the Black Act of 1723, because it signalled the trend in eighteenth-century law to protect individual property at the expense of general liberty. But woodland life also underwent changes reflecting broader changes in society. Woodlands were busy places in medieval and early modern Britain, despite the impression given by medieval romances and tales of Robin Hood. They were an important part of both rural and industrial economies and it is worth looking at how they were integrated with rural life in general.

The various woodland activities encompassed a range of special skills, some widely held, others more specialized, that documented a profound understanding of the properties of wood. In the medieval period uses of woodland varied little across the country, regardless of whether they were under Forest Law. Activity in the woods encompassed common rights as well as landowners' rights, employing sizeable numbers of people in gathering of fuel for monasteries, manors, villages and towns, providing a near universal market for the products of woodlands. A distinction was always made between timber, used for large projects like buildings, ships, bridges and mills, and smaller wood worked by turners, joiners and carvers. The smaller wood was the most important source of heat until it was superseded by the slow growth in the coal trade from the seventeenth century onwards, for which reason the underwood was until then usually regarded as more valuable than the timber trees. Periodic cutting, such as coppicing or pollarding, was the most effective way of managing the resource. Coppice cycles varied between seven and over twenty years, depending upon the species and the number of times it had been cut. In general the older the coppice the longer it takes to regenerate, so coppice cycles lengthen over time.[1]

When applied to the landscape, 'common' is a word sometimes used loosely, with connotations of timelessness and association with something inalienable. Common rights evolved gradually by customary use, so even in the thirteenth century their origin could be described as time-hallowed. Legal integrity was established by custom rather than statute. Common right did not mean universal right but local right, and never implied common ownership. In practical terms this meant that common rights differed from one parish to another. Tension often existed between commoners and landowners, erupting not infrequently into rancorous disputes, and it is in this context that most information about the practice of common rights can be gleaned. Scope for disagreement was wide. When commoners had a right to gather wood for domestic fuel, what constituted a reasonable quantity was open to question on both sides. It has been argued that competing claims on the use of woods like those of Hatfield Forest in Essex were the real cause of their preservation. The landowners could not grub up all the trees without infringing commoners' rights, while the commoners were not allowed permanent pasture for their animals because wood pasture would quickly have deteriorated into grassland with trees.[2]

Common rights, or 'estovers', to collect timber and wood for building, fencing and fuel had their own specific terms (housebote, hedgebote and firebote). These are known in detail in certain special cases only, such as in Needwood Forest in Staffordshire, where the rights were granted to tenants when the owner, Earl Ferrers, was attempting to establish a new town. Sometimes actual quantities were agreed, taking into account the extent of local woodland and the population that depended upon it. Study of common rights in thirteenth-century Staffordshire has shown that Burton Abbey allowed tenants three cartloads of wood per year for fencing and the same for fuel.[3] In some cases only fallen wood could be collected for fuel, while oaks were reserved for building timber with their felling usually supervised on behalf of the landowner. This left inferior and faster-growing species like willow, alder, thorn and holly for fencing. An enquiry at Stoneleigh in the Forest of Arden in 1273 found that, although pannage and game reserves were forbidden, tenants could gather enough oak and thorn branches between

Martinmas and Easter for fencing, to last for two years, and gathered dead wood for domestic heating, baking and brewing.[4]

The low density of much medieval woodland allowed pasture for cattle and pannage for pigs, particularly the latter, which were traditionally fattened up in the autumn. Commoners were often required to pay for pannage between Michaelmas (30 September) and Martinmas (11 November) – sokemen at Rugeley being required to surrender their third best pig to the Bishop of Lichfield – but pigs had no competitors in the consumption of acorns and beech mast.[5] Nature's bounty could be increased by the swineherds who used sticks to knock the mast from the trees. Rights of grazing cattle sometimes overrode a landowner's management of wood, for example in Epping Forest where the right to graze forced landowners to pollard their trees rather than coppice them.[6] Woodland was also a source of wild food in addition to poached meat, which was more often rabbit or wildfowl than venison. Bees provided honey and wax from forest hives, which usually took the form of natural or artificial holes in trees or hollowed-out logs. Surplus honey could be sold at market, but payments for honey also show up in the household accounts of larger houses. Woodland trees bore fruit – berries, apples, pears, cherries, sloes and bullaces were all taken from the Forest of Arden in the late middle ages, sometimes collected in sufficient quantities to be worth selling at market.[7] The hazel is a native British species and its nuts were widely collected as late as the nineteenth century. The importance of these trees is revealed in a petition to Edward I in 1290 from the men of Stoneleigh in the Forest of Arden. They claimed that their livelihoods had been threatened by the prevalence of assarting, undermining their rights, including the right to gather nuts.[8]

In the medieval Forest of Arden dressed timber such as laths and boards was prepared from timber collected under common rights and openly sold for profit. Wood was also used in the form of wattles and rods for fences and hurdles. Small wood was used for implements and tools, including carts, ploughs and harrows, spades and hoes. Smaller branches and trimmings were used in broom and basket making, and twigs and leaves were used for feed. While oak was considered the superior building material, other species had their favoured uses – ash for wheels, poplar for barrows, and alder for scaffold poles. Yew, or if unavailable elm, was favoured for making longbows. During the Hundred Years War the army was equipped with longbows from the majority of English and Welsh districts. In 1341, at the height of the first phase of the war, the crown ordered 7800 bows and 13,000 arrows.[9]

Timber was an essential building material until the mid nineteenth century. Even in areas where suitable stone was available, timber was required for roof trusses and partitions. In many places timber remained the most common form of building material for ancillary structures like farm buildings – cruck framing, for example, continued to be used for farm buildings after it had been superseded as a structural type for houses. Even large stone buildings utilized vast quantities of wooden joists. In some places, like the Severn Valley in Shropshire, timber became the building material of choice in the sixteenth and seventeenth centuries as it offered greater scope for carved ornament than stone. Direct evidence of the use of timber in local domestic contexts is sparse, usually occurring where there has been a dispute of some kind. For example, in Arden trees were taken in contravention of common rights. Fallen trees were often sold by the landowner, although in 1441 at Kingsbury it was reported that tenants had carried off trees that had fallen in stormy weather, an operation that required teams of men and not just an opportunist individual. Cases where theft of timber in Arden were brought to court show a consistent pattern of men taking timber for important domestic works rather than for profit: a man took timber to repair his house at Berwood in 1417; John Elys of Middleton felled an ash tree for his barn in 1408; and in 1415 John Warde of Nuneaton took oak to make three pairs of crucks.[10]

One of the richest districts in England for timber architecture, Suffolk, had comparatively few woodlands by the medieval period and therefore its timber was mainly imported. The Isle of Ely was similarly poorly endowed with timber, yet the octagon at Ely Cathedral is one of the largest and most spectacular medieval timber constructions in the whole of Europe. The inter-regional trade in timber also extended to smaller items. In 1524 a man named Glosse was sent from Stogursey in well-wooded Somerset to Wales in search of dressed timber suitable for making into benches for the church, timber that would have been transported across the Bristol Channel.[11] There is plenty of evidence that for large-scale projects timber was transported great distances. The fortress palace of Caernarfon in north-west Wales, begun for Edward I in 1283, used large quantities of timber imported by sea from north-east Wales and Cheshire.[12] The Forest of Dean supplied timber for very many large secular and religious buildings throughout south-east Wales and the west of England, and for the king's works in various places including the Tower of London.[13]

Wood provided the main source of domestic fuel, but for industrial applications where greater heat was required, for example in the smelting and refining of iron and lead, and in the burning of lime, charcoal was the best available fuel. Later, charcoal was also a component in gun-powder manufacture. Charcoal could be had from sustainable resources such as coppices, although this was not always the case in the medieval period when trees were felled for the purpose. Charcoal burners were traditionally untutored men living remote lives that were easy to char-acterize as savage or innocent, according to taste. There is something of the noble savage in the legend of John Walford, a hereditary charcoal burner in the Quantock Hills of Somerset, who lived for months on end in his isolated hut, only seeking human congress at weekends, and who murdered his wife less than a month after their marriage in 1789. Jenny Walford is said to have seduced him in his lonely woodland hideaway, just like the Devil ensnared the souls of isolated and vulnerable men in the medieval forest. Having fathered a child by her he was forced into a marriage he never wanted and tragically could not sustain. The law branded him savage; the noble part was folklore, of a man doomed never to marry Ann Rice, the woman he truly loved. His place of execution was his place of work and acquired the name Walford's Gibbet, a fittingly remote memorial of a man who lived semi-detached from civilization. At about the same time, in 1800, John Skinner came across a family of charcoal burners in Baglan, Glamorgan, living their isolated existence seemingly untainted by conventional morality. They were found

> inhabiting a mud cabin in the form of a sugar loaf. In the midst of this retirement they seem perfectly happy, tho almost all the children were in a state of their first parents, without covering, and seemed not ashamed. These people continue here all the summer for the purpose of making charcoal.[14]

Tanners, meanwhile, used stripped oak bark because it contained sufficient natural tannin to enable skins and rawhides to be converted into leather. In the tannery, bark was placed in alternate layers with hides, then immersed in water. Stripping bark from a tree is only feasible when the sap is rising, which meant that barking was a seasonal occupation from April to June. It was work that could occupy both men and women in isolation, as in this account of bark strippers at Newcastle Emlyn in Carmarthenshire:

> At the end of the spring, three women and two men would be seen going to the oak wood to bark the oak trees. The trees had been cut a week before ... Each one sits neatly on a tree, as if riding a horse side saddle. They start at the stump end, hitting the sharp iron to lift the bark ... They would spend three weeks or a month in a wood before finishing, and the only sound they would hear was the cart that came twice a week to take the bark to the tannery.[15]

Woodlands were an integral component of local life beyond the merely utilitarian. Their importance in gathering greenery for secular and religious festivals has already been described, as has claims that communal merriment often spilled over into sexual promiscuity. Even after such communal festivals declined, similar practices continued on a more private basis. In a famous rape case in the 1820s in Shropshire, the victim, Elizabeth Cureton of Coalbrookdale, was said by one witness to have been previously surprised with the defendant in the local Captain's Coppice.[16] Living in closely packed communities and small houses, the woodlands were a necessary private space and were thus part of the social landscape of a community. Potton Wood in Bedfordshire performed a similar function as it was said to be the resort of young lovers in a bowdlerized contemporary account:

> both sexes impatiently resort to this shady retreat, where the sportive game and sprightly dance give to the bloom of beauty additional tints ... they instantly repair to the Woodhouse, and there taste the neat baked cake, and sip the eastern herb; enlivened by this innocent repast they resume their pristine sport.[17]

Not everyone was fooled by this image of original innocence, especially in the moralizing and class-ridden nineteenth century. John Archer Houblon, whose family had owned Hatfield Forest since 1729, told his lawyer in 1826 that:

> Among the shrubbage growing upon the forest are an immense quantity of hazel stubs ... as soon as the nuts begin to get ripe persons of all descriptions

but consisting chiefly of the idle and disorderly men and women of bad character from [Bishops] Stortford ... and several neighbouring villages have come ... in large parties to gather the nuts or under pretence of gathering nuts to loiter about in crowds disturbing the deer and game, breaking down the trees ... and in the evening ... take beer and spirits and drink in the forest which affords them an opportunity for all sorts of debauchery.[18]

More arcane woodland rituals centred upon the supposed curative properties of certain trees. The tree that nineteenth-century folklore collectors found had the widest range of special properties was the ash. Branches of the ash were used to ward off snakes, which is similar to a tradition found in Somerset that 'ashen gads' protected cattle against fairies and witches.[19] Robert Plot was told in the seventeenth century that ash trees ward off 'fascinations and evil spirits' and that people made walking sticks from branches of ash and kept them beside their beds. The ash tree also possessed healing properties, a belief that persisted into the nineteenth century before it was superseded by modern medicine. Writers as diverse as James Frazer, Gilbert White and the mineral geologist Robert Hunt all found examples of similar rites. In 1776 a sceptical Gilbert White wrote from Selborne of a row of pollard ashes near the centre of the village:

> These trees, when young and flexible, were severed and held open by wedges, while ruptured children, stripped naked, were pushed through the apertures, under a persuasion that, by such a process, the poor babes would be cured of their infirmity. As soon as the operation was over, the tree, in the suffering part, was plastered with loam, and carefully swathed up. If the parts coalesced and soldered together, as usually fell out, where the feat was performed with any adroitness at all, the party was cured; but, where the cleft continued to gape, the operation, it was supposed, would prove ineffectual.[20]

White knew several people in Selborne who were supposed to have been cured in this way. He also remembered a much-venerated 'shrew ash' in the village. The twigs or branches of a shrew ash were supposed to relieve the pains felt by animals from a shrew running over their bodies. A shrew ash could be consecrated in the following way:

> Into the body of the tree a deep hole was bored with an auger, and a poor devoted shrew-mouse was thrust in alive, and plugged in, no doubt, with several quaint incantations long since forgotten. As the ceremonies necessary

for such a consecration are no longer understood, all succession is at an end, and no such tree is known to exist in the manor.[21]

Robert Plot gave similar account of the oaks, elms and ashes of Staffordshire. Here, once the mouse had been placed into a hole and then sealed by a wooden plug, cattle were whipped with the boughs of the tree to cure swelling. Plot had heard that, in Ireland, swelling in cattle was attributed to a certain kind of caterpillar which, once it had been placed in a tree and had died, the bark and leaves were stripped, steeped in water, then fed to the cattle as an antidote.[22] In nineteenth-century Cornwall Robert Hunt encountered a similar belief regarding the cleft ash tree, where after the ceremony the tree was bound together. If the bark grew back the child would grow healthy, but if the tree died the same fate would befall the child. In Cornwall the ash tree was only one such device – apertures in stones were equally effective, as was the practice of passing the child under the belly and over the back of a donkey.[23] What these practices had in common was that they were private rituals conducted by people who had no other recourse to medical treatment. They died out as medical care improved in the nineteenth century and as diseases of poverty like rickets declined. The origin of such rituals is uncertain, but it is no longer widely believed that they represent the last vestige of pre-Christian pagan worship, even though nineteenth-century writers wrote about such practices as 'primitive customs'.

Hunting was a different matter. In its illegal form it continued to irritate landowners and led indirectly to the passing of the Black Act. The Act derives its eerie title from deer stealers who blackened their faces as a disguise. The practice was known from the medieval period and was significant enough that in 1485 blacking and night hunting were made a felony. By the end of the seventeenth century a man was required to have an income of at least £100 to hunt game on his own land. In Richard Burn's *The Justice of the Peace and Parish Officer* (1772) it was explained that game laws were intended 'to prevent persons of inferior rank, from squandering that time, which their station in life requireth to be more profitably employed'.[24] But the poor were hardly fooled by laws to save them from themselves, and by the eighteenth century poachers differed little from their medieval counterparts except that with firearms they had at their disposal an indispensable tool far more effective than disguise.

There were two areas where gangs of blacked-up poachers were seen by landowners as a particular threat, in Hampshire and in Windsor Forest. Windsor Forest remained in part ownership of the crown and, despite the lapse of Forest Law in most areas of the country, was used as a royal hunting ground by those monarchs who still enjoyed the thrill of the chase. Even Queen Anne is said by Jonathan Swift to have hunted 'in a chaise with one horse, which she drives herself, and drives furiously, like Jehu, and is a mighty hunter, like Nimrod'.[25] The history of Windsor Forest in the seventeenth century was a turbulent one. Although the traditional protection for vert and venison had been retained in theory, its implementation had progressively weakened over the previous centuries – for example, deer who strayed from the forest or broke through its fences were considered fair game by local farmers, quite contrary to the law – and attempts at strict enforcement met with considerable resistance. The attempt by Charles I to revive forest laws was unsuccessful, but during his reign Windsor became so full of deer as to become overstocked. A complete reversal followed. The forest was denuded of trees and its deer were wiped out during the Commonwealth, only for Charles II to restore it to its former glory. A brief period of stricter legal enforcement followed the accession of William and Mary in 1689 but it soon lapsed, and remained in its relaxed state under Anne. George I first visited Windsor Castle and hunted in the forest in 1717, and subsequently ordered that no licences should be issued for hunting at Windsor, as he intended to hunt there himself. The forest regime hardened, bringing all manner of minor transgressions against venison and vert before the courts. The Reverend Will Waterson, vicar of Winkfield in the forest, was forced to conclude that 'liberty and Forest Laws are incompatible', but he overestimated the power of the ancient statutes. Forest Law was weak and needed to be supplemented by common law, which in 1719 made deer-poaching punishable by transportation and a year later introduced rewards of up to £100 for information leading to conviction. As a stamp of authority it backfired, as it provoked the formation of secret fraternities in Windsor who blacked up and undertook hunting expeditions in gangs, mounted and heavily armed. The blacks enforced their will by intimidation and occasionally by assault in an escalation that turned violent and claimed the life of a bystander, the son of a forest keeper.

A similar pattern emerged independently in Hampshire, where the crown still owned sizeable tracts of forest. Trouble erupted around the forests of Bere and Alice Holt where tenants of the see of Winchester objected to heavy-handed attempts to stamp out encroachments and transgressions. As the Surveyor General of Woods was to report in 1729, 'the country people everywhere think they have a sort of right to the wood and timber in the forests', based on tradition, 'and it is certain that they carefully conceal the spoils committed by each other, and are always jealous of everything that is done under the authority of the Crown'.[26] But, with local authorities being weak, nothing could prevent the organised culling of the deer, which was so brazen that the carcasses were being carried away from Alice Holt by day. Things came to a head in 1721 after a gang of poachers was arrested and sentenced to a day in the pillory. They formed a secret association and elected a leader who styled himself as 'King John'.

As soon as King John and his men were free from the pillory, the bishop's deer were slaughtered, lodges were burned and timber destroyed. Masked and mounted, the gang rode brazenly through neighbouring Farnham with their spoils. For over a year they acted with impunity, enforcing their will by intimidating informers and forest officials, like a latter-day Robin Hood and his merry men. The collapse of official law enforcement opened the door to other opportunists, news that reached London as a blur of anarchy. 'King John' in due course returned to his normal life and his true identity was never discovered, but other blacked gangs continued to operate and were eventually caught and punished.

The Black Act was the consequence of all this. It added many more capital offences to the statute book, which now included wearing a disguise in the forest, possessing an offensive weapon, sending threatening letters, arson, assisting in the rescue of prisoners and, of course, killing deer. In Windsor Forest at least the legislation appears to have had an immediate calming effect, for George I felt safe enough to hunt there in 1724. Deer stocks at Windsor were replenished from Woolmer, a 'treeless' forest adjacent to Alice Holt. In Hampshire, Alice Holt was described by a near neighbour Gilbert White in 1784. Although only an

infant in the days of 'King John', the countryside was still replete with
tales of the blacks. Their legacy was a continuing diminution of the
forest's deer, which were still hunted by night. One landowner, General
Howe, had tried to curb the practice by introducing German wild boar.
This achieved a temporary success in frightening the gangs until these
were hunted too.

Legislation to preserve hunting for the privileged classes is one
example of the distancing of patrician and plebeian cultures in the
eighteenth century, a trend that was already discernible in Renaissance
England. Venison symbolized the hunt and its consumption was a mark
of status. It denoted that a man possessed land in a society where power
and position was measured in such terms, while venison was 'a special
currency of class based on the solid standard of landed wealth, untainted
by the commerce of the metropolis'.[27] To serve venison to guests was
a mark of esteem, an indulgence granted occasionally to social inferiors
and a mark of respect to social equals and superiors. The black market
in poached venison debased this social currency and so the landed class
had a vested interest in stopping it. Where was the nobility of chasing
down a stag when a gang of mere labourers could do the same with the
same success?

Most poachers were, not surprisingly, poor. One man was sentenced,
in 1757, to fourteen years' transportation when, after going to Needwood
Forest in Staffordshire looking for deer but finding none, his dog killed
a sheep on the return home. He explained that with the scarcity of food
in that year he was reluctant to leave it behind and so carried it off.
Gilbert White and others explained that the rich man's desire to hunt
was no different from the poor man's, and that hunting was a test of
manhood:

> Most men are sportsmen by constitution: and there is such an inherent spirit
> for hunting in human nature, as scarce any inhibitions can restrain ... towards
> the beginning of this century all this country was wild about deer-stealing.
> Unless he was a hunter, as they affected to call themselves, no young person
> was allowed to be possessed of manhood or gallantry.[28]

The Black Act made it a capital offence 'unlawfully to ... cut down
or otherwise destroy any trees planted in any avenue, or growing in any
garden, orchard or plantation, for ornament, shelter or profit'. Although

the Act did not directly undermine rights of common, it failed to deal with legitimate complaints that when deer escaped from parks they damaged crops and gardens. It also gave landowners the upper hand in ensuing efforts to reduce or abolish common rights in the collection of wood. In his description of Alice Holt, Gilbert White also alluded to a dispute regarding its timber. The crown lands had been granted to Lord Stawell, who, following a large-scale felling of trees, also claimed the lop and top, countering the claims of the parish who said it was theirs by right. The parish took control: the local parishioners, 'assembling in a riotous manner, have actually taken it all away. One man, who keeps a team, has carried home, for his share, forty sacks of wood. Forty-five of these people his Lordship has served with actions.' [29]

Waltham Forest in Essex experienced several episodes of disputed access to wood, caused by a clash between commercial and traditional interests. The people of the neighbouring village of Loughton submitted a petition in the 1720s claiming the right to lop firewood. The lord of the manor did not dispute the right but sought to shift the terms of its application. Formerly wood could be taken from the forest on any wet day, a convenient arrangement as there would be less farm work on such days. He then tried to restrict wood gathering and lopping to Mondays only, whatever the weather, leaving the inhabitants unable to exercize their rights properly. The reason was commercial. The lord of the manor was overstocking with cattle, selling timber and ploughing the clearings to set coney warrens. [30]

Common rights to lop firewood in the winter months in Waltham Forest were said to have been established during the reign of Elizabeth I and were asserted by means of an annual perambulation of the forest on the night of 10 November. This was the right claimed by one member of the village when part of the forest was enclosed in the 1860s. Mr Willingale and his two sons broke down the fences and conducted the traditional perambulation, an offence which earned them a two-month sentence for malicious trespass. But Willingale was luckier than most. Enclosure of commons had been taking place for over a century and by the 1860s the Commons Preservation Society had been formed to fight a rearguard action. [31] The society was a defensive reflex aiming to counter widespread and profound changes in rural life in a period where the only constant was change itself. It had some notable successes, securing the London commons of Hampstead Heath, Wimbledon and Putney from what looked like certain enclosure. The commoners of Berkhamsted in Hertfordshire reacted vigorously when, in 1866, Lord Brownlow fenced off over four hundred acres of Berkhamsted Common. The commoners scored a notable victory by hiring 130 London labourers who, in the early hours, tore down three miles of iron railings.[32]

By the mid nineteenth century a large proportion of the rural people who no longer practised their common rights did so for the simple reason that they had left their villages and moved to the towns. Other changes in the rural economy chipped away at the reliance on local woodlands, such as the growing distribution of coal as a domestic fuel and an expanding market for timber and wood – Baltic softwood replaced many of the uses for local hardwoods. Woodlands were a necessary part of the rural economy when communities organized their lives on a local basis. The real decline in their use is a symptom of the more fundamental changes in country life, the social consequences of which are detailed in the work of Thomas Hardy and others.

12

Woodlanders

As the increasing power of property in Georgian England gradually encroached upon common rights, the psychology of rural England changed. The effects on commoners' rights can be tolerably understood, but the deeper impact upon individuals and communities is much more difficult to penetrate. The so-called 'peasant poets', labourers like Stephen Duck (1705–1756) and Robert Bloomfield (1766–1823), whose talents were taken up by the landowning class, might seem to promise to enlighten us in the humble ways of an illiterate class, but in the end they deliver what their patrons wanted to hear, namely derivative accounts of pastoral bliss dependent upon James Thomson's *The Seasons* (1724–30) and other similar works. Nor do the woodland eccentrics, men like the redoubtable Henry Hastings, son of the earl of Huntingdon, who lived in Dorset on the edge of the New Forest in the eighteenth century, tell us enough of what it was like to live an ordinary life in relation to woods.

The political and personal consequences of private property and woodland clearance are well expressed in the various works of William Cowper and John Clare, while the effect of a dwindling woodland economy was mercilessly recorded by Thomas Hardy later in the nineteenth century. In none of the cases was their livelihood woodland-based, but all three men were woodlanders in one important sense: they inhabited specific localities and never wrote of woodlands in the abstract.

This was not simply a class conflict. By the end of the eighteenth century forest dwellers attracted the scorn of a growing band of rural professionals – land agents, lawyers and surveyors – who spearheaded the drive for agricultural improvement and whose livelihoods depended upon rural development. Traditional woodland communities were a bar to such development and therefore became a favourite target of improvers. For example, Bere Forest in Hampshire was said to have been plagued with

> the worthless from all parts of the country ... constructing huts in concealed places, and living in a state of the utmost misery and depravity. There was scarcely a vice of which demi-savages can be guilty which these free-booters of the forest did not perpetrate.[1]

The principal mouthpiece of the rural professional was the Board of Agriculture, the semi-official body established in 1793 by Sir John Sinclair that spawned *General Views of the Agriculture* of the English counties. Charles Vancouver, in his study of the agriculture of Hampshire, thought the forests could do with a good dose of agricultural improvement: 'The appropriation of the forests would ... be the means of producing a number of additional hands for agricultural employment, by gradually cutting up and annihilating that nest and conservatory of sloth, idleness and misery.' He added that he hoped to see the abolition of every kind of common right.[2]

Improvement was closely associated with the enclosure movement that gathered pace in the latter half of the eighteenth century. Enclosure entailed the creation of a new pattern of fields and roads with the intention of increasing productivity by better land management. Like the landscape garden, enclosure imposed a preordained structure, regardless of topography, on landscapes that had slowly evolved quite different structures based on particular historical circumstances. Enclosure was therefore anti-historical and anti-individual. Its most prevalent form was to reorganize the open field systems that characterized a broad swathe of English countryside from County Durham to Dorset, where arable land was still cultivated in narrow strips. In its other form it appropriated common grazing land, which sometimes included wooded ground, instances of which are found throughout England. Enclosure required an Act of Parliament and was not therefore undertaken half-heartedly or without calculation of its material benefits.

Agricultural improvers had an ambivalent attitude to landscapes, praising the aesthetic qualities of wildness while also advocating the beauties of productivity. Similar ambivalence was pervasive in eighteenth-century literature, notably in James Thomson's *The Seasons*. Thomson could praise the industrious countryside while seeking in woodlands 'the haunt of meditation'. Improvers, in contrast, meditated on only one thing – how to improve the output of unproductive ground. They created a mood of rural utilitarianism that provoked a reaction from a sensitive intelligentsia who saw in their work a threat to nature itself. This took two forms, both of which have had a lasting impact on British culture. Naturalists like Gilbert White occupied themselves in observation and classification of flora and fauna, developing a respect for all living beings. In contrast, poets like William Cowper and John Clare meditated upon the personal and social consequences of changing nature and rural life, of which trees were a fundamental part.

In his youth William Cowper had had been a man about town, but he subsequently renounced his early lifestyle and moved to the country, settling at Olney in Buckinghamshire in 1776. His attempts to lead a quiet life were unsettled by changes in country life that disturbed his conservative instincts, although it could be argued that living at the margin of society gave his poetry a sharper edge. At Olney he was appalled by the needless destruction of trees in the name of progress that claimed material well-being was better than spiritual well-being. A plantation near Olney, through which Cowper had loved to walk, was felled in 1785 leaving Cowper bereft. It was the destruction of a sacred place in the name of utility, leaving him exiled from his own spiritual world and connection with the world of nature. He explained in a letter:

> I will never enter it again. We have both pray'd in it. You for me, and I for you, but it is desecrated from this time forth, and the voice of pray'r will be heard in it no more. The fate of it in this respect, however deplorable is not peculiar; the spot where Jacob anointed his pillar, and which is more apposite, the spot once honoured with the presence of Him who dwelt in the bush, have long suffer'd similar disgrace, and are become common ground.[3]

Woodland was the kind of place that Cowper needed not only to feel secure, but where he found a language of redemption that he and society needed for their spiritual health. The loss of it prompted him to attack the improvers as despoilers, and to accuse landowners of neglecting their paternalistic responsibilities. John Dashwood, inheritor of Norland Park in Jane Austen's *Sense and Sensibility* (1811), is accused of a similar dereliction of duty. And in *Mansfield Park* (1814) James Rushworth is considering employing Humphry Repton to improve the park. Having already cut down some fine old trees whose only crime was to grow too near to the house, Rushworth intends to cut down an avenue of trees leading up to the west front of the old Elizabethan mansion. 'Cut down an avenue!' replies Fanny Price. 'What a pity! Does it not make you think of Cowper. "Ye fallen avenues, once more I mourn your fate unmerited."'[4] Fanny Price was quoting Cowper's 'The Task', first published in 1785, where he ascribes insensitive attacks upon the familiar to the nature of landowning in the eighteenth century, upsetting a mythical age of stability:

> Mansions once
> Knew their own masters; and laborious hinds
> Who had surviv'd the father, serv'd the son.
> Now the legitimate and rightful lord
> Is but a transient guest, newly arriv'd,
> And soon to be supplanted. He that saw
> His patrimonial timber cast its leaf,
> Sells the last scantling, and transfers the price
> To some shrewd sharper, ere it buds again.
> Estates are landscapes, gaz'd upon a while,
> Then advertis'd, and auctioneer'd away.[5]

The poet mourned not merely the demise of nature but the decline of English society, as if that society needed a proper relationship with nature for its integrity. It cut to the heart of patrician hypocrisy, of a class that liked to associate old trees with the longevity of its own family and who were willing to pay Capability Brown to play up the association. But as Cowper unintentionally pointed out, how could new owners with no affinity or loyalty to their estates value them as anything but economic units? New money, in the form of Richard Payne Knight, had portrayed the oak tree as the symbol of the British constitution. Estate owners should

> Banish the fir's unsocial shade,
> And crop th' aspiring larche's saucy heads:
> Then Britain's genius to thy aid invoke
> And spread around the rich, high-clustering oak:
> King of the woods![6]

Cowper exposed such rhetoric as a shallow posture disguising

self-interest. Later, in his 'Yardley Oak' of 1791, the tree was turned into
a political symbol to oppose those ancient oaks that Brown and Repton
left for show in landscape parks. The Yardley oak could never be
appropriated by an individual landowner as it was part of a shared
heritage, a common culture that was otherwise being dismantled by
the developing of sophisticated tastes and individualising tendency of
Georgian Britain. The tree, identified like the poet as a witness to the
decline of rural virtues, is described as

> Survivor sole, and hardly such, of all
> That once liv'd here thy brethren, at my birth
> (Since which I number three-score winters past)
> A shatter'd veteran, hollow-trunk'd perhaps
> Now, and with excoriate forks deform,
> Relics of Ages! [7]

The slow-growing English oak is made to represent the organic development of England (in contrast to revolutionary France), while its
aged hollow centre represents the corruption at the heart of the establishment, notwithstanding its deep roots in history. As such the poem
is a traditional meditation on mutability but the tree had a special value
in expressing a shared ancestry and a place of sanctity:

> It seems idolatry with some excuse
> When our forefather Druids in their oaks
> Imagin'd sanctity ... [8]

The Yardley oak may have escaped the axe but it could not compensate
for the loss of trees to commercial expediency. Cowper was a powerless
onlooker. In choosing to live a life of seclusion and humility, he left
himself vulnerable to change that he could do nothing about. This at
least he shared with John Clare. But unlike Clare, Cowper was at first
just as much a newcomer to Olney as the new gentry were to their
country estates. His attachment to place was not won without a period
of acclimatization.

John Clare was born in 1793 in the not very remarkable village of
Helpston, then in the Soke of Peterborough and now part of Cambridgeshire, hardly a place thick with trees. The Act of Parliament for
the enclosure of Helpston and neighbouring parishes was passed in 1809

and its landscape had been more or less transformed by 1816 when Clare was twenty-three. So the landscape Clare found when he reached adulthood was in marked contrast to the landscape in which he had grown up. As a consequence, some of his poetry is overtly concerned with childish recollection, but a deeper current running through him is the importance of a sense of place and the deleterious effects of its disruption. Clare was a poet of place in that he wrote about the places he knew and these were confined to the area immediately around Helpston. He described his first journey out of his home patch – to Wisbech, some twenty miles east – as entering a foreign land, having no conception of what England could be like beyond the orbit of his daily life.[9] The point was that he could only be the person he was in the places that were his own. It was a source of strength in his poetry but limiting to other aspects of his life, such as the lack of literate companionship in his locality – he wrote to his publisher John Taylor in 1822 that 'I live here among the ignorant like a lost man'. It was his destiny to be a peasant poet relying on a gentleman class of reader, the very people whose insensitivity he was so scornful of. In fact his local patron Lord Radstock demanded the suppression of poems that displayed 'radical slang', a euphemism for views he disagreed with.

Enclosure forced Clare to look to the past and gave him little faith in the future, setting a tone that preoccupied many nineteenth-century authors in their attitude to nature and its exploitation. Irreversible changes to the landscape were personal losses, and he responded to them in personal terms – he never claimed to speak on behalf of the community and its economic hardships, or beyond the realm of his emotional and spiritual attachment to nature. In 'To a Favourite Tree' he rails against the 'accursed wealth' that has levelled whole woods. The same ecopolitics is found in a more famous poem 'The Fallen Elm', published in the second collection of Clare's work, *The Village Minstrel* (1821). The editor's introduction quotes a letter written by Clare on the impending demolition of a pair of trees:

> My two favourite elm trees at the back of the hut are condemned to die – it shocks me to relate it, but tis true. The savage who owns them thinks they have done their best, and now he wants to make use of the benefits he can get from selling them ... I have been several mornings to bid them farewel.[10]

The elm tree is made to symbolize the community as a companion of the community all its life, witnessing all the events that took place there:

> Old favourite tree, thou'st seen time's changes lour
> Though change till now did never injure thee.

The tree sheltered Clare's home, while 'The children sought thee in thy summer shade', but could do nothing against the axe. It was the corruption by the powerful, those men 'who bawl freedom loud and then oppress the free', creating a new world where 'wrong was right and right was wrong'.

> Such was thy ruin, music-making Elm.
> The rights of freedom was to injure thine.

The felling of trees forms the subject of several of Clare's poems of lament. In 'Round Oak and Eastwell' he describes two tree-shaded streams left 'naked to the sun' after enclosure has occasioned the felling of their green canopies:

> The fell destroyer's hand hath reft their side
> Of every tree that hid and beautified
> Their shallow waters in delightful clumps,
> That sunburnt now o'er pebbles skips and jumps.
> One where stone quarries in its hills are broke
> Still keeps its ancient pastoral name, Round Oak.
> Although one little solitary tree
> Is all that's left of its old pedigree;
> The other, more deformed, creeps down the dell,
> Scarcely the shade of what was once Eastwell,
> While the elm-groves that groaned beneath no tax
> Have paid their tribute to the lawless axe,
> And the old rooks that waited other springs
> Have fled to stranger scenes on startled wings.
> The place all lonely and all naked lies ...[11]

Lament at the destruction of nature in the wake of progress very much associates Clare with modern preoccupations, but there are other senses in which he could be living in the twenty-first century. Clare loved nature for its own sake and relished simple everyday experiences. 'The Summer Shower' begins:

> I love it well o'ercanopied in leaves
> Of crowding woods to spend a quiet hour
> And where the woodbine weaves
> To list the summer shower.[12]

'Walks in the Woods' describes his pleasure in ambling about, stopping to look at anything that catches his eye, in well-loved places that belonged to no one and everyone. Nor does anyone have any greater claim to their ownership than the birds who nest in them. He wants nothing from the woods but inner pleasures and has no ambition to profit from them in other ways. As a refuge from contemporary society a wood is not a place simply for solitary reflection, but the place of an alternative, more organic community. His first impulse is, however, one of escape, as the poem begins when he enters the wood and finds

> The brambles tearing at my clothes;
> And it may tear; I love the noise
> And hug the solitary joys.[13]

It is not long, however, before he comes across a woodman 'in leathern doublet', 'stickers' gathering rotten wood, poachers waiting for nightfall, and boys messing about. The woods have their own recognizable human geography in

> A little path that shadows plain
> That other feet have gone before;
> Yet through such boughs it creeps again
> As if no feet could find it more;
> Yet trodden on till nearly bare
> It shows that feet oft trample there.[14]

Clare's woodland, it has been observed, was not a natural landscape but a native place and he shared in the suffering that accompanied its destruction.[15] This place is shared with all manner of creatures that Clare describes not in an ordered fashion that a naturalist might frame them, but as they occur to him, flitting from jays to blackbirds, badgers, strawberries, ash trees, oaks and woodpeckers. Clare was well read in botanical sciences, owning copies of Linnaeus, James Lee's *Introduction to the Science of Botany* (1760) and Culpeper's *Herbal,* and was even persuaded to start a 'Natural History of Helpston' along the lines of Gilbert White. But the naturalist's approach was one of detached observation and classification, which did not suit Clare's temperament. There was no point in studying nature without the expression of feeling: 'I love to look on nature with a poetic feeling which magnifys the pleasure', and 'I love to see the nightingale in its hazel retreat and the cuckoo hiding in its solitudes of oaken foliage and not to examine their carcasses in glass cases'.[16] Clare shared an affinity with his fellow creatures and felt as displaced by enclosure as they did. So did the gypsies, who favoured the hollow tree known as Langley Bush and who Clare recognized as one of the native species of the woods. In 'the Gipsy Camp', Clare described a winter encampment in a snow-bound wood, of roasting mutton sheltered beneath an oak tree, where 'the half-roasted dog squats close' to the fire waiting for any morsel thrown away. Clare recognized an organic nature to the gypsy existence and the shared natural resource of common woodlands:

> Tis thus they live – a picture to the place;
> A quiet, pilfering, unprotected race.

The fact of enclosure and the consequent dislocation also affected Clare's judgement upon the nature of rural life when he was a child. In *The Shepherd's Calendar* (1827) he reminisces on the decline of May festivities as if the custom was as old as time and was abruptly curtailed by the 1809 Act:

> Old may day where's thy glorys gone
> All fled and left thee every one
> Thou comst to thy old haunts and homes
> Unnoticed as a stranger comes
> No flowers are pluckt to hail thee now
> Nor cotter seeks a single bough ...
> While the new thing that took thy place
> Wears faded smiles upon its face
> And where enclosure has its birth
> It spreads a mildew o'er her mirth.[17]

Elsewhere he is tempted to liken the pre-enclosure parish with Eden, and to identify himself as Adam within it. In 'Wanderings in June' he speaks of

> The whispering voice of woods and streams
> That breathe of Eden still.

It was a human birthright to 'muse in the greenwood' and there to 'meet the smiles of heaven', but this highly developed spiritual response was only possible by developing an intimate relationship with native places over time. Clare could not feel reverence for just any woodlands, it had to be certain known woods. No one is anyone in such a place, which is the ideal position to live in the world. In 'The Progress of Rhyme' he wrote:

> I felt it happiness to be
> Unknown, obscure, and like a tree
> In woodland peace and privacy.[18]

For all his love of seclusion and escape, and his reverence for nature, the woods, or any other aspect of the landscape, were never dehumanized. Nature had no meaning without its human imprint and the strength of his poetry is not simply his description of nature or expression of sentiment about nature, but how to live as part of it. This goes some way to explaining his sense of loss at enclosure and the valuation of nature in material terms. Of course the decline of nature was widely lamented in nineteenth-century Britain, but there are few writers who could express these losses in terms that transcend the personal. Clare stands as one of these writers, and in that sense he belongs with Thomas Hardy and specifically with Hardy's novels *Under the Greenwood Tree* and *The Woodlanders*.

Thomas Hardy's greenwood credentials are impressive. As early as 1883, well before the publication of *The Woodlanders*, the critic Havelock Ellis noted that 'Mr Hardy is never more reverent, more exact, than when he is speaking of forest trees', which he credited to Hardy's acquaintance with ancient tree worship still considered to have survived in isolated rural communities.[19] His birthplace at Higher Bockhampton in Dorset has an idyllic sylvan setting, but his native place was not a timeless one. The house had been put up by Hardy's great-grandfather in the early nineteenth century, and although Hardy remembered in 'Domicilium' the high beeches forming 'a veil of boughs' to 'sweep against the roof', the house had originally stood on an uncultivated heath. Its presence there with garden and orchard was a vindication of agricultural improvers like Arthur Young. The proximity of Higher Bockhampton to

Tolpuddle was an equally significant background to Hardy's work. But as Hardy's reputation as a novelist grew, so his sylvan birthplace was increasingly romanticised. In Charles Harper's *Wessex*, published in 1911, Hardy's cottage is described as if it was the last representative of an old rural England once suspended in time but now gone for good: 'there, where the blue wood-smoke from rustic chimneys ascends amid dense foliage, and where the swart heaths begin, he learned his "wood-notes wild"'.[20]

Hardy's early life was not as humble as his birthplace might suggest. His parents were reasonably well off and Hardy was lucky enough to enter the architectural profession, where he filled his spare time with study and gradually emerged as a new breed of intellectual, the auto-didact. He had, however, less fortunate relations living in poverty that exposed him to the coarseness of contemporary rural life. In 1896, writing a new preface to *Under the Greenwood Tree*, he referred to the cleansing of rural culture in the latter half of the nineteenth century, 'that ancient and broad humour which our grandfathers, and possibly grandmothers, took delight in, and in these days [is] unquotable'. In fact Hardy's early novels, as well as mature works like *Tess of the d'Urbervilles*, were sometimes criticized for their coarseness, a reflex that he was largely incapable of correcting and which marked the cultural divide between himself and literary London. Even though he had the advantage over Clare of a better education, he shared with him the curious social limbo of no longer fitting into his native class but of never being able to shake off his roots sufficiently to enter another class – Somerset Maugham once met him at a dinner party and remarked that 'he had still a strange look of the soil'. Hardy knew his place and settled permanently in Dorset rather than London. He inherited his mother's interest in local lore and his father's love of nature to create a body of work which he aptly described as novels of 'character and environment', an achievement that would not have been possible with-out a commitment to certain specific environments of Wessex.

Like Clare, Hardy's commitment to place would hardly have produced a remarkable body of literature if that place had not been undergoing significant changes. Hardy's Wessex is never a rural idyll suspended in time. It is undergoing change, in a tension between tradition and progress, while Hardy's references to barrows, hill forts and monuments in churches all make him conscious that the only constant in life is change itself.

Even though it is lighter in tone than much of his work, Hardy's second novel, *Under the Greenwood Tree* (1872), is concerned with just this tension in rural society. It was written partly at the family home in Higher Bockhampton and was his first successful work. The central character is Fancy Day, the new village schoolmistress whose father has risen from keeper on the earl of Wessex's estate to the lofty heights of 'head game-keeper, timber-steward and general overlooker'. Although Geoffrey Day, living in Yarlbury Wood and himself a fully-fledged woodlander, might have been regarded as living a traditional rural life, he does not want the same for his daughter. For her, education and marriage offer the means of escape from the rural working class and accordingly he has ambitions for her to marry a gentleman. For Fancy, education has opened her eyes to refinement and raised her expectations of life. Fancy is tempted by three suitors, Dick Dewy, Farmer Shiner and Mr Maybold, none of whom are quite on the same social level. As the vicar, Mr Maybold is of superior rank, while Dick Dewy is only the son of a tranter (a carrier) and little above the status of a labourer. Woodland and the parish church play host to the events of the novel. Woodland represents the traditional way of life, while that equally traditional in-stitution the church is the locomotive of change. The church brings the refinement of the outside world into the parish, played out in the novel's sub-plot, the replacement of the rustic Mellstock Quire by the more socially acceptable organ, played by Fancy Day. The group of string players is to be supplanted by a solitary player, equally significant for its social as its musical consequences. Events at the church therefore sym-bolise the conflict between vernacular and progressive culture.

The story begins in the woods:

> To dwellers in a wood almost every species of tree has its voice as well as its feature. At the passing of the breeze the fir-trees sob and moan no less distinctly than they rock; the holly whistles as it battles with itself; the ash hisses amid its quiverings; the beech rustles while its flat boughs rise and fall. And winter, which modifies the note of such trees as shed their leaves, does not destroy its individuality.[21]

Through this 'plantation that whispered ... distinctly to his intelligence' strode Dick Dewy, walking in the darkness as if it were daylight, singing a folk song, a native man emerging from his native environment. His main competition for Fancy comes in the person of the vicar. Mr Maybold is an outsider, never very comfortable with his rustic parishioners. His awkwardness unravels when his band of unwanted minstrels turn up unannounced at the parsonage, arguing that the old-fashioned choir should be retained. Maybold fends them off with a weak platitude that 'when we introduce the organ it will not be that fiddles were bad, but that an organ was better'. The events of the novel follow the course of the four seasons. Fancy Day is briefly tempted by the vicar's refinement but eventually confounds her father by marrying Dick. Even so, she cannot revert to traditional rustic values as if the world of refinement had never entered her head. Fancy is at first reluctant to take part in the wedding procession around the parish, saying that 'respectable people don't nowadays', but is persuaded to agree to it because her mother had done it on her wedding day. They set off for the church from the house in Yarlbury Wood 'every man to his maid': 'Now among dark perpendicular firs, like the shafted columns of a cathedral; now through a hazel copse, matted with primroses and wild hyacinths; now under broad beeches in bright young leaves they threaded their way into the high road over Yarlbury Hill' on the way to the church.[22]

The procession pays homage to their native parish and expresses their allegiance to the place and its people past and present. In accepting the tradition followed by her mother, Fancy is herself acknowledging the importance of cultural memory. The wedding breakfast takes place 'under the greenwood tree', an old tree near Geoffrey Day's house rich in associations of continuity, fertility and festivity, and further reinforcing the ties of the newly weds to their native place and their fellow creatures. The tree is

> horizontally of enormous extent, though having no great pretensions to height. Many hundreds of birds had been born amidst the boughs of this single tree; tribes of rabbits and hares had nibbled at its bark from year to year; quaint tufts of fungi had sprung from the cavities of its forks; and countless families of moles and earthworms had crept about its roots.[23]

It was here that the Mellstock Quire played their dance tunes, but where all the company was instructed 'never to be seen drawing the back of the hand across the mouth after drinking', an old English custom dying out 'among the better classes of society'. Tradition may have won the day but it is a qualified victory. The battle to save the choir is lost and Fancy can never go back to an innocent time when she knew nothing of the world beyond the parish boundary. The twist in the otherwise happy ending is that it is only a matter of time before the old way of life will be superseded. Hardy returned to same theme in his more mature novel *The Woodlanders*, published in 1887.

Great Hintock, the setting of the novel, is based on Melbury Osmund in Dorset, the place where Hardy's mother was born and grew up, while the outlying hamlet of Little Hintock is probably Hermitage, although Hardy blurred his geography sufficiently to create a convincing enough fictional place. Unlike many of his novels, it does not have an historical setting but is set in the 1870s. The plot is a vicious circle of love that draws in most of the main characters: the village labouring girl Marty South loves the apple dealer, cider-maker and woodsman Giles Winterbourne, who loves Grace Melbury, the daughter of a local timber merchant, who loves and eventually marries the educated outsider Dr Edred Fitzpiers. The themes are familiar from *Under the Greenwood Tree*, even if the treatment is darker, as well as from other Hardy novels like *The Return of the Native*. The clash of rural and urban civilizations is at the heart of what unfolds, and is personified by Grace Melbury, whose father has provided for her an expensive education. In this she is in a not dissimilar position to Hardy himself with his educated values struggling to stay connected with his childhood world. Her father points out that her education has rendered her socially superior to her childhood sweetheart Giles, who no longer makes a suitable match: 'He's lived our rough and homely life here, and his wife's life must be rough and homely likewise.' Winterbourne suffers the misfortune of losing his orchard and Grace breaks off her engagement with him and marries Fitzpiers, despite rumours linking Fitzpiers with another local girl. Her misgivings are vindicated when Fitzpiers takes up with a local widow, and Grace takes refuge by going to Winterbourne's cottage in the woods. As a man of propriety he gives Grace the cottage and sleeps outside. Already ill, he succumbs to exposure and is soon dead. Throughout the novel Marty South remains a silent admirer of Giles Winterbourne and continues to tend his grave after Grace has been tempted back by

Fitzpiers. The novel ends with the bleak future for the lonely maid Marty: 'I can never forget 'ee; for you was a good man, and did good things!'

Although the traditional rural life is presented as morally superior to polite society, it does not follow that the manifold sufferings endured by the characters are the result of corrupting a natural way of living by false values. But the characters are inescapably victims of their social position. The hopeless outlook for Marty South is made plain from the start. Her skill and intelligence can never be fulfilled because of her lowly social position. She is introduced, sitting in her cottage on a wooden chair before a wood fire, making 'smooth hazel-rods called spargads' for thatchers. She is a true daughter of the woods, but a poor and vulnerable one. The local barber has come to crop her hair to make a wig for the vanity of the widow Felice Charmond of Hintock House. Mrs Charmond is the owner of the woods around Hintock in which Marty labours and is the epitome of the detached landed interest: 'She's the wrong sort of woman for Hintock – hardly knowing a beech from a woak'. This characteristic is echoed in Fitzpiers. Whereas Giles first meets Grace under a tree, Fitzpiers first spies her through an eyeglass, and he remains an outsider looking in, never truly inhabiting the place like the native characters. At one point he exclaims 'My good God! So this is life!' when, looking out of his window in the 'grey grim dawn', he sees Melbury's men carrying away the large limb of a beech tree that has been blown off in the wind.

Trees are among the leading characters in the story, but not in any idyllic greenwood sense. The apparent long time-scale of the woods and the ensuing connotations of rural culture are illusions, as *The Woodlanders* deals mainly with plantations, not with wildwood. Marty's father lies ill in bed watching a tree out of the window. 'I should be alright by to-morrow if it were not for that tree', he exclaims, forewarning that it will be the death of him. Marty South explains to the doctor that her father 'says that [the tree] is exactly his own age, that it has got human sense and sprouted up when he was born on purpose to rule him, and keep him its slave'. Other villagers have similarly been ruled by specific trees, which is how John South knows that the death of the tree will coincide with his own death. It was exactly the kind of animistic belief that folklore collectors were scouring the countryside in search of, the kind of superstition that James Frazer would argue had roots in primitive tree worship and was now superseded by scientific rationalism. The doctor is disdainful of ignorant superstition and his diagnosis is as expected: 'the tree must be cut down; or I won't answer for his life', an event with predictable consequences.

Elsewhere in the novel Giles Winterbourne and Marty South are the wisest in the ways of nature – Giles Winterbourne is described as having 'a marvellous power of making trees grow' – but it is they who suffer most. They are powerless to take control over their own destinies:

> Marty South alone, of all the women in Hintock and the world, had approximated to Winterbourne's level of intelligent intercourse with Nature. In that respect she had formed his true complement in the other sex, had lived as his counterpart, had subjoined her thoughts to his as a corollary ... to them the sights and sounds of night, winter, wind, storm, amid those dense boughs, which had to Grace a touch of the uncanny, and even of the supernatural, were simply occurrences whose origin, continuance and laws they foreknew. They had planted together, and together they had felled; together they had, with the run of the years, mentally collected those remoter signs and symbols which seen in few were of runic obscurity, but altogether made an alphabet. From the light lashing of the twigs upon their faces when brushing through them in the dark either could pronounce upon the species of the tree whence they stretched; from the quality of the wind's murmur through a bough either could in like manner name its sort far off.[24]

Great sensitivity to nature is not regarded as the desirable moral attribute that the romantics and subsequently later conservationists thought it was. In any case, Hardy's comments about their lack of fear of nature at night demystifies the trees and makes their relationship with the woodlands far more profound. Giles and Marty inhabit the natural world rather than appreciate it aesthetically. Nature in *The Woodlanders* is a destructive force and Giles and Marty come to terms with nature only to become its victims. In his parallel of human and natural worlds, the trees are as locked in a Darwinian struggle for survival as any other species: As Grace Melbury looks out of the window of Winterbourne's cottage she sees 'trees close together, wrestling for existence, their branches disfigured with wounds resulting from their mutual rubbings and blows ... Beneath them were the rotting stumps of those of the group that had been vanquished long ago'. Early in the novel, as Winterbourne follows Grace Melbury and her father through the woods, the opportunity is taken to describe a woodland topography of spreading roots, mossed rinds and elbowed old elms and ashes, a place full of character and a past that the term 'natural history' is inadequate to capture:

> On older trees ... huge lobes of fungi grew like lungs ... The leaf was deformed, the curve was crippled, the taper was interrupted; the lichen ate the vigour of the stalk, and the ivy slowly strangled to death the promising sapling.[25]

The symbolic potential of such places was not lost on Hardy. The wind through trees is nature's Aeolian harp, whose tunes are invariably melancholy and harmonize with the dispositions of the characters. For Marty South, the trees begin to sigh as soon as they are planted, 'as if they sigh because they are very sorry to begin life in earnest', while John South is transfixed by 'the melancholy Gregorian melodies which the air wrung out' of the elm tree outside his house. Just as trees are deformed with age, so Hardy's human characters take on the features that their culture and environment bestow on them. The trees sigh in unison with the human characters. There is a symbiosis between humanity and nature, where evolution is not an ameliorating system.

The interconnectedness of trees and people is a regular Hardy theme. Hardy would have understood why John Clare was moved to bid a personal farewell to the two elm trees near his home. In his sensitivity to fellow creatures and the relationship of humans to nature Hardy also likens trees to people, although in a less precious sense than Clare. Hardy's poem 'Throwing a Tree' describes a morning's work for two woodmen in the New Forest. The woodmen with their axes are 'executioners' to a tree bearing a death-mark. Their axes made a 'broad deep gash in the bark' as if they are tearing through skin, then the tree 'shivers' as the two-handled saw starts to work through the trunk. Eventually the tree quivers and then crashes down, 'And two hundred years' steady growth has been ended in less than two hours'. Hardy's other tree poems like 'In a Wood', 'The Ivy-Wife', 'The Felled Elm and She' and 'Logs on the Hearth' also develop this theme. 'The Ivy-Wife' describes how the embrace of the ivy is resisted by beech and plane but is accepted by the ash tree. The ash is then strangled by the encroaching ivy, which also subsequently perishes. It is not clear whether the ivy should be regarded as substance or metaphor. 'In a Wood' was drafted in 1887 and rewritten in 1896 with the subtitle 'see *The Woodlanders*'. It is narrated by a city-oppressed individual looking for woodland peace, and is worth quoting in full:

Pale beech and pine so blue,
    Set in one clay,
Bough to bough cannot you
    Live out your day?
When the rains skim and skip,
Why mar sweet comradeship,
Blighting with poison-drip
    Neighbourly spray?

Heart-halt and spirit-lame,
    City-opprest
Unto this wood I came
    As to a nest;
Dreaming that sylvan peace
Offered the harrowed ease –
Nature a soft release
    From men's unrest.

But, having entered in,
    Great growths and small
Show them to men akin –
    Combatants all!
Sycamore shoulders oak,
Bines the slim sapling yoke,
Ivy-spun halters choke
    Elms stout and tall.

Touches from ash, O wych,
    Sting you like scorn!
You too, brave hollies, twitch
    Sidelong from thorn.
Even the rank poplars bear
Lothly a rival's air,
Cankering in black despair
    If overborne.

Since, then, no grace I find
    Taught me of trees,
Turn I back to my kind,
    Worthy as these.
There at least smiles abound,
There discourse trills around,
There, now and then, are found
    Life-loyalties.

In the poem Hardy develops the parallel between natural and human conflicts. The life loyalties of Giles Winterbourne end in his defeat, but the ending of the poem reinforces the bleak ending of *The Woodlanders* where, in a world of rapid change, Marty South is incapable of evolving, locked as she is in a closed world with only the trees and the dead for company. Woodland for Marty South is rich in personal memory, but the price she pays for it in her long-term material and emotional well-being is too high. Even her real woodlander skills and arcane culture will be overtaken by events and rendered worthless. Like an old person who has lived too long, Marty South will lose all the individuals who have shared her life, leaving no one who understands her. Hardy makes plain the outlook for the likes of Marty South in his essay on Dorset labourers, where he comments that while they are losing their individuality and their culture 'it is too much to expect them to remain stagnant and old-fashioned for the pleasure of romantic spectators'.[26]

Hardy exposes the illusion that we are connected to nature by sitting in our armchairs reading about it. The very act of reading *The Woodlanders* affirms that we have more in common with Fitzpiers than with Winterbourne, that we identify with nature through the medium of culture, and that culture filters out uncomfortable truths we would rather avoid. 'In a Wood' therefore disappoints the reader expecting to escape from human folly and to find something different in nature – which is after all why most people take woodland walks in the first place. But of course trees live by the same natural laws as people; and, if they have any value in teaching a wider lesson, it is to nurturing better relations with fellow humans. Hardy was therefore writing against the grain of most contemporary nature writing as he described the melancholy solitary reflections of the woodland walker. In both *Under the Greenwood Tree* and *The Woodlanders* it is impossible to live in the woodlands except in a community whose livelihood depends upon those places. For Marty South, and for John Clare, the woodlands are not a natural counterpoint to the social world, they are a landscape of personal memory and of lost community.

13

Dreamers

Solitude has long been associated with woodland experience. Sir Philip Sidney talked of 'sweete woods the delight of solitarinesse' to an Elizabethan audience, while in the middle of the following century Andrew Marvell found sanctuary in the woods of Lord Fairfax at Appleton House, where he was a tutor. The woods were essential to private thinking and for ruminating on the subject of nature, and the men and women who were equally bound by its laws:

> Thrice happy he who, not mistook,
> Hath read in Nature's mystic Book.

Marvell was a temporary visitor looking for mental recuperation. By the nineteenth century this was a commonplace experience and the solitary rambler had become the characteristic woodland visitor. Even a born and bred countryman like Richard Jefferies could write of Savernake Forest in Wiltshire in 1875 that it was a 'grand solitude' shared with the red deer, a forgotten landscape that had a past but no present, where 'the visitor may walk for whole days in this great wood and never pass the same spot twice. No gates or jealous walls will bar his progress.'[1] We have already looked at Clare and Cowper, two woodland solitaries who responded to rural change. Next we will look at a sequence of writers who retreated to the woods from urban and industrial society, and the ways in which that writing changed as the modern world penetrated every corner of daily life.

At the head of the romantic movement stands Jean-Jacques Rousseau, whose contemplative withdrawal from society provided some of the philosophical basis for romanticism. Detachment from his fellow beings initiated self-enquiry, essential in the quest for self-knowledge, and it also allowed him to think about his relationship to nature. Rousseau criticized those philosophers who had studied human nature to talk authoritatively about other people rather than to know themselves. In contrast, woodland was the ideal place in which to lose oneself in order to find oneself. Nature's independent time-scale set human progress in its proper relation with the natural world. Nature, as opposed to God, gave Rousseau a sense of original innocence that had been corrupted by progress and the social contract that alienated individuals from an authentic life. He learnt this by withdrawing from society to discover by patient intuition the nature of the first people to walk in the primeval woods.

In 1753 Rousseau visited the forests of Saint-Germain, where solitude and trees sparked a mental lightning. His sense of exhilaration is expressed in the account of those walks that appeared in *The Confessions* (completed in 1765 but published posthumously in 1781).

> I sought and I found the vision of those primitive times, the history of which I proudly traced. I demolished the petty lies of mankind; I dared to strip man's nature naked, to follow the progress of time, and trace the things which have distorted it; and by comparing man as he made himself with man as he is by nature I showed him in his pretended perfection the true source of his misery. Exalted by these sublime meditations, my soul soared towards the Divinity.[2]

That the miseries of mankind were self-inflicted was further expanded in his *Discourse on the Origin of Inequality* (1754). It described a period of prelapsarian innocence when men and women found their material needs in the forests, where they learnt self-preservation and the care of their fellow beings. The forest was presented as a monument more ancient than any relic of civilization and acquired at the same time an aura of timelessness. The search for natural man therefore needed a cultural forgetting of what the woods had been in recent history. Foresters had to go unnoticed and be replaced by imaginary primitives. As solitude in the forests prompted Rousseau to learn about his own true nature, so his place in the scheme of things helped him to appreciate nature for what it was. Appreciation of its beauties was not for Rousseau a matter of aesthetic tastes, but of his true inner self responding to his natural home.

Yet Rousseau's relationship to nature remained an ambiguous one, as it was based upon the disjunction between his material and philosophical worlds. From Saint-Germain he returned to Paris, where 'life among pretentious people was so little to my taste'. Unfortunately he had no skills that could be usefully employed in rural work, and he did not have the money that would allow him to lead a comfortable country life without working. The result was a compromise in the form of city life relieved by a daily and solitary walk in the Bois de Boulogne to order his thoughts. The Bois de Boulogne was for Rousseau like the forests beyond the boundary of Rome – an uncultivated wilderness that remained host to forces beyond the everyday world, where civilization could be understood by contemplating its opposite, and where nature was understood as the opposite of civilization. His search for the true lineaments of nature was conditioned by his experience of society and as a writer he was inescapably contributing to that society. Nature and history, forests and cities belong together just as the Bois de Boulogne belongs to Paris.[3]

In the English-speaking world one solitary observer of nature, William Wordsworth, took Rousseau's ideas further and established one of the contexts in which the natural world has been viewed ever since. While not especially noted for his tree poems or for the descriptive verse in which Clare and Cowper excelled, for Wordsworth contemplation of nature induced states of feeling that taught him what he was as a man, and gave him respect for all his fellow creatures. In the preface to *Lyrical Ballads* (1798) he had considered 'man and nature as essentially adapted to one another'. In one of the ensuing poems, he explained further that

> Therefore am I still
> A lover of the meadows and the woods,
> And mountains; and of all that we behold
> From this green earth; of all the mighty world
> Of eye, and ear, both what they half create
> And what perceive; well pleased to recognise
> In nature and the language of the sense
> The anchor of my purest thoughts, the nurse,
> The guide, the guardian of my heart, and soul
> Of all my moral being.[4]

Wordsworth's use of authentic everyday language in *Lyrical Ballads* was an attempt to strip away the artificial constructs of neoclassical poetry and reclaim the purity of natural sentiment. Simplicity in nature is found not in those breathtaking scenes for which Lakeland is famous, but in intimate proximity to living things; in short, in a wood.

> I heard a thousand blended notes,
> While in a grove I sate reclined,
> In that sweet mood when pleasant thoughts
> Bring sad thoughts to the mind.
>
> To her fair works did Nature link
> The human soul that through me ran;
> And much it grieved my heart to think
> What man has made of man.[5]

A contrast is set up opposing the world of nature, where 'every flower enjoys the air it breathes', and the artificial world of civilization, which has detached itself from the world of nature. Man may have been a product of nature, but man has subsequently taken over the role of creator and made a new artificial world of his own, the one that Wordsworth cannot but live in. The resulting sense of alienation is the discord between social reality and natural instinct that became one of the key attitudes to nature from the time of the industrial revolution. Wordsworth struck up a compromise between the two by returning to live in his native Lake District, where in later years he watched helplessly the unstoppable march of civilization as the railway crept its way into this hitherto remote corner of Britain. In other respects he was a man of his time writing about the concerns of his contemporaries, as did the other writers discussed, most of whom did not live permanently in the country.

Both Rousseau and Wordsworth struggled to find a compromise between nature and culture. Culture, the world of people, was urban in its focus and essential to fulfil their need for congress through the medium of poetry and prose. Such a compromise is an inherent char-acteristic of the romantic view of nature, although it has not always been acknowledged. The romantic tendency is to sustain nature's mys-tery, or at least to construct nature in such a way that it can be sensed but not explained, which meant that human sensibility about nature acquired greater authority than the experience of the rural labourer. Such a detached view was urban in its inspiration. The ability to divine nature's essence was the province of poets, who became unofficial 'high priests' preoccupied with the ineffable nature of nature. The tendency for solitary reflection in natural places self-evidently increased as the focus of society became more urban. Woodland became the haunt of thinkers and feelers, men like the Londoner John Keats, for whom woodlands were an other world of imagination where he never even dreamt of physical toil.

Woodland was vital to Keats's poetry. He once claimed, during a stay on the Isle of Wight, that its treeless landscape had sapped all his creative juices. His two major works, *Endymion* (1818) and the unfinished *Hyperion*, are both set in forests, and woods present a landscape of inspiration where he heard the nightingale, the 'light-winged Dryad of the Trees'. Yet Keats could never be mistaken for a countryman. In fact he was an occasional woodland visitor, and he went there to escape people rather than discover the alternative human communities of woodman and gypsy. Trees inspired him, but not any trees. His brother George emigrated to America and became, amongst other things, a timber merchant. Far from dreaming of an Eden across the Atlantic, the thought of the American forest horrified Keats:

> [its] rank-grown forests, frosted, black, and blind,
> Would fright a Dryad ...
> There flowers have no scent, birds no sweet song,
> And great unerring Nature once seems wrong.[6]

This aversion to the wild woods is entirely consistent and explains much of Keats's attitude to nature. Keats did not equate woodlands with wilderness, as a tree meant nothing unless it had a rich cultural heritage associated with it. Woodlands were therefore never uninhabited places. They were filled not with real rustic folk but with imaginary people and the ghosts of the poets who had been there before him. English woods embodied a rich cultural tradition for Keats that was expressed in folklore and in the works of Spenser and Shakespeare. But it was the classical pantheon that Keats drew upon most to people his woodland settings. In his sonnet 'Happy is England' he declared that a man may be happy knowing only the English woods, but confessed to occasionally longing for Italian skies, a landscape that he had never visited but that he had little trouble imagining. When his friend Leigh

Hunt moved to the edge of Hampstead Heath in 1816, this comparatively
suburban remnant of ancient Middlesex Forest sufficed for a woodland
retreat, and spawned the poem 'I Stood Tip-Toe'. In it Keats allied
himself with the ancient tradition as he compared himself with Ovid:

> So did he feel, who pulled the boughs aside
> That we might look into a forest wide
> To catch a glimpse of Fauns and Dryades
> Coming with softest rustle through the trees.[7]

Although Keats and John Clare never met, in John Taylor they shared
the same publisher and they became acquainted with each other's work.
Clare wrote perceptively of Keats's *Endymion* that when he

> speaks of woods Dryads and fauns are sure to follow and the brook looks
> alone without her naiads to his mind yet the frequency of such classical
> accomplishment makes it wearisome to the reader where behind every rose
> bush he looks for a Venus & under every laurel a thrumming Appollo [sic].

Keats wrote of Clare, equally revealingly, that Clare's 'images from
nature are too much introduced without being called for by a particular
Sentiment', and that his penchant for description stifled writing that
should be led by ideas.[8] Clare's woodland was one of personal association, Keats's of symbol and beauty.

Keats idealized nature, in particular as an idealization of beauty. In a
letter to Richard Woodhouse in 1818 he committed himself to writing
'from the mere yearning and fondness I have for the Beautiful', but
recognized that it came with the danger that he would set himself apart
from his fellow beings, remarking that 'All I hope is that I may not lose
all interest in human affairs'.[9] The archetypal setting of a Keats poem
is an arboreal one. Replete with ideas, it is nevertheless the place least
physically marred by human interference and as such could embody the
poet's truest thoughts and emotions, and provide him with the imagery
to symbolize the human spirit. In this sense nature could be seen to be
at one with humanity. It was a natural theology that prized beauty and
love above all else, and where, in the annual renewal of trees, immortality
could be glimpsed. In the 'Ode to a Nightingale' he can meditate on
suffering and the consolation of art through the bird in its greenwood
habitat. The nightingale

> In some melodious plot
> Of beechen green, and shadows numberless,
> Singest of summer in full-throated ease.[10]

This is contrasted with the world of men where 'to think is to be full of sorrow'. The only way to elevate himself to the beauty of the nightingale is on 'the viewless wings of poesy'. Keats, already diagnosed with the consumption that he described as his 'death warrant', confesses himself in such a heightened poetical state as 'half in love with easeful death':

> Now more than ever seems it rich to die,
> To cease upon the midnight with no pain,
> While thou art pouring forth thy soul abroad
> In such an ecstasy! [11]

Keats sought in trees and birds symbols that could help communicate his personal ideas and feelings. But not all of the feelings inspired by nature are necessarily transferable. William Hazlitt had argued that it was impossible for anyone to love nature simply for its own sake without their feelings being structured by personal memories. Hazlitt had been a lover of nature since his Shropshire childhood, at a time when sensitivity to nature went hand-in-hand with feelings of social justice and humanity.

> It is because natural objects have been associated with the sports of our childhood, with air and exercise, with our feelings in solitude, when the mind takes strongest hold of things ... [it is] because they have been one chief source and nourishment of our feelings, and a part of our being, that we love them as we do ourselves.

Intercourse with nature, it follows, is a way to revisit experiences without fear of contradiction or interruption. It becomes a safe refuge. Hazlitt went on to point out that the human form encompasses an infinity of motives, passions and ideas, to the extent that it was not possible to transfer one individual's personal experiences of a walk in the woods to another person. 'Each individual is a world to himself, governed by a thousand contradictory and wayward impulses.' [12] If this is true, then how can people converse with one another in relation to trees? It prompted the search for universal statements by poets and writers whose readership was urban. Hazlitt gave the example that, having once found shade and rest under a tree by a brook, he associated every combination of tree and brook with the same feelings, and suggested that this might have been the origin of Greek mythology. All such places were mystically personified by the dryad and naiad offering the cool fountain or tempting shade.

Keats adopted the classical as a symbolic shorthand, which had the additional advantage of a long and distinguished pedigree. The process was a legitimate search for common ground, although it was an inherent characteristic of that search that common ground could only be found by talking about nature in general ways. For example, Hazlitt's attachments came to be most strongly identified not with specific places but with seasons, be it the fresh foliage of spring or the 'dark massy foliage of autumn'. 'Thus Nature is a kind of universal home', and a stock of emotions and attitudes would eventually pall and turn into clichés.

Another manner in which nature became a generalised concept was in its association with religion. The American essayist Ralph Waldo Emerson (1803–1882) felt himself to be in the mystical presence of God when he walked in the woods, feelings that were shared with many contemporary British authors. According to Emerson woods are 'perpetual youth', 'plantations of God [where] decorum and sanctity reign' and where 'we return to reason and faith'. It was an intuitive belief, not something that could be gained from Bible study: 'The greatest delight which the fields and woods minister, is the suggestion of an occult relation between man and the vegetable. I am not alone and unacknowledged. They nod to me, and I to them.'[13] His theological approach to nature contradicted the secularized view of woodland prevalent in the eighteenth century, where it acted as a moral indicator. Emerson was proposing that nature formed part of a coherent plan or design, a view that would find itself in difficulty when it was brought into the wider debate about science and God. John Ruskin argued that science had 'thrown foolish persons into atheism', whereas 'to wise ones, [it provided] the most precious testimony to their faith yet given by physical nature'. The roots of a tree are in the earth and its branches reach up to the sky, so a tree is 'the animation of the dust, and the living soul of the sunshine'.[14]

To experience God as a mystical presence in nature had the effect of turning the woodlands into an abstract concept. In *The Poetry of Architecture* (1837) Ruskin wrote that 'the chief feeling induced by woody country is one of reverence for its antiquity. There is a quiet melancholy about the decay of the patriarchal trunks, which is enhanced by the green and elastic vigour of the young saplings.' [15] This is an idealised conglomerated image, not an actual wood where Ruskin had stood. It also implicitly states that the chief attraction of woods and other natural forms is that they are non-socialized places, a state of mind that could only be achieved by selective amnesia. It is in the woods that communion with nature is to be had, holding up a mirror to the solitary meditator. Ruskin likened an old forest tree as subject to the same laws of nature as himself,

> an energetic being, liable to an approaching death; its age is written on every spray; and, because we see it is susceptible of life and annihilation, like our own, we imagine it must be capable of the same feelings, and possess the same faculties, and, above all others, memory: it is always telling us about the past, never about the future. [16]

This is to see a tree entirely in philosophical terms. It is only a step away from veneration of nature, and from Wordsworth's comment that 'one impulse from a vernal wood' taught more human wisdom than the wisest philosopher. By writing about trees as sensitive beings Ruskin sought to identify the unity between all living beings in opposition to biological taxonomies that classified everything according to their differences. It urged respect for nature, but Ruskin did not recognize the social implications of his view, going so far as to claim absurdly that 'the man who could remain a radical in a wood country is a disgrace to his species'. [17] Ruskin has been described as one of those men having radical views but Tory tastes.

William Barnes (1801–1886), a friend and influence on Thomas Hardy, was a lifelong countryman and to that extent never idealized the country in the manner of Ruskin. His poems make sharp social comments about the interference of alien property owners. For example, in 'Picken o' Scroff' he deplores the fact that children are no longer allowed to gather the lop and top after felling, and in the self-explanatory 'Zellen Woone's Honey to Buy Zome'hat Sweet' claims that the value of a tree is greater than the sum of its timber, bark and small wood. But as well as being a man of the woods William Barnes was both a man of letters and an ordained priest. In an essay on 'Beauty and Art' written for *Macmillan's Magazine* in 1861, he described 'the beautiful in Nature' as 'the unmarred result of God's first creative or forming will'. The role of the poet of nature was clear to him: 'the beautiful in Art is the result of an unmistaken working of man in accordance with the beautiful in nature'.[18] The key word is 'unmistaken' as it introduces the notion of a right and a wrong way of interacting with nature. The logic of his statement is that, whatever twisted or distorted shape a tree may take, it is the result of God's will and to tamper with it is to besmirch God's creation. It was an absurd position and one that obliged him to contradict traditional woodland practice. When he had bought some wooded land near his birthplace, at Bagber in Dorset, a farmer was intent on pollarding the elm trees there. Barnes is said to have upbraided him with the comment that 'God made elms, and man made pollards'.[19] It encapsulates the problem of much nineteenth-century writing about nature that could only exist as escapism. Instead of writing about authentic woodlanders in the manner of Hardy, Barnes remained at one remove from his subject by recreating the woods in the language of the Dorset dialect.

Barnes was not, however, strictly speaking a dialect poet. His version of traditional local language was the fruit of philological study, not of fieldwork in local taverns. In his view the Dorset tongue was to the English language what the Doric order was to Greek culture. The language of the poems could not avoid sounding artificial, but Barnes had a legitimate point: 'In English purity is in many cases given up for the sake of what is considered to be elegance.' Barnes wanted to re-establish that purity and placed authenticity above social acceptability.

The use of dialect placed his relationship with nature in a cultural context, but his engagement with nature was normally a personal one – 'trees be company', as one of his poems put it. He never managed to live up to his ideal of praising nature simply as a divine creation, and his failure arguably saved his work from sterility. Like Keats and his preference for culturally rich European forests over barren American forests, woodlands meant nothing to Barnes without some form of personal engagement with specific trees. At times this can be stifled by convention. An idyllic time was had 'out a-nutten' – a rare example where Barnes had human company, and an innocent family one too, as the girls diligently went their own way to gather mushrooms. One of his most successful poems, 'The Woodlands', embeds his own personal experiences into specific places, and establishes the importance of seemingly everyday events in his personal memories:

> You gi'ed me life, you gi'ed me jaÿ,
> Lwonesome woodlands! zunny woodlands!
> You gi'ed me health, as in my playÿ
> I rambled through ye, zunny woodlands!
> You gi'ed me freedom, vor to rove
> In aïry meäd or sheädy grove;
> You gi'ed me smilèn Fannèy's love,
> The best ov all o't, zunny woodlands! [20]

Certain wooded places and certain trees mapped Barnes's own life. His own birthplace was shrouded by 'a lwonesome grove o' woak', and he remembered climbing 'the girt woak tree that's in the dell! There's noo tree I do love se well'. In 'Vellen o' the Tree' he laments the felling of an elm tree by reminiscing upon the mowers and hay-makers who have sought its shade in hot working weather.

If nature was a living being, in the rather vague and mystical sense described by Emerson and Ruskin, or the work of God that Emerson, Barnes and other clergymen maintained, then felling a tree was akin to sacrilege. Hardy's poem 'Throwing a Tree', already quoted, expresses some of the sensitively to the brutal act of felling, as did Gerard Manley Hopkins in his famous poem 'Binsey Poplars':

> O if we but knew what we do
> When we delve or hew –
> Hack and rack the growing green! [21]

After the poplars had been felled 'After-comers cannot guess the beauty been'. Hopkins was a great scholar of trees and woodland flora, a painstaking study that was sustained by his belief that he was contemplating the works of God. In 1866 he was engrossed in a study of oak leaves, trying to articulate their pattern of veins in a visual structure that had nothing to do with scientific classification. Based purely on its visual characteristics, Hopkins wanted to find the essence, or what he called the 'inscape', of the thing, in what was an inexhaustible and self-sustaining study. It was a sensory and not a scientific exploration. 'The bluebells in your hand baffle you with their inscape, made to every sense', he wrote in 1871 of bluebells he had collected near his Oxford college:

> If you draw your fingers through them they are lodged and struggle with a shock of wet heads; the long stalks rub and click and flatten to a fan on one another like your fingers themselves would when you passed the palms hard across one another, making a brittle rub and jostle like the noise of a hurdle strained by leaning against; then there is the faint honey smell and in the mouth the sweet gum when you bite them. But this is easy, it is the eye they baffle.[22]

But where could one go if there was not the sustaining belief of a Creator? For the country writer and poet Edward Thomas (1878–1917) nature replaced religion. Thomas rued the loss of a mythical view of the world, which left humanity aimless and incapable of reverence, but he could still detect it in 'the human tranquillity now to be seen only in a few old faces of a disappearing generation'.[23] His adult life began as a quest to recapture what lay behind those old faces, to find inner peace in the presence of nature. Thomas was profoundly attached to rural England and was especially at ease in wooded places, but he was also troubled by rural decline, and in being so he characterized much of the twentieth-century feelings about trees, and about nature and topography in general.

His love of nature and rural life was rhetorical. Its practical aspects were not suited to his temperament, which became apparent when Thomas moved with his family to Hampshire in order to send his son to Bedales School, while continuing with his career as a country writer. Bedales was one of the so-called New Schools established in the 1880s with its back-to-the-land philosophy and Arts-and-Crafts tastes. Unlike his wife Helen, Thomas never blended with the school staff with whom, on the face of it, he should have had much in common. Thomas was looking for personal freedom, a mix of pleasure and mystical communion, that was based on feeling rather than thought. It clashed with the school's philosophy of social improvement and practical solutions. Bedales and Thomas were opposite sides of the same coin, but they were not the first to turn their backs on the modern world.

William Morris dreamt of resurrecting the middle ages before he recognized that actions were more effective than idealizations. Richard Jefferies went in the opposite direction, beginning his career as an agricultural journalist but developing his writing to advocate nature as a source of spiritual strength and regeneration. In his influential confessional book *The Story of My Heart* (1883) he expressed his desire to discover 'soul-nature', 'to have from all green things and from the sunlight the inner meaning ... that I might be full of light as the woods of the sun's rays'.[24] Edward Thomas was a keen admirer, and wrote in his biography that Jefferies's work presented nature as 'a great flood of physical and spiritual sanity'. There was a readership ready to take this approach seriously, those who wanted religion but found its conventional forms undermined by modern science. They were the same readers who enjoyed Thomas Hardy's novels, but somehow seemed to miss the hardship of country life. Edward Thomas wrote for a similar audience. He represents a niche of English country writing in the late nineteenth and early twentieth centuries.

Among his contemporaries was W. H. Hudson, who in books like *The Green Mansions* (1904), about his childhood in Argentina, popularized the cult of a simpler life. To a certain extent so did Lady Chatterley's lover Mellors, who has left the army and taken a job as gamekeeper, living in a cottage in the woods 'alone, and apart from life, which is what he wanted'. It was in the woods that Lady Chatterley escapes the stifling social conventions of the country house, in favour of the simpler, more honest world of the gamekeeper. The escape paralleled D. H. Lawrence's own flight from the artificial, mechanized society that he hated, in search of something more earthy and more fulfilling, a search that led him half way around the world to Sicily, Sri Lanka, Australia and New Mexico. Edward Thomas sought a similarly fulfilling alternative life closer to home.

Thomas made a name for himself as a nature writer with his first book, *The Woodland Life* (1897), published when he was just nineteen and still a student. Born in London, and educated at Oxford, Thomas henceforth quit the town and the suburbs for the country in search of an ideal. In the process he achieved the near impossible task of earning a living as a country writer. Thomas was commissioned to write a series of illustrated country books servicing a growing market for rural reflection. Essays provided an outlet for more serious work, where Thomas exercized his talent for prose-poetry, a genre both popular and highly regarded in the first decade of the twentieth century. Communication of the qualities inherent in nature depended upon the qualities of the writer, and Thomas was undeniably good at it. In the *Rose Acre Papers*, a collection of essays published in 1904, he described a wood in the dead of winter in a highly wrought manner typical of its author: 'a bleak day in February, when the trees moan as if they cover a tomb, the tomb of the voices, the thrones and dominations of summer past. The rabbits are housed. Dead as soon as born, the first lesser celandine puts forth one flower'.[25] For all its wordiness this was still only commercial writing, however, and neither his essays nor his country books achieved any special critical acclaim until the publication in 1909 of *The South Country*, an exploration of Thomas's favourite places, including childhood holidays spent in Wiltshire near the home of his chief influence and benchmark, Richard Jefferies.

The work reveals the contradictions in his approach to nature. He rarely took maps when he walked, he cared little for grand historical monuments like cathedrals, and even tried to convince himself that he was 'pure of history'. Admitting that he was a modern man whose condition was to belong nowhere, he did not recognize a sense of place in much of his writing. This was a weakness, of course, as his description of the richly varied south of England tended to merge toward a conglomerated image. For a man who wanted to see the world around him in an unhistorical manner, woodland was natural territory because it offered the possibility of a universal landscape. In *The Heart of England* (1906) he described woodland as a land of soft compulsion to meditation. Only by meditation will the visitor become attuned to his surroundings. A sensitive and solitary rambler finds such places companionable and reassuring and 'soon has a feeling of ease and seclusion there'.[26] Helen Thomas later confessed that, like Lady Chatterley and her lover, she and her husband had a penchant for making love in woods.[27]

Alone in Cornwall Thomas stepped into a wood that for this London-born, Oxford-educated writer was not a Cornish wood but another world:

> And there was no sound in the caverns of foliage except one call of a cuckoo
> as I entered and the warbling of a blackbird that mused in the oaks and
> then laughed and was silent and mused again and filled the mind with the

fairest images of solitude – solitude where a maid, thinking of naught, un-
thought of, unseen, combs out her yellow hair and lets her spirit slip down
into her tresses – where a man fearful of his kind ascends out of the deep
so that his eyes look bravely and his face unstiffens and unwrinkles and his
motion and gesture is fast and free – where a child walks and stops and runs
and sings in careless joy that takes him winding far out into the abysses of
eternity.[28]

The idealization of women, especially as an analogue of nature, is
typical of Thomas (as it was also of Morris and Jefferies), but the figures
are all here idealized. Just as his landscapes tended to group around a
single unifying image, so his country folk merge into a single universal
figure. The place is characterized by its freedom from any social or
historical context, allowing the author to reconstruct society purely in
his own imagination. The passage opens up its author's deep love of
woodlands and he goes on to describe why he likes trees, for the sensual
pleasures they offer and their 'kindliness and their serene remoteness
and inhumanity'. The woodland, then, was a certain kind of uninhabited
landscape separate from places where human congress normally takes
place. But Thomas had nothing against people. He was gregarious
enough in his daily life, but he liked to experience nature alone. His
wife Helen Thomas remarked that 'almost his greatest pleasure, and
certainly his greatest need, was to walk and be alone' in the southern
English counties.[29]

Isolation from his normal life made it easier to interact with people
of other social classes and his nomadic impulse gave him an affinity
with gypsies. He could converse easily with rural folk, could discern the
wisdom they tried to convey to him and had a natural affection for
them. He frequently met and described poachers, as in *Cloud Castle*
(published posthumously in 1922), where he meets an old man who has
been in turns poacher, gamekeeper and soldier. 'His eyes have the cold
pale-blue brightness, suggestive of weak or short sight, which is almost
always noticeable in men whose eyes are much used out of doors.' The
real man in front of him soon turns imperceptibly into a mythical
woodman:

His dress, though he knows it not, by a curious but natural adaptation to
surroundings, has become of unspeakable hues; slowly he has taken the
colours of the wildwood in autumn's grey and brown. He is an expert poacher,

an essential qualification for a good gamekeeper, has a superstitious belief in herbal remedies, can mimic the cries of birds, and his vocabulary is mixed with Romany.[30]

In short, the old man is a personification of all those essences that Thomas sought in country life. But Thomas was always an onlooker, never a participant. He could never become like the old man of the woods, never think like him or share the same instincts, or be his friend on equal terms. His livelihood depended upon an urban readership that expected to find the peace and simplicity in nature that they could not find in their own lives, and in many cases whose reading was a substitute for the actual experience. His sensitive observations of rural folk served to accentuate his alienation from them. His act of writing country books was a symptom that the primal relationship with nature had been disrupted and needed to be administered in this artificial form.

Ultimately Edward Thomas came to realize that his idealism needed reconciliation with the real world. He did so partly by resolving his greatest problem as a country writer – that he should give up prose and that his natural medium was poetry. But he did not give up his quest for communion with nature, or celebrating what was left of it. In the poem 'The Unknown Bird' (1915), to single out one of many examples, the unseen bird lost among the canopy of beech trees in early summer is a metaphor for the elusive essence of nature that could be discerned after careful attention but never quite pinned down and preserved. Indeed it was a song of a bird that could never succumb to the classifying impulses of the naturalists:

> I told
> The naturalists; but neither had they heard
> Anything like the notes that did so haunt me.[31]

That essence of nature was the fugitive ideal irreducible by the scientists.

The rural Britain that Edward Thomas had set out to idealize was changing and Thomas knew it. His longest poem, 'Lob' (1915), is ostensibly about the search for an old countryman, but Lob is really a metaphor of traditional life now vanished. This realization, together with his adoption of the medium of poetry, coincided with what threatened to obliterate European culture, the Great War. It was in 1914 that Thomas stopped observing and started participating, joining the army even though he was now in his mid thirties and above the age of men expected to serve. Killed by shrapnel in 1917, his talent as a war poet was not to write from the trenches but to link the large-scale events of the war with the small world of the countryside. One of his most successful war poems, 'As the Team's Head Brass' (1916) was written, like all his war poems, before he was sent out to the Front and is filled with foreboding. In it the narrator watches the team of horses work through the field with military precision – like cavalry – and yet they stumble along in tired fashion and Thomas knows that their days are numbered. Whatever the outcome, the war will see an end to this way of life. He is sat on a fallen elm, emblem of those who had already fallen, and specifically of the ploughman's mate, when the ploughman remarks that 'Now if he had stayed here we should have moved that tree'. The poem begins with two lovers entering a wood, and they remain a pervasive presence throughout the poem, emerging at the end. While death looms ominously over the poem – the death of a traditional way of life and the likelihood acknowledged by the narrator of his own personal death – the lovers have been initiating a new generation, and the poem ends on a note of rejuvenation. It was Thomas's main achievement as a mature poet to set his world within a larger compass, and to find hope for the future rather than merely mourning the past.

The artist who best managed to express the devastation that Edward Thomas felt was coming was Paul Nash (1889–1946). Nash had a similar affinity with nature, and sought its latent meanings as if they were a transcript of private human sensibility. His stark portrayal of the field of battle is one of the memorable images of the conflict. *The Menin Road*, commissioned by the Imperial War Museum, is a scene of scurrying soldiers, craters and fallen masonry, and a road passing through a wood. The wood has been flattened by the heavy guns from who knows which side, leaving only the mutilated trunks devoid of branches, a metaphor of the old world that had been shattered and would be scarred for evermore.

Edward Thomas and other poets who escaped to nature from the industrialized and urban worlds acknowledged that in part they were lamenting a lost childhood. It associated nature with a safer and simpler world than the one they lived in. Richard Jefferies mined the rich vein of childhood in his mature work, while his belief in the mystical properties of nature took him away from the farmsteads and into the woods. In South Yorkshire he wrote that

> I wish that the men now serving the great polished wheels, and works in iron and steel and brass could somehow be spared an hour to sit under this ancient oak in Thardover South Wood, and come to know from the actual touch of its rugged bark that the past is living now, that Time is no older, that Nature still exists as full as ever, and to see that all the factories of the world have made no difference.[32]

This kind of rhetorical writing took him away from the real world into the world of the private imagination, exemplified by his novel *Wood Magic* (1881). In it the farmer's son Bevis befriends the wild animals he encounters around the farm and they introduce him to a parallel society of animals, to which Bevis is admitted by a secret way in the woods. But it is not a sentimental view of nature. The hare complains bitterly that her son, the leveret, has been consumed by the weasel. The alternative society is fraught with conflict just like the real world. The king of the wild animals is the magpie Kapchack, whose rival, the wood pigeon Choo-Hoo, has assembled a motley band of fellow outcasts, and tries to seize power. Jefferies presents the animal world as parallel to the human world and thereby emphasises that the human race is a part of nature. Bevis learns that if he wants to live as part of nature and understand the world he lives in he must learn direct from nature itself, echoing Wordsworth's 'vernal impulse', in contrast to the reductive mode of the sciences. The chief novelty of the story, however, was that apart from Bevis the characters are all animals, the formula adopted by Kenneth Grahame for his *Wind in the Willows*. But whereas Jefferies presented nature as an analogue of society, Grahame's idealized society was not what he thought it was or had ever been, but what he thought it should be like.

Kenneth Grahame was a man of his times. A London-based civil servant whose conservative instincts made him outwardly conform to the prevailing social code, he inwardly found relief in the world of childhood, animal fable and fantasy. The countryside was the world of escape which he found on walking holidays. By the end of the nineteenth century the countryside had become established as a holiday destination. It was the heyday of the wayfarer, and of country diaries and wildflower illustrations. The latter half of the nineteenth century also saw the establishment of countywide natural history and archaeological societies that structured group activities such as wildflower expeditions and fungus forays. For Kenneth Grahame and others of his generation the countryside was aristocratic and pre-industrial, a place somehow immune from material prosperity and the threat of socialism, and a world much removed from that of Edward Thomas. Nature and the experience of nature through art became a cloistered refuge from the real world. But, as has been pointed out, although Kenneth Grahame was often *in* the country he was never *of* it.[33] Like so many of his contemporaries, he was addicted to the country and had a notional interest in its people, but there was never any danger of him wielding an axe or a fork.

The Wind in the Willows (1908) served to sublimate its author's fear of a changing, degraded world, and perhaps even his disillusionment with adult life. The characters in the story are desexualized, and none of them works, each living an aristocratic bachelor's idyll. The Wild Wood symbolizes the chaos and anarchy at the margin of civilization, as demonstrated when the Mole and Rat tread fearfully through it at night. Its denizens, the stoats and weasels, are the malevolent and threatening proletariat who briefly triumph when they capture Toad Hall. In the end natural justice prevails over anarchy and the wild-wooders see their proper place in the scheme of things. A. A. Milne, who took up the baton after Grahame, ostensibly set his Pooh stories in Ashdown Forest and its Hundred Acre Wood, but created a timeless and enchanted world familiar from Grahame but not so different from the enchanted forest of the Grimm brothers in Germany. Rabbit 'stopped and listened, and everything stopped and listened with him, and the forest was very lone and peaceful in the sunshine'. The real world was far away.

The alternative to using animals was to invent creatures, as did J. R. R. Tolkien. Tolkien's mythology was not a wholly invented world but the adaptation of a rich tradition of English (not classical) literature by a Professor of Anglo-Saxon in the University of Oxford, a practising Christian and veteran of the Great War. His literary reputation is based on three works, *The Hobbit* (1937), its three-volume sequel *The Lord of the Rings* (1954–55), and a prequel published five years after his death, *The Silmarillion* (1977). Under the supervision of the wizard Gandalf,

Bilbo Baggins leaves his comfortable home in the Shire and travels with
a company of dwarfs through mountain and forest and eventually
rescues a magic ring that is the key to evil and corruption. The hobbit
endures danger, hardship and sacrifice to win freedom from the tyranny
of evil. The sequel chronicles the history of Middle Earth in the Great
Year of the Third Age, and the adventures of another hobbit, Frodo,
who has inherited the ring from Bilbo. His task, with his fellow hobbits,
is to cast the ring into the Cracks of Mount Doom in Mordor to stop
Sauron, the evil lord of Mordor, from getting hold of it. Their adventures
in a hostile world of elemental wonder and peril recall the Devil in
medieval sermons and the knights testing their mettle in the medieval
forest. But here the villain is the modern mechanized world and its
corrosive effects on nature and humanity.

Tolkien drew on his knowledge and love of *Beowulf, Sir Gawain and
the Green Knight,* Malory and other works, sending him out deep into
the imaginary greenwood, sustained by his own love of trees. A Tolkien
forest is therefore a mixture of personal memory and cultivated myth.
In one of his early stories, 'Leaf by Niggle', written in 1938–39, he
confessed it was prompted by the felling of a favourite poplar tree. Its
only crime was to have been 'large and alive', and 'I do not think it had
any friends, or any mourners, except myself and a pair of owls'.[34] Tolkien
knew what he was about when he tried to resurrect English mythological
literature in his novels. He was one of the first scholars to recognize the
importance of mythology as a version of the truth, not as the province
of the ignorant. In 1938, a year after *The Hobbit* was published, he argued
that myths are not the opposite of history as they reveal underlying
realities, citing the Gospels as the supreme example. Tolkien was also a
man of his times. The tone of his work is anti-modern, anti-industrial
and anti-urban, and in that sense he is of a generation of men that
could not help looking back to a sunnier age before the Great War and
before they grew up. The avoidance of sexuality and lack of credible
female characters are the most commonly cited flaws in the work,
although his defenders might counter that *The Lord of the Rings* fails
politically because it is primarily religious. His fantasy world is a critique
of modern society, and his ideal is a kind of ecological Christianity.[35]

Trees and forests never stray far out of Tolkien's imagination. In an
epic battle against evil, the fate of trees is a moral indicator of those

who act upon them. Gandalf, the wise and moral wizard, is a lover of trees, whereas his counterpart Saruman, the head of the order of wizards, becomes blinded by self-interest and is a destroyer of trees, making 'wastes of stump and bramble where once there were singing groves'. His fortress is eventually overcome by the Ents, half-men and half-trees, whose roots penetrate the rocks of Saruman's fortifications and break them up, a hopeful symbol of the rejuvenating power of nature. Ents are the most ancient race in Middle Earth. In their remote beginnings they were indistinguishable from actual trees and they age at the same rate. Tolkien later described the invention of the Ents as an unconscious act, and said that he wrote a whole chapter on Treebeard the Ent in a single draft, as if he were divinely inspired.

The character Tom Bombadil, who is introduced into the story when he frees the hobbits from the grasp of a malevolent willow tree, is a personification of ancient wisdom and a benevolent forest spirit, who teaches the wisdom of learning from living things as the way to take one's place in the world. This wisdom imbues a respect for all living things and also of the otherness of those living beings. The hobbits feel themselves to be strangers in a forest where all other creatures are at home, a humbling experience. It entails a belief in trees as parallel beings with souls and loves and hates:

> Tom's words laid bare the heart of trees and their thoughts, which were often dark and strange, and filled with a hatred of things that go free upon the earth, gnawing, biting, breaking, hacking, burning: destroyers and usurpers. It was not called the Old Forest without reason, for it was indeed ancient, a survivor of vast forgotten woods; and in it there lived yet, ageing no quicker than the hills, the fathers of the fathers of trees, remembering times when they were lords. The countless years had filled them with pride and rooted wisdom, and with malice.[36]

If there is an Eden in Middle Earth it is the golden wood of Lothlorien, the ancient forest where the wood-elves believe all their kindred once dwelt. It is here that the supernatural mallorn trees grow, a place where the elves find it enough to eat, drink, rest and walk among the trees. It is a place of recuperation on the hobbits' adventures, a place to delight in living things, and perhaps a recollection of its author's childhood woodland rambles. Lothlorien is not a permanent escape from the outside world but a temporary refuge and a source of hope for the future. The nut of the mallorn tree is eventually planted to repair the damage done to the Shire, the home of the hobbits, during the War of the Ring between Sauron the Great and the free peoples of Middle Earth. 'The trees were the worst loss and damage' sustained by the Shire and 'Sam [Gangee] grieved over this more than anything else. For one thing, this hurt would take long to heal, and only his great-grandchildren, he thought, would see the Shire as it ought to be.'

Trees are important in Tolkien's work because they stand for attitudes to nature in general, and as growing things they contrast with the mechanical things he resented. As a place of escape, woods for Tolkien therefore offered temporary respite from the modern world, whether they were actual lived experience or the stuff of myth. Nostalgia for a simpler world might be a commonplace reaction, but it nevertheless is an important mechanism for coping with a rapid rate of change, and in Tolkien's case may express the disillusionment with the world felt by men of his generation. Nostalgia links the Old Forest of Middle Earth with the Wildwood of Kenneth Grahame, and it is a link that goes back through Edward Thomas to the pre-enclosure woodlands of John Clare. The woods took on a new role throughout the nineteenth century that contrasted with its political cast in the eighteenth. As the mechanized world expanded, symbolized so well in Thomas Hardy's novels as the creeping tendrils of the railway penetrating every corner of Wessex, so the woods had to be reinvented as a place of wildness. Keats's woods alive with dryads, Barnes's woods with reconstructed native talk, Hopkins with God, Thomas with a countryside ideal, Grahame and Tolkien with a fantasy land. We can only travel there in the imagination. None of the writers discussed here found much fresh insight into nature that they had not brought with them when they set out from the town. Even Edward Thomas could never find the fulfilment he craved, remaining always a bystander in the scenes and the people he described. As a place of escape, the mental and physical forest was one of shrinking comfort in the century after Keats. Its native inhabitants faded away into a more and more abstracted ideal, a symptom of the incompatibility of this vision with the outside world. The company of trees was one of increasing urgency for people who went there to contemplate loss, in a vision of the world that could see only a bleak future and could only comfort itself by looking backwards, the sigh of the soul in an increasingly treeless world. Looking inwards eventually ceases to be healthy. The alternative, of course, was to take practical steps to establish a more realistic relationship with nature.

14

Experts

The hornbeam is one of Britain's native species. Confined mainly to woodlands in south-east England, it is a tree with a long history of pollarding. Before the advent of coal, the wood was sold to London as domestic fuel and it produced a good quality of charcoal. It was a tree well suited to wood pasture because grazing animals like deer did not inhibit its growth, but it did not yield suitable timber for building. Its alternative name 'hardbeam' explains why carpenters have always found it a difficult material to work with, and why it was only ever employed where resilience was needed, for instance for the cogs of wind and water mills. The hornbeam is a characteristic species of Essex woodlands including Epping Forest and yet it is among the least known of British trees. Poets have never singled it out for praise and it never had the honour of supplying timber to build the mighty Royal Navy. In short the hornbeam is a handsome tree with few champions.

William Morris was brought up at Walthamstow in Epping Forest and when he was a young boy and young man he knew it 'yard by yard from Wanstead to the Theydons, and from Hale End to the Fairlop Oak'. In his youth the pollards were still cut every five or six years. As a man over sixty, Morris drew on his childhood haunts to put up a stout defence of the hornbeam, when he entered the debate about the future of the forest. By the end of the nineteenth century it was threatened by the spread of the commuter belt and by that other malaise of the suburban landscape, the golf course. His account of the forest contrasts with that strain of country writing that presented woodlands as another world, the conglomerated image that was everywhere and nowhere. The woods of his childhood were the biggest hornbeam woods in Britain, a place where holly grew in thickets between the pollards to create a 'curious and characteristic wood', and a distinctive place that should be preserved as such. He argued that its preservation would allow subsequent generations to appreciate what the ancient forests were like. Although that argument is more complicated than Morris realized, it was call to act rather than simply lament.

William Morris was scathing about the experts charged with deciding the future of his beloved hornbeams – 'we do not want to be under the thumb of either a wood bailiff, whose business is to grow timber for the market, or of a botanist whose business is to collect specimens for a botanical garden; or of a landscape gardener whose business is to vulgarise a garden or landscape to the utmost extent that his patron's purse will allow of'.[1] And yet the state of woodlands in the twenty-first century is to a large extent the work of experts from businessmen to ecologists, and of economic and conservation policies. Meanwhile what these woodlands mean to us has become more the province of naturalists than of poets, who no longer habitually look to the natural world for analogy and metaphor of contemporary life.

Contrary to the myth widely held in Edwardian England, a timeless rural England was not undergoing a terminal decline like a biblical fall. Ancient woodlands had undergone significant changes over many centuries, although it is fair to say that the nineteenth and twentieth centuries brought the most dramatic of those changes. Economy, society, technology and culture have changed and continue to change since the industrial revolution at an accelerating pace. The woodlands are no different. The decline of traditional woodland was counterbalanced by a new approach to commercial forestry that was as significant for its social and economic impact as for its impact on the landscape.

Commercial forestry had a slow start and a long period of incubation. The Scottish Arboricultural Society (now the Royal Scottish Forestry Society) was formed in 1854 and in 1882 two foresters in northern England – Henry Clark and J. W. Robson – were instrumental in the founding of the English Arboricultural Society (now the Royal Forestry Society of England, Wales and Northern Ireland). Both societies rekindled interest in forestry and gave momentum to government initiatives to introduce a more scientific and systematic approach to forest management. British forestry was also influenced by the improvements in German forest practices and by the establishment in 1855 of an Indian Forest Service. The expertise for the latter institution was largely imported from Germany. Dr William Schlich (1840–1925), one of three successive German

Inspector Generals employed in India, was responsible for *The Manual of Forestry*, published in five volumes between 1889 and 1896, of which the final two volumes were translations of previously published German texts.

New forestry practices were pioneered in Britain in the small crown woodlands where, for example, bark stripping was abandoned as uneconomical. Open-grown oaks that could only flourish by periodic thinning of surrounding undergrowth were no longer required by the Royal Navy and were relinquished as economically worthless. Poorer stands of oak were cleared and the ground was replanted with conifers. The crown also actively sought to increase its stock of woods, as in the purchase of Tintern Woods in 1901–2 as an extension to its woodlands in the Forest of Dean, an indication that not all private woodlands were pulling their economic weight.

Fast-growing conifers may have come to symbolize the worst excesses of the forest economy in the twentieth century but they were also widely planted in the nineteenth. It is worth remembering that Thomas Hardy described his two famous woodlanders, Giles Winterbourne and Marty South, as the 'pine planters' in the title of his poem about them. Conifer plantations have suffered a bad press for as long as they have been in existence. As early as 1810, the travel writer Richard Fenton could complain of the hill behind Gwydir Castle in north Wales, 'magnificently wooded with the thriving aftermath of a most venerable forest that once clothed the hillside to its very summit ... now disfigured by a strait belt-planted line of grim firs. Why will not men in such cases leave Nature as they found her?' [2]

A Royal Commission established in 1906 recommended afforestation in Britain on the approximately nine million acres of ground that it claimed could be planted with trees without affecting agricultural production, at a time when only three million acres of ground were regarded as economic forestry. In the event, the 1924 census of woodlands in Britain showed that the total area of woodland, still just under three million acres, did not actually increase in the ensuing decade, mainly because progress in planting was cancelled out by the unforeseen need for felling. Afforestation was intended to provide rural employment and to increase the supply of home-grown timber. Britain had taken for granted that timber could be brought from the Empire or imported cheaply from Scandinavia, but it was to receive a rude awakening.

The strategic need for home-grown timber became apparent after 1914 when the British Expeditionary Force in France had to purchase its timber from French forests. Henceforth the organisation of timber supplies came under centralized administration. It led directly to the Forestry Act of 1919 and the founding of the Forestry Commission, which took over the administration of the crown forests in 1923. To replenish stocks of timber felled during the war, coniferous species like the Sitka spruce, Douglas fir, silver fir and larch, all of which had become familiar in the nineteenth century, now came to the fore. One of the Forestry Commission's first acts was to plant beech and larch at Egges-ford Forest in Devon, a event commemorated by the erection of a self-congratulatory plaque at the site. In 1956 a stone was laid in Egges-ford Forest to commemorate the planting of one million acres of trees in Great Britain. The Forestry Commission was not therefore primarily concerned with managing existing woodlands, but with new planting.

Economic forestry ushered in a new breed of forester quite distinct from the traditional woodmen who had worked on coppice woods. A. C. Forbes, a member of the government's Forestry Sub-Committee in the war, betrayed a characteristic doublethink when he lamented the old British woodland worker:

> Many of these men could tell at a glance the number of cubic feet in a rough-headed oak, ash or elm, not perhaps with mathematical accuracy but as near as was necessary to estimate its value ... Many of them knew what an acre of underwood could turn out to within a dozen hurdles or bundles of peasticks.[3]

Economic forestry brought new skills, and led to the modern forest worker with his chainsaw and conifers, heavy machinery and even helicopters for spraying fertiliser. But the comparison was based upon the fallacy that the two breeds of workman were in competition, which they were not. Forests were managed for timber, not underwood. Coppicing declined because there was a shrinking demand for its product, not because coppices were superseded by new plantations. Wood declined as a source of domestic fuel when the railway allowed coal to be sold throughout rural districts. Specialized wood industries survived longer

– as in the manufacture of hurdles, rakes and withies for basket making – but most of them perished in the agricultural depression of the 1930s.[4] The rural economy also adapted to the decline in traditional woodland products by diversifying. Shooting pheasants and other game had become fashionable in the nineteenth century. Uncut woodlands provided cover for game and lodges were built for gamekeepers, in a sport that was economically as well as socially significant. At Burnham Beeches, Buckinghamshire, pollarding of its common wood pasture ceased about 1820 when coal became available, and rhododendron and azaleas were planted in the 1860s to provide cover for game, leaving a woodland rich in ecology but based upon its specific and changing land use. Other coppice woodlands, however, were not necessarily grubbed up and replaced with plantations. Most of them fell into neglect, the kind of woodland that is now common in many places like the Kent Weald.

Contrary to some misapprehensions, the large-scale planting of coniferous forestry did not occur until after 1945. A woodland census conducted in the mid 1960s showed that the area under forestry had increased to over 4.3 million acres. Of the 77 million trees planted in 1970, 44 million were Sitka spruce, 15 million pine, 3.5 million larch; only some 280,000 were broad-leaved deciduous trees.[5] State-led policies had a marked impact on the scale of Britain's woodlands and plantations. Grants were given to private owners to increase their acreage under timber and manage their existing stocks, while the Forestry Commission also expanded its stocks, which had been depleted during the 1939–45 war. The policy was to achieve maximum yield.

In some areas this had a dramatic impact on the landscape. Large parts of industrial South Wales were planted with conifers when large tracts of estate farmland were sold off and tenant farms became enveloped by plantations. Ancient woodland also suffered for this policy, as it was replanted with conifers on a large scale after 1945. It has been claimed that destruction of nearly half of Britain's ancient woodlands in the three decades after 1945 was mostly attributable to afforestation.[6] In 1953 a virus *Myxomatosis cuniculi* was first diagnosed in Britain. Although natural in South America, it had been introduced into Britain via France as a means of rabbit control. It proved very effective, killing off 99 per cent of Britain's rabbit population, aided by the establishment by the Ministry of Agriculture of rabbit clearance committees in every region.[7] It ultimately failed but, like DDT, reveals an incredible arrogance that scientists could control nature so ruthlessly in the name of economic growth.

Because of the planting policy in post-war Britain, early campaigners against the mass felling of trees for short-term commercial benefit, like John Stuart Collis, gave Britain a relatively easy ride. America, by contrast, was castigated for its tree-felling by Collis, who pointed out the consequences of felling trees, leading to soil erosion, the loss of a means to stabilize ground water, and ultimately to serious floods.[8] Not until the 1970s was there a softening of policy in Britain that recognized the recreational potential of woodlands, and the public's unfulfilled interest in them. 1973 was designated 'The Year of the Tree' and the public was urged to 'plant a tree in 73' not for its economic benefit but to enhance the environment. As ancient woodland was given over to afforestation, interest in the woodlands as historical phenomena grew.

Academic study of woodland history takes an opposite approach to the mystifying ideal images of Edwardian country writers like Edward Thomas. It explains why woodlands exist in the form they do and considers how 'natural' nature is. It is this open-eyed approach to the natural world that underpins strategies for conservation, and it is this expertise that has acquired the greatest authority in placing a value upon the natural environment. After so many self-serving myths about the survival of the natural world, it was time to sober up.

By the time archaeology developed as a discipline in the early twentieth century it was established that the post-glacial environment of Britain was well-wooded, and that human development was the result of successive waves of immigrants from the Continent. In its most extreme, or purist, form, this theory pictured the first settlers crossing the English Channel to a pristine, complete and self-contained world, for which the term wildwood has been coined to distinguish it from natural woodland altered by human activity. The task of the first settlers was the clearing, reshaping and pacification of virgin woodland, and with their descendants slowly transformed nature into the topography of towns, villages and fields that are now familiar. In the 1950s, when W. G. Hoskins argued that the English landscape was the product of a long evolution rather than the relatively recent effect of parliamentary enclosure, it was still considered to be a heroic achievement. Hoskins ascribed the greatest period of forest clearance to the Anglo-Saxons, and cited evidence from

Saxon place-names to support the argument. Swithland on the edge of Charnwood Forest in Leicestershire was 'the land cleared by burning', while Brentwood – 'burned wood' – in Essex was also thought to be evidence of how the wilderness was cleared.[9] Place-name interpretation is a precarious business and since Hoskins's time, when the historian relied largely upon written sources, the scientific study of trees has developed immeasurably, allowing information on the landscapes of prehistory to be reconstructed using new forms of excavated evidence including snail shells, nut shells, pollen grains and fragments of trees embedded in peat bogs. Recent research has pushed the myth of the wildwood even further back into prehistory. What we know of the prehistoric landscape is also informed by the kinds of structures that were built by prehistoric societies, especially the large and conspicuous funeral and other monuments that characterized the Neolithic and Bronze Ages. It has already been remarked that large-scale landscape features like Avebury and Silbury Hill in Wiltshire could only have been set up in relatively open country that offered distant prospects.

What passes for native in the British Isles is the ecology that became established after the retreat of the last ice age some 13,000 years ago. As the climate steadily warmed, so new species found the climate and soil suitable, leading eventually to the 'climax' vegetation of our temperate climate, predominantly wildwood. A map of native British tree species is a complex one as it depends upon a variety of factors, such as soil and local variation in climate, as well as competition between species. Birch and pine were most prevalent in the north of Scotland. Southern England was characterized by lime woods, with patches of ash, elm, beech, hazel, hornbeam and oak woods. Although oak is now regarded as the quintessential English tree, it was not the dominant species on its most fertile soils. That the lime tree is not now regarded as characteristic of English woods is largely due to the fact that its wood was deemed less useful than other species. The true province of the oak was Wales which, together with the west and north of England, was characterized by oak and hazel woods. Beneath these vast canopies of trees were a variety of brambles and plants like dog's mercury, bluebell and wood anemone, although they grew best where light penetrated the canopy and later when woodland clearings became more common.

Tree clearance began before farming, but it is now known that the 'slash and burn' technique practised in Africa and North America could not have taken place in the same way in Britain. The method was certainly known in Britain, however, as it is referred to in the medieval Welsh tale of 'Culhwch and Olwen'. Ysbaddaden Chief Giant sets a task for Culhwch, who seeks the hand of his daughter Olwen. Pointing to a great thicket he says, 'I must have it uprooted out of the earth and burnt on the face of the ground so that the cinders and ashes thereof be its manure'.[10] In reality this was easier said than done. Of native species in Britain, only the pine produces a resin that makes it susceptible to destruction by fire when green, and even then the most likely beneficiary of a forest fire is the pine itself, as it quickly establishes itself on burned ground. The axe was the tool of forest clearance, but killing a tree was not a straightforward business: nearly all native species will either send up new shoots from the stump (coppice) or roots (sucker) and therefore have to be grubbed out completely. The task was probably achieved slowly (therefore the rapid clearance of the world's rainforests does not provide a ready parallel) and was probably aided by grazing animals which eventually killed trees by eating the saplings, and which elsewhere created the definitive and most common form of woodland by the medieval period, the relatively open wood pasture.

Once a tree has been felled it has to be cut up and removed, itself a formidable task. Nevertheless, clearance was more rapid than was once presumed – as the case of large ritual monuments shows – even if it is difficult to explain, and was accompanied by non-human factors. The sudden decline of the elm from about 4000 BC, coincidentally near the time when farming was adopted in Britain, is most likely to have been caused by some form of elm disease similar to the Dutch Elm Disease of the twentieth century, which was spread by bark-beetles. The deterioration of the climate to wetter conditions also speeded up the decline of woodlands on poorer upland soils and helped in the creation of the now familiar moorlands. Places where prehistoric wood has survived in abundance, like the Somerset Levels, show that techniques of coppicing had already been developed by the third millennium BC.[11] Poles used in the wooden trackways in Somerset demonstrate an understanding that coppiced wood is far more useful than branches in their natural state because it produces much straighter poles in greater abundance. The prehistoric landscape was not, therefore, a simple divide between agriculture and wilderness, as even the surviving native woodland was affected by human agency. It was the place where men hunted, cut wood for tools and fuel, and where people gathered hazelnuts, as well as being the gateway to the supernatural world.

Large areas of lowland Britain were open country in the first millennium BC, contrary to earlier opinion, as has been shown in East Anglia where unnoticed large-scale field systems have been identified.[12] It has been estimated that half of the natural wildwood had disappeared by about 500 BC; or, to put it in another way, the Romans conquered an island that was still 50 per cent wilderness.

The Romans brought industry, urban living and agricultural improvement, and also a sophisticated knowledge of woodland management. The Romans were great builders of military installations, towns and villas, and so needed large quantities of timber, which they found by the clearance of ancient woodland and by new planting. Many sites of wooden buildings have been excavated, including a number in the port and city of London. At New Fresh Wharf a third-century wooden quay has been discovered, the timber for which had relatively narrow growth rings which suggest it had been cut from dense woodland. The Roman penchant for hypocausts and baths also meant an increasing market for domestic fuel. Pollen analysis proves that the sweet chestnut is not a native but a naturalized species and was probably introduced in the Roman period as a coppice tree. The Roman author Columella, writing in the first century AD, singled out oak and chestnut as the most suitable species for coppicing.[13] Roman organization saw extensive woodland management to provide charcoal for the iron industries of the Forest of Dean and the Weald. Woodland management involved the identifying and bounding of specific woods, often delineated by wood banks, which is the manner in which woodland is understood today, not as limitless wildwood but with boundaries and a name.

The arrival of Anglo-Saxons, far from being just a period of tree felling, is now known to have coincided with some woodland regeneration as the structure of Roman farming and rural life suffered from recession, especially in the vicinity of Hadrian's Wall. The north Hampshire district, for example, was well-wooded in the medieval period but overlay earlier Celtic fields. In some places, like the Welsh Marches, woodland regeneration was a deliberate policy to provide hunting grounds. Knowledge of Anglo-Saxon woodlands can be gleaned from charters, over eight hundred of which contain descriptions of the boundaries of woodlands that describe a topography that is recognizably English. The Domesday survey of England found that woodland covered some 15 per cent of the country, concentrated in a few densely wooded areas, including the Weald, Essex and the Chilterns in south-east England and a woodland belt from Dorset to the Peak District. The landscape of the medieval hunter, therefore, was a mixture of semi-ancient woodland, wood pasture grazed with livestock to produce its open character, and secondary woodland. None of it could be regarded as wildwood. Even densely wooded regions like the Forest of Dean had been altered by coppicing and livestock grazing over a long period.

Study of woodland history has enabled historians to argue that woodlands are cultural phenomena, which has helped to ensure that coppices in places like Hatfield Forest are revived rather than being cleared to make way for conifer plantations. The character of woodland has an historical dimension, a fact that allows us to understand the changing nature of nature itself. Sycamore was introduced into Britain in the late middle ages and subsequently spread into woodlands, sometimes at the expense of native species. Its speedy growth is a nuisance in some contexts, but, as it can be cut in an eight-year rotation, a bonus where it is coppiced. An odourless wood with a fine grain, sycamore produces the best kitchenware, including rolling pins, bread boards and wooden spoons. The horse chestnut, introduced into Britain from Turkey in the early seventeenth century, has been slower to naturalize and spread from its original context as a parkland tree that offered a beautiful broad canopy and a good cool shade. The game of conkers also emerged later. It is first recorded in the Isle of Wight in 1848 and remains the most popular children's game with plants, superseding similar games played with cobnuts and hazelnuts.[14] The fashion for conkers developed when the most common experience of trees was no longer in woodland or in country estates but in the open spaces of Victorian towns. Of garden escapees, the rhododendron has been the most successful naturalising shrub, usually but not always resented. It provides spring colour, replacing the colour of hawthorns and other blossoms that once characterized the native woodlands. The rhododendron is an introduced species, but it was a native species before the last ice age.

What of wild flowers, of which British woodlands are traditionally so rich? The beauty and variety of woodland flowers is a factor of human interaction. When wood is cut, light can penetrate through the canopy and allow flowers to flourish, while the eventual regrowth of wood prevents the ground becoming overrun with grass. The coppice is fertile ground for classic English flowers like the primrose, bluebell, oxlip, dog's mercury, wood sorrel and anemone. A wood is likely to have a greater range of woodland flora the greater its age, because the spread into secondary woodland of many species is inhibited by the presence of open land between scattered areas of woodland, although there are many variations based on region and soil. Oxlip is abundant in the ancient woods of Cambridgeshire, Suffolk and Essex, but not outside these areas and is rare in even secondary woodlands. In its wild form, coralroot is confined to only a few specific areas, including the Kent and Sussex Weald and the beech woods of the Chilterns. Where plantation trees are grown for timber rather than coppice, like the closely spaced rows of conifer that are now thankfully less common than they once were, the understorey is usually devoid of interest, gloomy and unsuitable even for sheep to graze. Lack of light and a carpet of acidic pine needles allow nothing to grow and consequently the forest floor is barren of insect and bird life. However, even beech plantations have fewer understorey species because they are not cut on a periodic basis that allows flora to establish itself. The native flora is therefore one of the indicators of the use of woodland in historic times and has never been a timeless natural inheritance.

The systematic study of woodlands undermines many of the myths that have grown up about the natural world. Oliver Rackham calls them 'factoids', dismisses them as pseudo-history and argues that they prevent a proper understanding of nature that is there to be understood if we take the trouble to learn its language. He has a point, citing the hysterical reaction to the storms that damaged parts of south-east England in October 1987. Many trees were toppled in a night of hurricane force winds. Photographs taken the morning after show one of the tidiest regions of Britain strewn with debris and uprooted tree trunks. 'Our Darkest Hour' was the headline in the *Sevenoaks Chronicle,* as six of its seven symbolic oaks had fallen in the storm, an event that was described as nothing less than the destruction of the town's heritage, even though the trees had only been planted in 1902.[15] But Oliver Rackham pointed out that a society that equates a fallen tree with a dead tree knows nothing about trees. (Nor, for that matter, is a tree felled by the axe or chainsaw a dead tree.) The immediate reaction was that nature would never recover without a policy of planting new trees to replace those that had been lost, a policy that with pause for thought would have been recognized as unnecessary and a little ridiculous.[16] The storm of 1987 was not a natural but a cultural disaster. Its effect on ancient woodland was completely misunderstood, since most of the trees that were killed were young planted trees. Even trees that had fallen continued to live and thrive as horizontal organisms, and where trees fell and allowed light to pour in other flora were able to flourish. Nature's ability for self-regeneration ensured that gaps in the woodland canopy were soon filled by other trees without any human intervention.

Just as woodland is irrevocably the outcome of human interaction, so our knowledge of woodland is culturally based. What we know about trees is almost entirely learned from books, whether we follow history or pseudo-history. Nobody now learns to identify trees in the empirical fashion that was once universal in rural life. We learn it from the plethora of available guide books, including guides to wildflowers and fungi that index their material, without a trace of irony, under the heading 'common names'. The forestry industry itself abandoned empirical knowledge of tree management in favour of the classroom and lecture hall where new practices could be taught. The English Arboricultural Society began examinations in forestry in 1897 and in 1905 a School of Forestry was established at Oxford University, with William Schlich as its first professor. Ecological science has informed the management of woodlands as wildlife habitats by national bodies like the Woodland Trust, founded in 1972, English Nature (formerly the Nature Conservancy Council) and the county wildlife and nature conservation trusts that have emerged in the latter half of the century. When poets moved elsewhere the woods became habitats where ecosystems could be studied and preserved. Myths had been thrown off, but it was not quite the dawn of a new enlightened age. New myths simply sprang up in unexpected places.

15

Green Men

It was in the 1930s that Lady Raglan described a carving in Llangwm church in Monmouthshire, depicting a man sprouting foliage from his mouth and ears, as a Green Man.[1] The name was a lucky choice, given the connotations of greenness in alternative ideologies in the latter half of the twentieth century. Overturning its previous association with innocence, it has become the colour of the ecological resistance to consumer society. 'Greenpeace' has become the best-known brand of ecological protest. The German artist Joseph Beuys named his ecological political movement the 'Greens', and so successful were they that in Britain the Ecology Party changed its name to the Green Party. To be green is to be environmentally sensitive and the historical figure of the Green Man has been engaged in the argument that an environmental awareness was possible in western civilization before the industrial revolution.

Lady Raglan, a folklorist rather than an art historian, was the first person to try to explain what Green Man carvings meant. Thousands of them are found in British, French and German churches, although, despite their profusion, they were only ever minor subject matter. The fact of being minor subject matter, and therefore relatively incon-spicuous, encouraged the argument that the Green Man was a subversive figure in Christian art. Lady Raglan associated the figure with paganism and with figures from popular culture like the Jack-in-the-Green, Robin Hood and May King of summer games, drawn largely from the pages of Frazer's *Golden Bough.* It was widely believed in Lady Raglan's time that Christianity had failed to wipe out paganism and that in medieval Britain the two religions existed side by side. The belief was greatly influenced by Margaret Murray's flawed thesis that witchcraft survived in parallel with Christianity and was the survival of pre-Christian pagan religion.[2] Although the theory is no longer tenable it retains a considerable following as what Oliver Rackham would term a 'factoid'. It has subsequently been shown that the Jack-in-the-Green is not a manifestation of the ancient Green Man but was a creation of the eighteenth century.[3] It was the use of the pub name 'Green Man', with signboards depicting a Jack-in-the-Green, that prompted Lady Raglan in her naming of the carvings in the first place. But the Jack-in-the-Green has turned out to be another example of the urban myth that time moves on in the town but stands still in the country.

Kathleen Basford discovered that the foliate head, some examples of which disgorge foliage, is found in the form of leaf masks in the western and eastern Roman Empire in the first century AD, and argued that it was associated with the cult of Bacchus. The carving appears on a Christian tomb of the fourth or fifth century at Poitiers, the earliest Christian context for the motif. The figure emerges again in twelfth-century architecture, at which time it makes its first appearance in Britain. Green Men appear in more profusion in the later middle ages until the Reformation in the mid sixteenth century, usually lurking in inconspicuous locations such as roof bosses, bench ends and misericords.[4]

What does the figure mean? The medieval Green Man has a wholly Christian context, and is not a figure known from pagan art in Britain or anywhere else. The Green Man was not a figure familiar to Anglo-Saxons and Celts before or immediately after their conversion to Christianity and therefore is not indigenous to Britain. The figure does not even appear in medieval bestiaries, in which fabulous creatures and their moral attributes are described. This lack of evidence is a hindrance to some, but carte blanche for others. Its architectural context and human characterization, however, both express something of its general meaning. The Green Man emerged in the twelfth century when the iconography of Christian architecture was taking shape, appearing usually as a peripheral figure on doorways, crossing arches inside churches, and fonts, upon which it was common to portray grotesque visual incarnations of the sinful life. Not all of these Green Men are recognizably men, as some are clearly masks while others are just grotesque faces. The Norman crossing arch of Melbourne Priory in Derbyshire has a carving on one of the capitals depicting a contortionist squatting down with a hideous smile, splayed legs and hands holding the branches spewing out of his mouth. This ugly and primitive-looking contortionist is a device to suggest sin and a lack of spirituality. At Kilpeck in Herefordshire, where there is also a Green Man on the doorway, one of the shafts flanking the door is decorated with a related image of foliage in which two knights are entangled. The foliage represents the snares of the Devil, ready to entrap unwary men who stray from the straight and narrow path of virtue, a theme familiar from medieval literature.

The association of the Green Man with sin was further developed in the later middle ages, when a profusion of Green Man carvings show a sinister figure disgorging naturalistic foliage, usually oak or vines. The life of the spirit was eternal, but Green Men chose the way of the flesh and therefore went the way of all flesh, to death and decay, providing the food on which plants grow. Green Men are the medieval equivalent of dead men pushing up daisies. At Crowcombe, Somerset, is a vivid and well-known bench-end depicting a gaunt face, with hair of leaves, that disgorges vines from his mouth, a standard motif of local wood carvers. From his ears emerge two club-wielding mermen, representing the demons in his head.

The Green Man has subsequently been reinvented as a symbol of nature's life force, a modern and not a medieval idea. In this guise he stands in opposition to western civilization and as a figure from the past that suggests all is not lost for the future. The most influential prophet of this new environmentalism is the late William Anderson, whose book *The Green Man* (1990) placed the Green Man as the male counterpart to the Great Goddess, the central tenet of James Lovelock's Gaia hypothesis. Lovelock, a British scientist, proposed that the physical and chemical condition of Earth actively made the planet fit for life, a self-correcting system that humanity disturbed at its peril. In the chance naming of his hypothesis Gaia, after a Greek Earth goddess, he inadvertently turned a cybernetic system into a living organism. Although he later retreated from the connotation of the title, its spurious association with ancient religion was an attractive proposition to unorthodox thinkers. By claiming that the Green Man was the male counterpart of the goddess Gaia, William Anderson drew Lovelock's hypothesis into a modern belief system, and allied that belief system with the authority of science.

The tone of Anderson's writing is of religious conviction rather than

historical analysis, and is awash with meaningless purple prose in the
tradition of Victorian romanticism: the Green Man 'symbolises the
union of humanity and the vegetable world', 'is the guardian and revealer
of mysteries', and in him 'we see the dark garden of the imagination
woken up by the rays of the sun of consciousness'.[5] Anderson wanted
the Green Man 'to give simplicity and clarity to the confusion and
complexity of modern technological society, and to point us towards
renewing the harmony and unity to the world of Nature'.[6] The growth
of interest in the Green Man is psychological. Anderson argued, after
Jung, that the Green Man is an archetypal figure that has risen up in
our consciousness to counterbalance our present negative attitude to
nature. The Green Man cult is, by contrast, proof that we invent the
Gods we need.

This is not all bad news. Myths about male spirituality offer an
alternative role model of masculinity, and focus the mind on attempts
to bring nature closer to our lives and to contemporary culture. No one
can dispute that it is healthy to think about trees. The Green Man is a
rhetorical myth that does not lead us directly to trees, but taps the
emotional need for something beyond a society that has divorced itself
from nature. It belongs with the romantic tradition of trees as timeless
and universal organisms, not of trees as places, with which this book is
chiefly concerned.

The material foil to the spirituality of the Green Man in contemporary
society are the tropical rainforests. It is significant that, although trees
and forests have a high profile in conservation politics, it is in this global
context that they have achieved it. Rainforests cover widespread territory,
including the Amazon basin, equatorial West Africa and south-east Asia.
They have long been at the service of the West, supplying it with
mahogany and teak, and are the ultimate source of coffee and bananas,
not to mention peanuts, avocados, mangoes and more, which have
become such staple foods they have lost their exotic tag. In 1950 rainforests accounted for 15 per cent of the Earth's land surface, an area
that was halved over the ensuing twenty-five years and whose decline
has subsequently accelerated. Few people would declare themselves
indifferent to trees yet, when westerners look to Brazilian and Indonesian
forests as the salvation of the planet, it demonstrates how distant we
have become from nature in our daily lives.

Trees became a major currency in environmental politics in the wake of the worst excesses of rainforest destruction. Whereas the decline of European and North American forests was a protracted process, the pace of rainforest losses has devastated native communities and left a landscape scarred. In the late 1980s some 150,000 square kilometres of virgin forests, approximately the area of England and Wales, was being lost each year. Cleared forest opened up land for mineral exploitation, to be flooded for hydroelectric power schemes, and to make way for cattle ranches, all in the name of a global economy that forces poorer countries to look for ways to generate cash in the short term. But what do these losses mean?

On the whole, material arguments have prevailed in our estimation of the value of the rainforests. Loss of trees contributes to global warming and, especially in the case of the tropics, diminishes what is rapidly being understood as the world's great medicine cabinet. Reserpin, for instance, is used to treat cardiac problems; and curare, which contains the valuable muscle relaxant tubocurarine, is used in heart and lung surgery. Tropical rainforests contain most of our planet's biodiversity but their plant life has yet to be fully studied; it may never be if present rates of felling are maintained. The Madagascar periwinkle is used in the treatment of leukaemia, yet it disappeared from the wild when its habitat was destroyed. Destruction of the traditional ways of life in the forest has its drawbacks too. It was native Amerindians who made an infusion from cinchona bark, the derivation of quinine used to treat malaria, and who discovered the analgesic and narcotic qualities of the coca plant. Yet the salvation of the rainforests and their people can never compensate for our need to be among trees in the normal cycle of our lives. Nor can the love of nature for its own sake be enough if it values nature most when it is remote and exotic. We need a more direct reconnection with trees.

It is debatable where the modern engagement with woodlands really began. Perhaps it should be with John Clare who, owning nothing and minding his own business ambling among the trees, could easily be pictured in today's world, where his lifestyle would be branded alternative. But Clare was rooted in his native place, which is no longer the experience characteristic of even a majority of rural dwellers. This psychological dislocation from nature is endemic in a peripatetic society and can only be restored by actively taking steps to engage with a specific locality. This is what Henry Thoreau did when he went to live in woods owned by his friend Ralph Waldo Emerson.

On Independence Day in 1845 Thoreau took up residence in the woods of Walden in Massachusetts 'because I wished to live deliberately, to front only the essential facts of life'. Thoreau submerged himself in the infinity of nature while coming to terms with his mortality, the essential fact of his life. He built himself a wood cabin, settled himself to looking, listening and wandering about the woods familiarizing himself with its animals and trees, and reading and writing. In his two-year search for what mattered in life, he could learn from nature in a manner that no one could teach him, and consequently learned lessons that he would never be able to pass on to others. Thoreau did not therefore merely isolate himself from everyday community relationships – his nearest neighbour lived a mile away – but the woods of Walden also cut the reader off from what are incommunicable experiences. Reading is not a substitute for experience. Thoreau cannot explain everything but he can be a guide and inspiration to others to do what he has done and find out for themselves. One of his principal lessons is that we learn more about nature by living it ourselves than we do through literature or art, following the philosophy of his friend Ralph Waldo Emerson, who argued that intuitive personal experience was more valuable than the institutional spirituality of the church or other collective movements. Thoreau was a champion of personal freedom. He wanted to reawaken the promise of a New world, which had been the American dream in the first place, not simply recreate the Old world of Europe in a new place. His experiment with simplicity influenced utopian socialists like Edward Carpenter at the end of the nineteenth century and, a century later, interests the proponents of 'deep ecology'. But it was not a project for Thoreau's whole life, only an experiment to ground himself in reality. Sooner or later he knew he would have to return to normal social relations and he did not delude himself that he could escape from society, which is just as well as his sojourn in the woods was ended by his imprisonment for non-payment of a poll tax during the Mexican war.

Thoreau's reputation as a writer fluctuated but eventually became established, and *Walden* is now regarded as a classic of American literature. The woods of Walden have also become something of a shrine to Thoreau, and thereby have been brought into the cultural world in a manner that Thoreau would never himself have experienced. His lasting reputation is based upon his living with nature and the ability to think aloud about living with nature. As E. L. Doctorow remarked, we need both the book and the place because 'we are not all spirit any more than we're all clay; we are both and so we need both'.[7]

Thoreau has been variously described as the vanguard of the modern conservation movement and as the first hippie. His text, like a religious tract, encouraged other Americans to depart for the woods and think for themselves, and in so doing have produced minor literature such as Bradford and Vena Angier's *At Home in the Woods: Living the Life of Thoreau Today* (1951) and Charles Seib's *The Woods: One Man's Escape to Nature* (1971). In Britain, there has been less literary interest in nature in the twentieth century, although it is central to the works of some poets like Ted Hughes and Andrew Young. The most interesting question is what role should places like woodlands have in our lives, and what is the place of humankind in nature. It has been said that humans are 'natural aliens' because we have long since ceased to live in any natural habitat, and no longer readily associate ourselves with any primary habitat, whether the primeval forest or the dry African Rift Valley.[8] History has also exposed the myth of nature as a work of art. Nature is not a finite object with an end to its creation and then an afterlife of interpretation, but a living organism that is continually changing and annually renews itself. Ancient woodland does not remain ancient woodland as Stonehenge remains Stonehenge, but only if the activities that define it as ancient woodland are continued. Nor is nature an entity that humans do unnatural things to. As humans are part of nature, the products of the human mind are as natural as a squirrel storing nuts. If this is accepted, then human dominion and even stewardship over nature are questionable philosophical positions.

What is not questionable is that, for humanity's sake, we need to keep the woodlands we have and to plant new ones. The recent trend for creating community woodlands has tried to accommodate a perceived need for accessible woodlands for urban populations, as well as to generate community spirit. The ecological value of woodlands is widely recognized and the most familiar friends of wooded places still include ornithologists and mycologists with the dog-walkers and photographers. What is more difficult is to develop a way in which we can reconnect with such places.

A post-war generation of artists has sought a more intimate and physical relationship with nature, at the same time challenging the notion that art is the product of a studio and is presented in a gallery. The importance of forests to Anselm Kiefer and Joseph Beuys has already been described. The Italian sculptor Giuseppe Penone (1947-) immerses himself physically and mentally in the elements of nature before commencing a sculpture. He lays himself on the ground and then opens his arms to enjoy 'the coolness of the ground and attain the necessary degree of peace for the accomplishment of the sculpture'.[9] For one of his works, made from 1968 in woods at Garessio south of Turin, he grabbed a sapling and then fastened a cast-iron model of his hand on to that point. In the ensuing decade the tree grew and bulged around the hand, a changing work of art to which nature contributed. Active engagement and contribution to the natural world in Britain has been the province of a small band of artists, including Richard Long (1945-), David Nash (1945-) and Andy Goldsworthy (1956-), and has been taken up by the charity Common Ground. To conserve or plant a woodland on purely ecological grounds is to leave out one of the fundamental conditions in which all woodlands live, their relationship to the human race. This is the lesson of Oliver Rackham's studies, and it is Common Ground's aim to promote the cultural interface with local nature. The Forestry Commission has also recognized this, and has established sculpture parks in the Forest of Dean and Grizedale in Cumbria, which in turn accepts the broader argument that a woodland is more than a wildlife habitat or economic unit. Woodlands are places, in the sense that, once they are invested with human emotions and can be seen as repositories of human memory, they cease to be environments. Essentially we are all looking for places, not environments.

David Nash is actively engaged in the landscape, and with trees in particular, as a source of inspiration and materials, but also as a stage upon which his works grow. Born in Surrey, Nash gave up the swinging London of the 1960s for depopulated North Wales, settling at Blaenau Ffestiniog. To help establish himself he took a job with the Economic

Forestry Group planting trees, giving him a familiarity with trees and
the properties of wood. As a sculptor who now specializes in wood,
Nash has acquired many of the skills that used to be the property of
woodmen but have now vanished: to estimate the volume of timber in
a fallen tree and the works that could be created from them, of knowing
the grain of wood and which trees make the best charcoal, and which
wood is right for a particular object. His works allude to the uses that
were once made of wood, like ladders, vessels of various descriptions,
spoons, bowls, tables and chairs. He uses unseasoned timber worked
into shapes by the chainsaw, then relinquishes control, allowing his
sculptures to warp naturally. The work is finished, therefore, when the
wood stops its growing and changing. The importance of the artist is
that he is not seeking to control nature, but instead is acting as a
facilitator and then a witness to the natural vitality of the material. His
Black Dome of 1986, made for the Forestry Commission's sculpture park
in the Forest of Dean, more directly pays homage to an ancient craft,
laid out like a charcoal clamp in a clearing. The work was inspired by
the author's experience of working at Grizedale in Cumbria, where old
charcoal burning sites are discernible if you know how to interpret them.
Black Dome comprised a low dome of 900 short charred stakes of larch,
sharpened to look like coals (real charcoal would have been too brittle).
The intention was to allow the work to become reintegrated with its
environment, rotting down in about forty years to leave only a low
hump.

His larger works are outdoor installations, some of which are in urban
spaces, others in sculpture parks. Some, however, have woodland locations where the work makes a positive contribution to the sense of place.
Where this is accompanied by gathering fallen wood – much of his early
work was made from gathered dead wood as he could not afford to
shop at the timber merchants – the process of making the work is more
intimately associated with place. In 1971 Nash began working on a small
wood at Caen-y-Coed near Maentwrog in Gwynedd. None of his work
is more representative of his interest in integrating the growth and
change of nature into his art, and of acknowledging the importance of
place, than the *Ash Dome* planted here in 1977. Twenty-two ash saplings
were planted, with the intention that they should be tended for thirty
years to create a sculpture for the twenty-first century. The time of

inception was one of gloom and pessimism, so the work was conceived as a deliberate act of faith in the future. Ash trees were chosen because they will lean away from the roots without falling, and have been pruned and grafted into their overall shape with sinuous trunks below a canopy enlarging like the shaping of a pot on a potter's wheel. It is rare among outdoor sculptures in being a living organism that takes the earth, air and rain into its being, and one that needs its specific environment to grow, in contrast to most outdoor sculptures whose material is chosen for its durability in an alien environment.

Andy Goldsworthy established his reputation as a land artist by making rapid sculptures with natural found materials, usually in one of a series of well-established forms like arches, spirals, lines and spheres, then photographing them before they disintegrate naturally. The materials are those found close at hand, earth and stones, sticks, leaves and stalks, and ice and snow. The transience of the sculptures reflects the transience of human interaction with nature, and explains the need to keep on making. The collection of materials locally for each work contributes to their sense of place, and can often only be made at certain specific times, tying them to a specific set of circumstances. Often the structures collapse or are blown away before they are finished, bringing an element of unpredictability and recognition that the artist is not always in total control. The making is an essential part of the meaning of the sculptures, and explicitly establishes the artist as a part of nature. The emphasis on making also answers the most common criticism of this kind of work, that it relies for its dissemination on photography, and in doing so falls within the pictorial tradition of western painting, which it does not. Like David Nash, Goldsworthy is able to ground his work in a wood near his home in Dumfriesshire, aptly titled Stonewood, given the relationship between inert mineral and fragile living matter so often explored in his work. He has likened the life of a tree to the life of a sculptor, because 'a tree is an active part of its place, it makes that place richer and is an indication of the way something can change a place'.[10]

Selection of materials allows the artist to build up an intimate knowledge of the locality and its trees. His work gathering leaves exposes him to the kind of isolation once experienced by woodmen and to experience the character of a woodland that only the wood cutters, barkers and charcoal burners ever got to know. For example, 'there is a strangeness in leaves dropping to the ground on a calm day' that is quite distinct from the experience of being 'in woods after a hard frost in autumn with trees noisily shedding their leaves'. The quality of leaves is also variable. 'To understand leaves, I need to work the dry brittle windblows, the cold wet frost-fallen, and the fresh green growing.' Such an approach taught the artist about the structure of leaves upon a tree, where the thick leaves are found on the outer branches that receive more sunlight, in contrast to the leaves closer to the trunk, which are more delicate, and that larger leaves are found on smaller trees, especially those that have been coppiced. Different species have the potential to make different kinds of work. Just as once sycamore was for tableware, hornbeam for charcoal and so on, sycamore leaves can be worked into box shapes, but chestnut leaves make spirals and horns.[11]

Much of this intimacy with the landscape is incommunicable, in which context the artists have an inspirational role in encouraging others to explore the woodlands in their own individual ways. We no longer expect poets to offer a substitute for experience in the way that Edwardian country writers like Edward Thomas were expected to do. The self-consciously lyrical style of Thomas in his essay-writing days implies a morality of feeling, but they were really only commonplace feelings that Thomas as a good writer had a special talent for conveying. It is their skill with words that we admire more than the depth of their feeling for trees.

In the retrospective study of David Nash's work *Forms into Time*, the most revealing comment by the artist was not made in the service of explaining any of his works but in the dedication of the book to his older brother 'who took playing seriously and let me join in'. Artists like David Nash and Andy Goldsworthy are part of a long tradition of cultural engagement with trees and woods, within the context of the contemporary world they live in. Ironically it is they who are the upholders of the tradition of woodland interaction that gave us the May festivities of gathering greenery, decking with garlands and crowning a May Queen. Revivalists who have sought to resurrect and sustain these 'traditional' events, after they were revived in the nineteenth century, are really commemorating a piece of social history. The engagement with nature has been left to the artists in a manner that marks the change in society.

The way of the modern world is to celebrate the individual's personal expression. In the late medieval world the celebration of the community fulfilled a role in a transient society that developed after the Black Death but was dwindling by the time of Shakespeare. Both individual and communal engagement with nature share a concern for marking the passage of time. What makes them seem so different is not so much a different attitude to nature, but the radical changes in society. The significance of John Clare and Thomas Hardy is that they recognized that a way of living with nature, and the culture consequent upon it, was a fragile thing and would soon be lost, not that humans would never be able to establish contact with nature again.

The struggle to establish a new and independent relation to nature outside the terms already set by science and sentimentality is encapsulated in John Fowles's *The Tree* (1979). As a young man Fowles was an ardent naturalist, but came to realize that naming species is implicitly categorising them and bringing them under human control, another form of ownership. This habit he blamed on the harmful legacy of Victorian science that demanded that our relationship with nature is 'purposive, industrious, always seeking greater knowledge', which is ultimately a dreadfully serious and puritanical approach. In his attempt to unlearn the lessons of science, Fowles came to like 'a kind of wandering wood acquaintance, and no more; a dilettante's, not a virtuoso's; always the green chaos rather than the printed map'.[12] John Fowles's experience parallels the experience of Edward Thomas in moving from commercial country prose to poetry. Nor is the approach that Fowles has adopted new – his 'green chaos' recalls John Clare's 'Walks in the Woods' that describes its inhabitants in a haphazard fashion, and perhaps also echoes 'The Unknown Bird' by Edward Thomas, which meditates on the irreducibility of bird song. Its significance is that it demonstrates how individual appreciation of nature does not change as rapidly as society changes. The notes written by Andy Goldsworthy bear a striking resemblance to the journals of Gerard Manley Hopkins. Both are self-generated structures that break free from orthodox thinking about nature. In relying on the senses they are more human than any cool scientific classification. The close study of natural objects is an appreciation that is shared by the artist and botanical illustrator alike, with quite different outcomes.

The modern myth of the Green Man is like the medieval myths of the romantic forest and the rural muse of late Victorian and Edwardian writers. It establishes not so much a physical as a psychological space structured by the need for whatever is not found within the compass of ordinary life. No previous society has relinquished all self-serving myths about its relation to nature. Hard facts do not always tell us what we want to hear, or give a coherent and unequivocal message. This world is not any different, but it is as well to remember that romantic literature adopted a tone of lament and mystification because its authors felt alienated from the society they lived in. There can be no healthy relationship to nature in the twenty-first century without coming to terms with our technological and consumer environments. To do this we must admit the debit side of the scientific revolution and acknowledge that consumerism is no more than a short-term fix. We will always need woodlands because we need places outside everyday life. It is this that links us with the medieval and prehistoric worlds, not the survival of old customs. Its history will be always be manipulated because what we think of our stewardship of nature is intimately bound up with what we think of ourselves. Today's artists and naturalists do not perform quite the same function as nineteenth-century writers and the priests of pre-Christian cults, who were the individuals charged with paying special attention to these places and mediating them for us. In a world of dwindling faith in institutional culture, the role of Thoreau and Goldsworthy is to make us go to the woods for ourselves.

Notes

Notes to Chapter 1: Roots and Branches

1. W. Blake, 'The Ecchoing Green', lines 11–14.
2. *The Prose Edda of Snorri Sturluson*, translated by Jean Young (1954), p. 45.
3. W. G. Hoskins, *The Making of the English Landscape* (1970), p. 86.
4. Ibid., pp. 17–18.
5. Lucretius, *De rerum natura*, translated by W. H. D. Rouse (1937), v, lines 954–61, 966–72.
6. R. P. Harrison, *Forests: The Shadow of Civilization* (1992), pp. 47–49.
7. Quoted in S. Schama, *Landscape and Memory* (1995), p. 237.

Notes to Chapter 2: Gods

1. J. Frazer, *The Golden Bough* (abridged edition, 1922), p. 2.
2. *The Geography of Strabo*, translated by H. L. Jones (1923), iv, c. 5.2.
3. Pliny, *Natural History*, translated by J. Healy (1991), xvi, cc. 245–51.
4. Julius Caesar, *The Conquest of Gaul*, translated by S. A. Handford (1951), vi, c. 16. Strabo, *Geography*, iv, c. 5.2.
5. Tacitus, *Germania*, translated by H. Mattingly (1948), chapters xxxix, xl, xxvii.
6. Tacitus, *Annals of Imperial Rome*, translated by M. Grant (1977), xiv, c. 30.
7. Pausanias, *Guide to Greece*, i, translated by P. Levi (1979), ix, 3.1–4.
8. Ibid., vii, 18.7.
9. Frazer, *Golden Bough*, p. 111.
10. Pliny, *Natural History*, xii, c. 3.
11. M. Low, *Celtic Christianity and Nature* (1996), p. 82.
12. P. H. Sawyer, *Anglo-Saxon Charters* (1968), S311.
13. R. Hutton, *The Pagan Religions of the Ancient British Isles* (1991), p. 329.
14. Ibid., pp. 297–300.
15. Judges, 6, vv. 11–24.

16. D. Farmer, *The Oxford Dictionary of Saints* (1997), pp. 63–65.

17. Frazer, *Golden Bough*, p. 111.

18. Low, *Celtic Christianity and Nature*, pp. 83–84, 91–92.

19. T. Pakenham, *Meetings with Remarkable Trees* (1996), pp. 99–100, 121.

20. R. Morris, *Churches in the Landscape* (1989), pp. 78–79.

21. R. Mabey, *Flora Britannica* (1996), pp. 32–33.

22. Low, *Celtic Christianity and Nature*, pp. 84, 89–90, 92.

23. R. Hutton, *The Stations of the Sun* (1997), pp. 182–83.

24. C. Morris (ed.), *The Journals of Celia Fiennes* (1949), p. 242.

25. Low, *Celtic Christianity and Nature*, pp. 87–88.

Notes to Chapter 3: Harts and Boars

1. J. Cummins, *The Hound and the Hawk* (1988), p. 67.

2. *The Geography of Strabo*, translated by H. L. Jones (1923), iv, c. 5.2.

3. M. Swanton, *Anglo-Saxon Prose* (1975), p. 109.

4. D. Hooke, *The Landscape of Anglo-Saxon England* (1998), pp. 154–59.

5. C. Young, *The Royal Forests of Medieval England* (1979), p. 35.

6. Ibid., p. 11.

7. Ibid., p. 98.

8. W. L. Warren, *Henry II* (1973), p. 390.

9. Ibid.

10. Young, *Royal Forests*, p. 81.

11. M. Keen, *The Outlaws of Medieval Legend* (1977), p. 197.

12. J. Birrell, 'Who Poached the King's Deer? A Study in Thirteenth-Century Crime', *Midland History*, 7 (1982), pp. 11–12.

13. Young, *Royal Forests*, p. 39.

14. Cummins, *Hound and Hawk*, pp. 2–3.

15. Ibid., pp. 10–11.

16. F. Barlow, *William Rufus* (1983), p. 419.

17. Ibid., pp. 420–32.

18. R. Fitznigel, *Dialogus de Scaccario*, translated by C. Johnson (1950), pp. 59–60.

19. T. Malory *Le Morte D'Arthur*, viii, c. 3.

20. Cited in Barlow, *William Rufus*, p. 120.

21. R. Barber, *Bestiary* (1999), pp. 70–71.

22. Ibid., p. 65.

23. Cummins, *Hound and Hawk*, pp. 107–8.

24. Barber, *Bestiary*, p. 87.

25. D. Farmer, *The Oxford Dictionary of Saints* (1997), pp. 176, 242.

26. Cummins, *Hound and Hawk*, p. 53.
27. Ibid., p. 70.

Notes to Chapter 4: Exiles

1. C. Saunders, *The Forest of Medieval Romance* (1993). The influence of the Bible and classical literature on medieval romance literature is discussed in more detail on pp. 10–34.
2. Augustine, *Confessions*, translated by R. S. Pine-Coffin (1961), x, c. 35.
3. Chaucer, *The Friar's Tale*, lines 1380–83, 1636–38.
4. Saunders, *Medieval Romance*, p. 17.
5. D. Farmer, *The Oxford Dictionary of Saints* (1997), p. 463.
6. Virgil, *The Aeneid*, translated by W. F. Jackson Knight (1956), iv, lines 117–25.
7. Ovid, *Metamorphoses*, translated by Mary Innes (1955), iii, lines 137–253.
8. M. Keen, *Chivalry* (1984), p. 227.
9. T. Malory, *Le Morte D'Arthur*, vi, c. 1.
10. Ibid., vi, c. 10.
11. Ibid., vi, cc. 19–20.
12. Ibid., xviii, c. 9.
13. *Sir Gawain and the Green Knight*, lines 2187–88.

Notes to Chapter 5: Outlaws

1. Tacitus, *Agricola*, translated by H. Mattingly (1948), cc. 34, 37.
2. W. Linnard, *Welsh Woods and Forests* (1982), pp. 25–27.
3. E. L. G. Stones, 'The Folvilles of Ashby Folville', *Transactions of the Royal Historical Society*, fifth series, 7 (1957).
4. R. Mabey (ed.), *The Oxford Book of Nature Writing* (1997), pp. 11–12.
5. M. Keen, *The Outlaws of Medieval Legend* (1977), pp. 74–75.
6. *A Gest of Robyn Hode*, stanza 347.
7. Ibid., stanza 447.
8. R. Hutton, *The Rise and Fall of Merry England* (1993), pp. 31–33.
9. Ibid.

Notes to Chapter 6: Lovers

1. M. Low, *Celtic Christianity and Nature* (1996), p. 127.
2. *A Celtic Miscellany*, translated by K. Jackson (1971), p. 63.
3. Ibid., pp. 68–69.

4. Ibid., pp. 73–74.

5. Ibid., p. 254.

6. Ibid., pp. 75–76.

7. Ibid., p. 76.

8. Ibid., p. 99.

9. Chaucer, *The Knight's Tale*, lines 1506–11.

10. R. Hutton, *The Stations of the Sun* (1997), pp. 230–31.

11. Quoted in R. Hutton, *The Rise and Fall of Merry England* (1993), p. 28.

12. Quoted in J. Frazer, *The Golden Bough* (abridged edn, 1922), p. 123.

13. Hutton, *Merry England*, pp. 56–57.

14. Jackson, *Celtic Miscellany*, pp. 82–84.

15. Hutton, *Stations of the Sun*, pp. 233–35.

16. W. Shakespeare, *A Midsummer Night's Dream*, act 4, scene 1.

17. Ibid., act 2, scene 1.

18. W. Shakespeare, *As You Like It*, act 1, scene 1.

19. Ibid., act 2, scene 1.

20. Ibid.

21. W. Shakespeare, *Macbeth*, act 4, scene 1.

22. E. Spenser, *Shepheardes Calendar*, v, lines 9–14, 27–31.

23. R. Herrick, 'Corrina's Going a-Maying', lines 43–58.

Notes to Chapter 7: Patriots

1. J. Evelyn, quoted in S. Schama, *Landscape and Memory* (1995), p. 161.

2. The subject of Restoration Day and Royal Oak Day is discussed at length in R. Hutton, *The Stations of the Sun* (1997), pp. 288–94.

3. R. Mabey, *Flora Britannica* (1996), pp. 75–77.

4. J. Evelyn, *Sylva* (1664), frontispiece and p. 1.

5. Ibid., preface.

6. Ibid., p. 108.

7. Ibid., pp. 65, 91.

8. Ibid., p. 25.

9. O. Rackham, *Trees and Woodland in the British Landscape* (1990), pp. 94–97.

10. D. Defoe, *A Tour Through the Whole Island of Great Britain* (1962), ii, p. 146; i, p. 140.

11. A. Pope, 'Windsor Forest', lines 29–32.

12. Ibid., lines 60, 64.

13. Ibid., lines 385–88.

14. Quoted in Schama, *Landscape and Memory*, p. 161.

15. J. Ruskin, *The Poetry of Architecture* (1837), in *The Works of John Ruskin*, i (1903), p. 120.

16. P. Keating, *Kipling the Poet* (1994), pp. 163–64, 171.

17. R. Kipling, 'A Tree Song', from *Puck of Pook's Hill* (1906).

18. H. Brogan, *Mowgli's Sons: Kipling and Baden-Powell's Scouts* (1987).

19. J. Jenkins and P. James, *From Acorn to Oak Tree: The Growth of the National Trust* (1994) p. 115.

Notes to Chapter 8: Altdeutsche Wälder

1. Quoted in M. Williams, *Americans and their Forests* (1989), p. 409.

2. Tacitus, *Germania*, translated by H. Mattingly (1948), bk ii.

3. Ibid., bk iv.

4. Tacitus, *Annals of Imperial Rome*, translated by M. Grant (1977), i, cc. 60–61.

5. Ibid., i, c. 51.

6. Quoted in S. Schama, *Landscape and Memory* (1995), p. 93.

7. J. Ellis, *One Fairy Story Too Many: The Brothers Grimm and their Tales* (1983).

8. Quoted in J. Zipes, *The Brothers Grimm* (1988), p. 60.

9. R. Nash, *Wilderness and the American Mind* (1982), p. 141.

10. J. Taylor and W. Shaw, *A Dictionary of the Third Reich* (1987), p. 175.

11. Schama, *Landscape and Memory*, pp. 75–81.

Notes to Chapter 9: Big Trees

1. M. Williams, *Americans and their Forests* (1989), p. 33.

2. Ibid.

3. A. de Tocqueville, *Democracy in America*, translated by Henry Reeves (1838), ii, p. 74; idem, *Journey to America*, translated by George Lawrence (1960), p. 335.

4. Williams, *Americans and their Forests*, p. 19.

5. Ibid., pp. 11–12.

6. R. Nash, *Wilderness and the American Mind* (1982), p. 69.

7. Quoted in R. Hughes, *American Visions* (1997), p. 139.

8. S. Daniels, *Fields of Vision* (1993), pp. 155–56; Nash, *Wilderness*, p. 67.

9. Williams, *Americans and their Forests*, pp. 14, 16.

10. A. Walloch, 'Thomas Cole: Landscape and the Course of American Empire', in W. Truettner and A. Walloch (eds), *Thomas Cole: Landscape into History* (1994), p. 55.

11. Ibid., p. 51.
12. Williams, *Americans and their Forests*, p. 13.
13. Quoted in Walloch, 'Thomas Cole', p. 67; Daniels, *Fields of Vision*, p. 157.
14. Nash, *Wilderness*, p. 79.
15. S. Schama, *Landscape and Memory* (1995), pp. 185–87.
16. G. Catlin *North American Indians* (1841), i, pp. 294–95.
17. Nash, *Wilderness*, pp. 125–88.
18. R. Mabey (ed.), *The Oxford Book of Nature Writing* (1997), p. 143; D. Lowenthal, *George Perkins Marsh* (2000), p. 295.
19. Lowenthal, *George Perkins Marsh*, pp. 418–19.
20. Williams, *Americans and their Forests*, p. 405.

Notes to Chapter 10: Patrician Trees

1. S. Daniels, 'The Political Iconography of Woodland in Later Georgian England', in D. Cosgrove and S. Daniels (eds), *The Iconography of Landscape* (1988), p. 51.
2. Dudley Metropolitan Borough Council, *William Shenstone and the Leasowes* (1984).
3. J. Thomson, *The Seasons* (1724), 'Summer', lines 522–25.
4. J. Austen, *Northanger Abbey* (1818), chapter 14.
5. Quoted in Daniels, 'Political Iconography', p. 69.
6. Quoted in S. Daniels, *Humphry Repton* (1999), p. 54.
7. S. Daniels, *Fields of Vision* (1993), p. 92.
8. Daniels, 'Iconography of Woodland', p. 59.
9. M. Cormack, *The Paintings of Thomas Gainsborough* (1991), p. 140.
10. R. Payne Knight, *The Landscape* (1794), ii, lines 43–46.
11. Ibid., iii, lines 395–400.

Notes to Chapter 11: Plebeian Underwood

1. O. Rackham, *Hayley Wood* (1975), pp. 29–31.
2. O. Rackham, *The Last Forest* (1989), pp. 90–91.
3. J. Birrell, 'Common Rights in the Medieval Forest: Disputes and Conflicts in the Thirteenth Century', *Past and Present*, 117 (1987), p. 30.
4. A. Watkins, 'The Woodland Economy of the Forest of Arden in the Later Middle Ages', *Midland History*, 18 (1993), p. 26.
5. Birrell, 'Common Rights', p. 38.
6. Rackham, *The Last Forest*, p. 12.
7. Watkins, 'The Woodland Economy of the Forest of Arden', p. 28.

8. Birrell, 'Common Rights', pp. 48–49.
9. J. Munby, 'Wood', in J. Blair and N. Ramsay, *English Medieval Industries* (1993), p. 400.
10. Watkins, 'The Woodland Economy of the Forest of Arden', pp. 26–27.
11. R. Hayman, *Church Misericords and Bench Ends* (2000), p. 10.
12. A. Taylor, *Caernarfon Castle* (2001), pp. 9–10.
13. C. Hart, *Royal Forest* (1966), pp. 26–27, 263–66.
14. W. Linnard, *Welsh Woods and Forests* (1982), p. 74.
15. Ibid., p. 89.
16. V. Gatrell, *The Hanging Tree* (1994), p. 488.
17. Anon., *c.* 1806, quoted in Rackham, *Hayley Wood*, p. 41.
18. Rackham, *The Last Forest*, p. 136.
19. K. Briggs, *Fairies in Tradition and Literature* (1967), p. 82.
20. G. White, *The Natural History of Selborne*, edited by P. Foster (1993), p. 172.
21. Ibid., pp. 172–73.
22. R. Plot, *Natural History of Staffordshire* (1686), pp. 222–23.
23. R. Hunt, *Popular Romances of the West of England* (1881), pp. 415, 420–21.
24. Quoted in D. Hay, 'Poaching and the Game Laws on Cannock Chase', in D. Hay, P. Linebaugh and E. P. Thompson (eds), *Albion's Fatal Tree* (1975), p. 191.
25. E. P. Thompson, *Whigs and Hunters* (1975), p. 29. I have drawn on this standard work for much of what follows on the Black Act.
26. Ibid., p. 136.
27. Hay, 'Poaching and the Game Laws on Cannock Chase', p. 246.
28. White, *Selborne*, p. 23.
29. Ibid., p. 28.
30. E. P. Thompson, *Customs in Common* (1991), p. 102.
31. Ibid., pp. 142–43.
32. R. Mabey, *The Common Ground* (1980), p. 250.

Notes to Chapter 12: Woodlanders

1. R. Mudie, *Hampshire* (1838), quoted in E. P. Thompson, *Whigs and Hunters* (1975), p. 121.
2. C. Vancouver, *General View of the Agriculture of Hants* (1813), p. 496.
3. Quoted in T. Fulford, 'Cowper, Wordsworth, Clare: The Politics of Trees', *John Clare Society Journal*, 14 (1995).
4. J. Austen, *Mansfield Park* (1814), chapter 6.
5. W. Cowper, 'The Task', lines 746–56
6. R. Payne Knight, *The Landscape* (1794), iii, lines 59–63.

7. W. Cowper, 'Yardley Oak', lines 1–6.

8. Ibid., lines 9–11

9. J. Barrell, *The Idea of Landscape and the Sense of Place* (1972), p. 121.

10. M. Storey, *Clare: The Critical Heritage* (1973), p. 138.

11. J. Clare, 'Round Oak and Eastwell', lines 3–17.

12. J. Clare, 'The Summer Shower', lines 1–4.

13. J. Clare, 'Walks in the Woods', lines 4–6.

14. Ibid., lines 43–48.

15. R. Williams, *The Country and the City* (1973), p. 138.

16. Storey, *Clare*, p. 24.

17. J. Clare, *The Shepherd's Calendar*, 'May', lines 429–34, 458–61.

18. J. Clare, 'The Progress of Rhyme', lines 286–88.

19. M. Seymour-Smith, *Hardy* (1994), p. 368.

20. P. Beer, *Wessex* (1985), p. 90.

21. T. Hardy, *Under the Greenwood Tree*, book i, chapter 1.

22. Ibid., book v, chapter 1.

23. Ibid., book v, chapter 2.

24. T. Hardy, *The Woodlanders*, chapter 44.

25. Ibid., chapter 7.

26. Williams, *The Country and the City*, p. 207.

Notes to Chapter 13: Dreamers

1. R. Jefferies, *The Hills and the Vale* (1909), p. 34.

2. J. J. Rousseau, *The Confessions*, translated by J. M. Cohen (1953), p. 362.

3. R. P. Harrison, *Forests: The Shadow of Civilization* (1992), p. 133.

4. W. Wordsworth, 'Lines Composed a Few Miles Above Tintern Abbey', lines 102–11.

5. W. Wordsworth, 'Lines Written in Early Spring' (1798), lines 1–8.

6. J. Keats, 'Lines to Fanny', lines 39–40, 41–42.

7. J. Keats, 'I Stood Tip-Toe', lines 151–54.

8. A. Motion, *Keats* (1997), p. 480.

9. Ibid., p. 319.

10. J. Keats, 'Ode to a Nightingale', lines 8–10.

11. Ibid., lines 65–68.

12. W. Hazlitt, 'On the Love of the Country', *Examiner* (November 1814), reproduced in G. Keynes (ed.), *Selected Essays of William Hazlitt* (1970), pp. 4–5.

13. R. W. Emerson, *Nature* (1836), chapter 1.

14. J. Ruskin, *Fors Clavigera*, vi (1876), in *The Works of John Ruskin*, xxviii (1907), p. 541.

15. J. Ruskin, *The Poetry of Architecture* (1837), in *The Works of John Ruskin*, i (1903), p. 69.

16. Ibid., p. 68.

17. Ibid., p. 69.

18. L. Baxter, *The Life of William Barnes* (1887), pp. 184–86.

19. Ibid., p. 105.

20. W. Barnes, 'The Woodlands', lines 9–16.

21. G. M. Hopkins, 'Binsey Poplars', lines 9–11.

22. Quoted in R. Mabey (ed.), *The Oxford Book of Nature Writing* (1997), p. 84.

23. Quoted in J. Marsh, *Edward Thomas: A Poet for his Country* (1978), p. 36.

24. R. Jefferies, *The Story of My Heart* (1883), p. 35.

25. Quoted in Marsh, *Edward Thomas*, p. 42.

26. R. Gant (ed.), *Edward Thomas on the Countryside* (1977), p. 61.

27. A. Motion, *The Poetry of Edward Thomas* (1980), p. 112.

28. E. Thomas, *The South Country* (1932), p. 172.

29. H. Thomas, 'Introduction' to *The South Country* (1932).

30. Gant, *Edward Thomas*, pp. 108–10.

31. E. Thomas, 'The Unknown Bird', lines 16–18.

32. Jefferies, 'A King Of Acres', *The Hills and the Vale*, pp. 97–98.

33. P. Green, *Beyond the Wild Wood: The World of Kenneth Grahame* (1982), p. 96.

34. J. R. R. Tolkien, *Tree and Leaf* (1964), introduction.

35. This is the argument set out in K. Taplin, *Tongues in Trees* (1989), pp. 191–97.

36. J. R. R. Tolkien, *The Fellowship of the Ring*, book 1, chapter 7.

Notes to Chapter 14: Experts

1. *Daily Chronicle*, 23 April 1895.

2. R. Fenton, *Tours in Wales, 1804–13* (1917), pp. 172–73.

3. Quoted in N. D. G. James, *A History of English Forestry* (1981), p. 213.

4. O. Rackham, *Trees and Woodland in the British Landscape* (1990), p. 99.

5. James, *English Forestry*, p. 257.

6. Rackham, *Trees and Woodland*, p. 104.

7. O. Rackham, *The History of the Countryside* (1986), p. 48.

8. J. S. Collis, *The Triumph of the Tree* (1950).

9. W. G. Hoskins, *The Making of the English Landscape* (1970), pp. 57–58.

10. *The Mabinogion*, translated by T. Jones and G. Jones (1974), p. 113.

11. B. Coles and J. Coles, *Sweet Track to Glastonbury: The Somerset Levels in Prehistory* (1986), pp. 86–88.

12. T. Williamson, 'Early Co-Axial Field Systems on the East Anglian Boulder Clays', *Proceedings of the Prehistoric Society*, 53 (1987), pp. 419–32.

13. K. Dark and P. Dark, *The Landscape of Roman Britain* (1997), pp. 38–40.

14. R. Mabey, *Flora Britannica* (1996), p. 262.

15. *Sevenoaks Chronicle*, 17 October 1987.

16. Rackham, *Trees and Woodland*, pp. 201–3.

Notes to Chapter 15: Green Men

1. Lady Raglan, 'The Green Man in Church Architecture', *Folklore*, 50 (1939), pp. 45–57.

2. M. Murray, *The Witch Cult in Western Europe* (1921).

3. R. Judge, *The Jack-in-the-Green* (1979).

4. K. Basford, *The Green Man* (1978).

5. W. Anderson and C. Hicks, *The Green Man* (1990), pp. 14, 33, 163.

6. Ibid., p 163. A similar approach is taken in J. Matthews, *The Quest for the Green Man* (2001), where the Green Man is interpreted as one manifestation of a universal symbol. Other manifestations include shamans, druids, Robin Hood and Edward Thomas.

7. Quoted in L. Buell, *The Environmental Imagination* (1995), p. 311.

8. N. Evernden, *The Natural Alien* (1985).

9. Quoted in M. Andrews, *Landscape and Western Art* (1999), p. 206.

10. A. Goldsworthy, *Wood* (1996) p. 6.

11. Ibid., p. 69.

12. J. Fowles, *The Tree* (2000), p. 61.

Further Reading

What follows is not an exhaustive list of what is arguably an inexhaustible subject. I have divided the works into primary and secondary sources for convenience, although some of them could belong to either. The list of secondary works gives the main sources that I have consulted in writing the book, while the section of primary works lists accessible editions of the most important texts that have been discussed.

PRIMARY WORKS

A Celtic Miscellany, translated by Kenneth Jackson (Harmondsworth, Penguin, 1971).

Barber, Richard, *Bestiary* (Woodbridge, Boydell Press, 1999).

Barnes, William, *Selected Poems* (Harmondsworth, Penguin, 1994).

Bédoyère, Guy de la (ed.), *The Writings of John Evelyn* (Woodbridge, Boydell Press, 1995).

Chrétien de Troyes, *Arthurian Romances*, translated by William W. Kibler (Harmondsworth, Penguin, 1991).

Clare, John, *Selected Poems* (London, Dent, 1997).

Emerson, Ralph Waldo, *Selected Essays*, edited by Larzer Ziff (Harmondsworth, Penguin, 1982).

Fowles, John, *The Tree* (London, Vintage, 2000).

Frazer, Sir James, *The Golden Bough: A Study in Magic and Religion* (London, Macmillan; abridged edition 1922; reprinted London, Wordsworth Editions, 1993).

Gant, Roland (ed.), *Edward Thomas on the Countryside: A Selection of his Prose and Verse* (London, Faber and Faber, 1977).

Geoffrey of Monmouth, *Life of Merlin: Vita Merlini*, edited by Basil Clarke (Cardiff, University of Wales Press, 1973).

Goldsworthy, Andy, *Wood* (London, Viking, 1996).

Grahame, Kenneth, *The Wind in the Willows* (Harmondsworth, Penguin, 1994).

Grimm, Jacob and Wilhelm, *Complete Fairy Tales of the Brothers Grimm*, translated by Jack Zipes (London, Econo-Clad Books, 1988).

Hardy, Thomas, *Collected Poems* (London, Macmillan, 1930).

Hardy, Thomas, *Under the Greenwood Tree* (Oxford, Oxford University Press, 1985).

Hardy, Thomas, *The Woodlanders* (Oxford, Oxford University Press, 1985).

Hardy, Thomas, *Selected Poems* (Harmondsworth, Penguin, 1993).

Hopkins, Gerard Manley, *Poems and Prose* (Harmondsworth, Penguin, 1953).

Jefferies, Richard, *The Story of my Heart* (London, Quartet, 1979).

Jefferies, Richard, *The Hills and the Vale* (Oxford, Oxford University Press, 1980).

Keats, John, *The Complete Poems* (Harmondsworth, Penguin, 1977).

Kipling, Rudyard, *Puck of Pook's Hill* (Harmondsworth, Penguin, 1994).

Lucretius, *De rerum natura*, translated by W. H. D. Rouse, Loeb Classical Library (London, William Heinemann, 3rd edn 1937).

Mabey, Richard (ed.), *The Oxford Book of Nature Writing* (Oxford, Oxford University Press, 1997).

Mabinogion, The, translated by Gwyn Jones and Thomas Jones (London, Dent, 1974).

Malory, Sir Thomas, *Works*, edited by Eugene Vinaver (Oxford, Oxford University Press, 2nd edn, 1971).

Marryat, Captain, *Children of the New Forest* (Harmondsworth, Penguin, 1995).

Nash, David, *Forms into Time* (London, Academy Editions, 1996).

Ovid, *Metamorphoses*, translated by Mary Innes (Harmondsworth, Penguin, 1955).

Pausanias, *Guide to Greece*, i, *Central Greece*, translated by Peter Levi (Harmondsworth, Penguin, 1979).

Pliny the Elder, *Natural History: A Selection*, translated by John F. Healy (Harmondsworth, Penguin, 1991).

Pope, Alexander, *Poetical Works* (Oxford, Oxford University Press, 1966).

Shakespeare, William, *A Midsummer Night's Dream* (Harmondsworth, Penguin 1994).

Shakespeare, William, *As You Like It* (Harmondsworth, Penguin 1994).

Sir Gawain and the Green Knight, edited by J. A. Burrow (London, Penguin, 1972).

Spenser, Edmund, *Poetical Works* (London, Oxford University Press, 1970).

Tacitus, *On Britain and Germany*, translated by H. Mattingly (Harmondsworth, Penguin, 1948).

Tacitus, *The Annals of Imperial Rome*, translated by Michael Grant (Harmondsworth, Penguin, 1977).

Thomas, Edward, *The South Country* (London, Dent, 1932).

Thomas, Edward, *Selected Poems* (London, Dent, 1997).

Thoreau, Henry David, *Walden and Civil Disobedience* (Harmondsworth, Penguin, 1984).

Tolkien, J. R. R., *The Hobbit* (London, Allen and Unwin, 3rd edn, 1966).

Tolkien, J. R. R., *The Lord of the Rings*, 3 volumes (London, Allen and Unwin, 2nd edn, 1966).

Virgil, *The Aeneid*, translated by W. F. Jackson Knight (Harmondsworth, Penguin, 1956).

White, Gilbert, *The Natural History of Selborne*, edited by Paul Foster (Oxford, Oxford University Press, 1993).

SECONDARY WORKS

Anderson, William, and Hicks, Clive, *The Green Man: The Archetype of our Oneness with the Earth* (London, Harper Collins, 1990).

Andrews, Malcolm, *Landscape and Western Art* (Oxford, Oxford University Press, 1999).

Ballantyne, Andrew, *Architecture, Landscape and Liberty: Richard Payne Knight and the Picturesque* (Cambridge, Cambridge University Press, 1997).

Barlow, Frank, *William Rufus* (London, Methuen, 1983).

Barrell, John, *The Idea of Landscape and the Sense of Place, 1730–1840: An Approach to the Poetry of John Clare* (Cambridge, Cambridge University Press, 1972).

Basford, Kathleen, *The Green Man* (Cambridge, D. S. Brewer, 1978).

Bate, Jonathan, *The Song of the Earth* (London, Picador, 2000).

Baxter, Lucy, *The Life of William Barnes* (London, Macmillan, 1887; reprinted Routledge/Thoemmes Press, 1996).

Bellamy, John, *Crime and Public Order in England in the Later Middle Ages* (London, Routledge & Kegan Paul, 1973).

Bradley, Richard, *An Archaeology of Natural Places* (London, Routledge, 2001).

Buell, Lawrence, *The Environmental Imagination: Thoreau, Nature Writing and the Formation of American Culture* (London, Harvard University Press, 1995).

Cardinal, Roger, *The Landscape Vision of Paul Nash* (London, Reaktion Books, 1989).

Collis, John Stuart, *The Triumph of the Tree* (London, Jonathon Cape, 1950).

Cormack, Malcolm, *The Paintings of Thomas Gainsborough* (Cambridge, Cambridge University Press, 1991).

Cosgrove, Denis and Daniels, Stephen (eds), *The Iconography of Landscape* (Cambridge, Cambridge University Press, 1988).

Cox, J. Charles, *The Royal Forests of England* (London, Methuen, 1905).

Cummins, John, *The Hound and the Hawk: The Art of Medieval Hunting* (London, Weidenfeld and Nicolson, 1988).

Daniels, Stephen, *Fields of Vision: Landscape Imagery and National Identity in England and the United States* (Cambridge, Polity Press, 1993).

Daniels, Stephen, *Humphry Repton: Landscape Gardening and the Geography of Georgian England* (London, Yale University Press, 1999).

Doel, Fran and Geoff, *Robin Hood: Outlaw or Greenwood Myth* (Stroud, Tempus, 2000).

Doel, Fran and Geoff, *The Green Man in Britain* (Stroud, Tempus, 2001).

Ellis, John, *One Fairy Story Too Many: The Brothers Grimm and their Tales* (London, University of Chicago Press, 1983).

Ferris-Kaan, Richard (ed.), *The Ecology of Woodland Creation* (Chichester, John Wiley, 1996).

Green, Peter, *Beyond the Wild Wood: The World of Kenneth Grahame* (Exeter, Webb and Bower, 1982).

Harrison, Robert Pogue, *Forests: The Shadow of Civilization* (London, University of Chicago Press, 1992).

Hart, Cyril E., *Royal Forest: A History of Dean's Woods as Producers of Timber* (Oxford, Clarendon Press, 1966).

Harvey, Nigel, *Trees, Woods and Forests* (Princes Risborough, Shire, 1981).

Hay, D., Linebaugh, P. and Thompson, E. P. (eds), *Albion's Fatal Tree: Crime and Society in Eighteenth-Century England* (London, Allen Lane, 1975).

Holt, J. C., *Robin Hood* (London, Thames and Hudson, revised edn 1989).

Hoskins, W. G., *The Making of the English Landscape* (Harmondsworth, Penguin, 1970).

Hughes, Robert, *American Visions: The Epic History of Art in America* (London, Harvill Press, 1997).

Hutton, Ronald, *The Pagan Religions of the Ancient British Isles: Their Nature and Legacy* (Oxford, Blackwell, 1991).

Hutton, Ronald, *The Rise and Fall of Merry England* (Oxford, Oxford University Press, 1993).

Hutton, Ronald, *The Stations of the Sun: A History of the Ritual Year in Britain* (Oxford, Oxford University Press, 1997).

Irwin, Michael, *Reading Hardy's Landscapes* (Basingstoke, Macmillan, 2000).

James, N. D. G., *A History of English Forestry* (Oxford, Blackwell, 1981).

Keating, Peter, *Kipling the Poet* (London, Secker & Warburg, 1994).

Keen, Maurice, *The Outlaws of Medieval Legend* (London, Dorset Press, revised edn, 1987).

Keith, W. J., *Richard Jefferies: A Critical Study* (London, Oxford University Press, 1965).

Linnard, William, *Welsh Woods and Forests: History and Utilisation* (Llandysul, Gomer Press, new edn, 2000).

Low, Mary, *Celtic Christianity and Nature: Early Irish and Hebridean Traditions* (Edinburgh, Polygon, 1999).

Lowenthal, David, *George Perkins Marsh: Prophet of Conservation* (London, University of Washington Press, 2000).

Mabey, Richard, *The Common Ground: A Place for Nature in Britain's Future?* (London, Phoenix, 2nd edn, 1993).

Mabey, Richard, *Flora Britannica* (London, Sinclair-Stevenson, 1996).

Marsh, Jan, *Edward Thomas: A Poet for his Country* (London, Elek, 1978).

Matthews, John, *The Quest for the Green Man* (Newton Abbot, Godsfield Press, 2001).

Motion, Andrew, *The Poetry of Edward Thomas* (London, Routledge and Kegan Paul, 1980).

Motion, Andrew, *Keats* (London, Faber and Faber, 1997).

Nash, Roderick, *Wilderness and the American Mind* (London, Yale University Press, 3rd edn 1982).

Pakenham, Thomas, *Meetings with Remarkable Trees* (London, Weidenfeld and Nicolson, 1996).

Pakenham, Thomas, *Remarkable Trees of the World* (London, Weidenfeld and Nicolson, 2002).

Rackham, Oliver, *Hayley Wood: Its History and Ecology* (Cambridge, Cambridgeshire and Isle of Ely Naturalists' Trust, 1975).

Rackham, Oliver, *The History of the Countryside* (London, J. M. Dent, 1986).

Rackham, Oliver, *The Last Forest: The Story of Hatfield Forest* (London, J. M. Dent, 1989)

Rackham, Oliver, *Trees and Woodland in the British Landscape* (London, Weidenfeld and Nicolson, 2nd edn 1990).

Saunders, Corinne, *The Forest of Medieval Romance: Avernus, Broceliande, Arden* (Cambridge, D. S. Brewer, 1993).

Schama, Simon, *Landscape and Memory* (London, Harper Collins, 1995).

Seymour-Smith, Martin, *Hardy* (London, Bloomsbury, 1994).

Storey, Mark, *The Poetry of John Clare: A Critical Introduction* (London, Macmillan, 1974).

Taplin, Kim, *Tongues in Trees: Studies in Literature and Ecology* (Bideford, Green Books, 1989).

Thomas, R. George, *Edward Thomas: A Portrait* (Oxford, Oxford University Press, 1985).

Thompson, E. P., *Whigs and Hunters: The Origin of the Black Act* (London, Allen Lane, 1975).

Thompson, E. P., *Customs in Common* (Harmondsworth, Penguin, 1993).

Truettner, William and Walloch, Alan (eds), *Thomas Cole: Landscape into History* (London, Yale University Press, 1994).

Tubbs, Colin R., *The New Forest: An Ecological History* (Newton Abbot, David and Charles, 1968).

Tyler, J. E. A., *The Tolkien Companion* (London, Macmillan, 1976).

Warren, W. L., *Henry II* (London, Eyre Methuen, 1973).

Williams, Merryn, *Thomas Hardy and Rural England* (London, Macmillan, 1972).

Williams, Michael, *Americans and their Forests: A Historical Geography* (Cambridge, Cambridge University Press, 1989).

Williams, Raymond, *The Country and the City* (London, Chatto and Windus, 1973).

Wood, Christopher S., *Albrecht Altdorfer and the Origins of Landscape* (London, Reaktion Books, 1993).

Young, Charles, *The Royal Forests of Medieval England* (London, University of Pennsylvania Press, 1979).

Zipes, Jack, *The Brothers Grimm: From Enchanted Forest to the Modern World* (London, Routledge, 1988).

Index